LONGMAN LINGUISTICS LIBRARY
Title no 24

GRIMM'S GRANDCHILDREN
CURRENT TOPICS IN GERMAN LINGUISTICS

LONGMAN LINGUISTICS LIBRARY

General editors
R. H. Robins, University of London
G. N. Leech, University of Lancaster

PF 3051 HER

Grimm's Grandchildren

Current topics in German linguistics

Thomas Herbst
David Heath
Hans-Martin Dederding

LONGMAN

LONDON AND NEW YORK

LONGMAN GROUP LIMITED LONDON

Associated companies, branches and representatives throughout the world
Published in the United States of America by Longman Inc, New York
© Longman Group Ltd 1979

First published 1980
Cased ISBN 0 582 55487 X
Paper ISBN 0 582 55489 6

British Library Cataloguing in Publication Data
Herbst, Thomas
    Grimm's grandchildren. — (Longman linguistics
library; no. 24).
    1. Linguistics
I. Title   II. Heath, David   III. Dederding,
Hans-Martin
410'.943   P123   78-41007

ISBN 0-582-55487-X
ISBN 0-582-55489-6 pbk.

Printed and bound in Great Britain by
Butler & Tanner Ltd, Frome and London.

for Ute
Brigitte
Angelika
Hermann
Manuela
Thea
Bianca
Bettina

Preface

All Germans could fairly be called Grimm's grandchildren because almost all German children have enjoyed being told many of the famous fairy tales known as *Grimms Märchen*. However the label Grimm's grandchildren serves particularly well for the description of linguists in Germany since it was Jacob Grimm who, in the early nineteenth century, created an interest in language which went far beyond that of those scholars who had at the time already written grammars of German. Whilst these grammarians often used the terminology of traditional Latin grammar and others, or the same scholars, tried to keep the German language free from all foreign influences, Jacob Grimm ridiculed this normative prescriptive approach. He established *Sprachwissenschaft* as a descriptive science in Germany, but his interest in language went far beyond merely writing grammars, as Professor Ganz pointed out in his inaugural lecture at Oxford (*Conception*, 1973: 10–11): 'For Grimm German language and literature, German law and institutions, and German history formed a natural triad based on the unity of the nation ("Volk") which most obviously manifests itself in the language. It is this "Spirit of the Nation" which, through its language, somehow creates its own cultural superstructure.'

It is not only the interest in the historical side of language study and the principle of the descriptive character of linguistics which we have inherited from Grimm, it is the preoccupation with the relationship between language and culture, language and nation and with the role of language in society, all matters which since Grimm's days have played a great part in linguistic work in Germany. This is especially true of the work undertaken during and after the Second World War which this book will focus on.

This volume does not present an outline of the German School of Linguistics, simply because there is no such school, no bright star in the sky of linguistic theory showing the way to the promised land where all our questions about language will be answered. It is not in spite of this, but because of this that the research done in Germany may be of interest to the English-speaking world.

The worldwide boom in transformational linguistics has not passed Germany by, but transformational linguistics has been met with considerable criticism, for two main reasons: firstly, as we shall show in Chapter 7, some of the insights of transformational grammar lose their conviction when applied to languages other than English; secondly, and perhaps more importantly, this scepticism has its roots in the firm link between modern German linguistics and the work of Bühler, Trier and the Prague School. This has led to a situation in which many varied approaches to language description have been followed up; since today more and more linguists in the English-speaking world are also searching for alternatives to TG, this fact may be particularly significant. Dependency grammar is just one of these competing theories.

Thus a book on German linguistics will automatically serve as an introduction to various approaches to the study of language in general; it will also involve the discussion of some typical aspects of the role of linguistics in German society. On the one hand, Germany has a strong prescriptive tradition, the 'normed' standard language being codified in the various volumes of the *Duden*, a grammar accepted by most native speakers as the norm; on the other hand, some German linguists have insisted on a close connection between their research and a sociological and political analysis, and these socio- and pragmalinguists have had considerable influence both on German mother-tongue teaching and on foreign language pedagogy.

The strong linguistic tradition and the place of the linguist in society may explain some of the characteristics of the theories developed, but it is the structure of the German language which is the prime factor in this context. For this reason we have, in the second part of this book (Chapters 10 to 16), examined a number of problems of German grammar – not so much as an aim in itself, but mainly as a further illustration of the approaches discussed in Part 1. (We hope, however, to have chosen our examples in such a way that the reader without a good command of the language can also read these chapters with profit.)

It is regrettable, but inevitable, that a book of this length cannot discuss all the questions that are of interest or outline all the theories that deserve mention, if it is intended to be read and understood by those with a general interest in linguistic matters. We hope, however, that the professional scholar will find that this book not only gives him a general idea of the development of contemporary German linguistics but that it supplies him with sufficient references and bibliographical material to enable him to follow up any approaches or questions which may be of particular interest.

The fact remains that a survey of this type must always remain incomplete, otherwise it could never be written (or read). In any case, the choices made are subjective, although we have done our best to give a representative account of the progress of Grimm's grandchildren. If our outline of *Current Topics in German Linguistics* should not have failed to achieve this aim completely, it is due to the friendly assistance we received from many advisers. We should like to express our thanks to Dr Seiffert of Hertford College, Oxford, and to Professor Palmer of Reading; and especially to Dr B. Naumann and Dr E. Burgschmidt for commenting on some of the chapters and for their constant help throughout the writing of the book. We are equally indebted to our general editors, Professor Robins and Professor Leech, who have very generously made suggestions for improvements and have given us every encouragement. Finally, we wish to express our gratitude to Peggy Drinkwater of Longman, our extremely patient and benevolent guardian angel.

Nürnberg   T H
October 1979   DH
                                                                                                HMD

Acknowledgments

We are grateful to the following for permission to reproduce copyright material:

Max Hueber Verlag for a simplified table from *Untersuchungen zur Struktur der Bedeutung* by G. Wotjak; Hermann Luchterhand Verlag for 'Erinnerung an eine Landschaft am Mittelmeer' by Peter Härtling from *Anreden, Gedichte aus den Jahren 1972–77* by Peter Härtling © 1977 by Hermann Luchterhand Verlag, Darmstadt und Neuwied.

Contents

Part 1

Chapter 1

German linguistics to 1900

1.1 From the beginnings to K. F. Becker

What happened in the study of language throughout the Middle Ages does
not fit into our modern categories of national schools. In the Middle Ages
science, bound together by the common language Latin, was even more international than it is today. Language, for the medieval grammarians, meant
Latin, irrespective of their practical or philosophical purposes. In Germany,
as in other countries, practical grammar was based on Donatus and Priscian,
who lived in the fourth and fifth to sixth centuries respectively, and, later, on
the *Doctrinale* of Alexander de Villa Dei (1199).

As far as philosophical grammar is concerned, in Germany Thomas of
Erfurt contributed to the *grammatica speculativa*, whose aim it was to in-
corporate the study of language into scholastic thought. Unlike the practical
grammars, which were confined to the teaching of forms and formal categories
of Latin, speculative grammar discussed problems of meaning, for example
the question of what the grammatical categories correspond to in reality.[1]
Although speculative grammar was rejected by the Renaissance together with
everything medieval, some of its results, such as the distinction between noun
and adjective, and the term object, were embodied in later practical grammars.

The new appreciation of the vernaculars in the Renaissance had shifted the
emphasis towards practical grammar. Due to the political and cultural dis-
union of the Holy Roman Empire this practical trend lasted in Germany
longer than in the more centralized European countries, where the language
used at the court was adopted as the standard considerably earlier. While in
England F. Bacon (*De dignitate*, 1623) and Locke (*Essay*, 1690) continued
working in philosophical grammar, and universal grammars were developed
in France, in Germany most of the energy devoted to the study of language
was taken up by the question of DAS GEMEINE DEUTSCH (common German,
see Eggers, *Sprachgeschichte*, 1969: 152–60), the only notable exception being
Leibniz. All German grammars from Schottel (*Haubtsprache*, 1663) to Ade-

lung (*Lehrgebäude*, 1782) deal with the question of the standard in one way or other. Schottel and Adelung also mark the two positions between which opinions varied at different times: Schottel held the view that there was no dialect on which the common language was based, but rather that it made use of the best of all dialects (see Jellinek, *Geschichte I*, 1913: 131). Adelung, on the other hand, regarded the type of language spoken by educated people in upper Saxonia as its model.[2] Wieland, in opposing Adelung, came close to our modern view, stating that *Hochdeutsch* was mainly a literary language, and, as a spoken norm, existed only as an ideal (see Jellinek, 1913: 360–74, see also Introduction).

The other important development in German grammar was the albeit incomplete departure from the Latin model, which had been followed almost slavishly by the earliest grammars (see Jellinek, 1913: 21). Categories, such as the ablativus or the optativus – the latter even taken from Greek – were gradually abolished. The most important step, however, was probably the distinction between syntactic categories (noun, verb, etc) and syntactic functions (subject, predicate, object, etc), which was finally established in K. F. Becker's grammar (1836–9).[3] The *syntaxis* found in older grammars had been based on the parts of speech and would have analysed the sentence

[1] Vater raucht Pfeife.

as noun + verb + noun instead of subject + predicate + object. A sentence such as

[2] Dass du heute kommst, freut mich.

shows that these terms are not always equivalent. In [2] the subject is a *dass*-clause. Becker made the term OBJECT, which is taken from scholastic metaphysics, an unambiguously grammatical term. In combining it with the classical SUBJECT and PREDICATE as well as his own terms ATTRIBUTE and BESTIMMENDES OBJEKT (later: adverbial) he established what we call traditional syntax today. His system had an exceptionally long life in school-teaching, and was not challenged by other models of syntax until the twentieth century.

Before Becker's all German grammars had been normative grammars in that they saw their aim as promoting correct speaking and writing. In this connection it is immaterial whether they took their norm from the inherent basic correctness of language, using analogy as a corrective criterion (Schottel, 1663) or from its use by educated speakers (Adelung, 1782). However, when Becker's grammar appeared, linguistics had already taken another turn. The historical investigation of language made language change appear as a natural process. This led to a fervent rejection of normative grammar (see Grimm, *Grammatik*, 1819: IX). The dichotomy between the philosophical and the practical study of language continued in the form of scientific grammar and school grammar. The former was, by definition, historically oriented.

1.2 Historical linguistics

1.2.1 *The topics*
Historical considerations in the study of language were not entirely new. Many
of the questions which were to become the focus of nineteenth-century linguistics had traditionally been objects of linguistic thought. These were, above
all, the question of the original language, the question of the relationships
between languages and the question of 'what words really mean', that is to
say etymology.

THE ORIGINAL LANGUAGE: Throughout the Middle Ages and the Renaissance it was generally believed that Hebrew, being the language of the Old
Testament, was the original language, and that all other languages had succes-
sively descended from it (see Arens, *Sprachwissenschaft*, 1969: 73). This, grammarians thought, could be proved by setting up lists of words corresponding
formally and semantically in Hebrew, Greek, Latin and German. The large
number of loan-words made this method appear conclusive. Apart from these
words, many genuine correspondences were found, but very often a vague
similarity was considered sufficient to prove their derivation from Hebrew.

THE RELATIONSHIP BETWEEN LANGUAGES: Apart from outstandingly successful attempts at classifying the languages of Europe (see Arens, 1969: 74–
6) the notions concerning the relationships between them were rather unclear.
Secure statements as to relationship and origin were only possible in the case
of the Romance languages, which had been recorded since the days of the
Roman Empire and which were discussed in Dante's *De vulgari eloquentia*
(about 1305, see Robins, *History*, 1967: 100–1). But in general the methods
of comparing languages did not provide lasting results. Still, the material
gathered in works such as Adelung and Vater's *Mithridates* (1806–17) and
the reflections about the criteria of comparison, which are found, for example,
in Kraus ('Rezension', 1787), were important steps towards more accurate
investigation.

ETYMOLOGY: Only a small number of words reveal an obvious link between
sound and content, for example *cuckoo*. Etymology tries to account for all
other words, as well. The method traditionally employed was to derive a word
from other words or phrases of the same language, but before stricter methodological rules were introduced and the history of the word as well as related
words in other languages were taken into account, the explanations given were
mostly far-fetched and arbitrary (see Robins, 1967: 22–3 and 78).

1.2.2 *Herder and Humboldt: language and mind*
The idea implied in etymology is that a word is not a purely conventional
sound-string chosen arbitrarily to denote a phenomenon of the world, but
that there is some natural link between the phenomenon and the word. Such
was also the belief expressed by Herder (*Abhandlung*, 1776). He claimed that
there was a close connection between language and mind. Words were created

by the operation of the mind,[4] which assigned sounds to the phenomena of the world according to acoustic analogies, that is to say all words were thought to have originally been of the *cuckoo* type, having undergone in the course of time various changes with the result that the analogy became obscured. For the study of language this meant that the old forms were more revealing than the extant ones.

It is necessary to appreciate this in order to understand the enthusiastic reception given to William Jones's discovery of the close similarity between Sanskrit and the European languages. The ancient texts of Sanskrit provided an opportunity to go several centuries further back in history, and thus, perhaps, come closer to the real meaning of the words in Herder's sense. One should bear in mind that, for the early comparative and historical linguists, the study of the old texts and the work of comparison, however fascinating in itself, was not only an investigation of forms, but by doing so they hoped to gain greater insight into the mind they saw working behind the forms.[5]

This aim is most clearly expressed in the works of Wilhelm von Humboldt. Like Herder he assumed that there was a close connection between language and the mind. For him, however, it was not necessary to go back to the origins of language. He conceived of language as a continuous mental process: language is not ERGON, *ie* an object once formed and then used mechanically like a tool, language is ENERGEIA, a permanent mental activity (Humboldt, 'Verschiedenheit', 1830–5:418). Language acquisition, and also every instance of speaking and understanding, is an attempt at analysing and mastering the world of phenomena. The sum total of these attempts is reflected in language. However, the analysis of reality is not uniform all over the world, different language communities produce different analyses. Thus, each language has a particular content structure – Humboldt called it INNERE SPRACHFORM – reflecting its speakers' particular view of the world, and, in turn, influencing it.[6] The difference between languages is not so much a difference in sounds or formal structure as a difference in the *innere Sprachform*.[7] The task of linguistics is the investigation of language and its influence on man supported by empirical comparative studies (Humboldt, 'Thesen', 1810–11: 20).[8]

Humboldt was well aware of the difficulty of establishing the *innere Sprachform* of a language. Therefore, he had recourse to a formal criterion for his classification of languages. Following A. W. Schlegel (*Observations*, 1818) he based it on the changes words may undergo for syntactic purposes in different languages and arrived at three types:

(i) isolating languages (no change at all, for example Chinese)
(ii) agglutinating languages (strictly regular and unequivocal affixes added to the root, for example Turkish)
(iii) inflecting languages (change of root vowels and use of affixes carrying several meanings, for example Latin)[9]

These types are idealized, for real languages are never pure realizations of one type. They are always mixed to some degree (Humboldt, 'Verschiedenheit', 1827–9: 301).

The example of Humboldt's classification of languages alone shows that the scope of his work went far beyond that of his contemporaries who concentrated on just one language family: the Indo-European. This is even more true of Humboldt's philosophy of language, which we have only touched upon above. With the exception of the work of a few linguists, the ideas of language as *energeia* and *innere Sprachform* were not taken up again until the end of the century (see 1.3).[10] It was Humboldt's wish to lay the foundations for a comprehensive study of language comprising both philosophy of language and empirical work. For the rest of the century, however, the latter predominates over works investigating language from a psychological or philosophical point of view.[11]

1.2.3 *Historical and comparative linguistics: first phase, from Bopp to Schleicher*

The great achievement of the first half of the nineteenth century is the identification of the Indo-European family of languages. As early as 1776 W. Jones had attributed the striking similarities between Sanskrit words and those of various Indo-European languages to a common original language, which had probably ceased to exist. In the second decade of the nineteenth century several linguists determined to investigate the relationships prevailing between the languages (once) spoken in Europe and from Asia Minor to India.

Bopp's pioneering study of the conjugation systems of several Indo-European languages was published in 1816. The Dane Rask's work on the origin of Old Norse and Icelandic followed two years later. In 1819 the first volume of J. Grimm's *Deutsche Grammatik* appeared, the second edition of which (1822) contained the sound-shifts.

By comparing old stages of Germanic languages and other Indo-European languages Grimm realized that guttural, labial and dental plosives on the one hand and fricatives and affricates on the other showed regular correspondences, which he stated to be a result of historical development (*cf* Greek *pater* – OHG *fater*, Greek *deka* – Gothic *taihun* – OHG *zehan*). This sound-shift is one of the most important differences between the Germanic languages and the other Indo-European languages.[12]

The method employed was the established one of finding words (or morphemes, as in Bopp, *Conjugationssystem*, 1816) which correspond in different languages. However, stricter rules were applied. Sound-change was only accepted if it showed some regularity, and, as the knowledge of the correspondences increased, meaning was more and more left out of consideration: the sound-change was more reliable.

In the following years more and more languages were shown to belong to the Indo-European family.[13] Many of the studies betray a biological view of language. Humboldt had compared it to an organism (Humboldt, 'Sprach-studium', 1820: 3), Grimm saw comparative anatomy as the model for comparative grammar (Grimm, *Grammatik*, 1819: XII). Languages were even thought to have times of growth and decay. Even if this terminology was only metaphorical at the beginning, it exerted great influence on the way language was seen. The culmination of this biological view can be seen in Schleicher (*Compendium*, 1861–2). Basing his work on the results of the previous fifty years he tried to reconstruct the Indo-European language, and, perhaps under the influence of Darwin's *The Origin of Species* (1859), presented the development of the Indo-European languages as an evolutionary process, which he depicted in a tree diagram:[14]

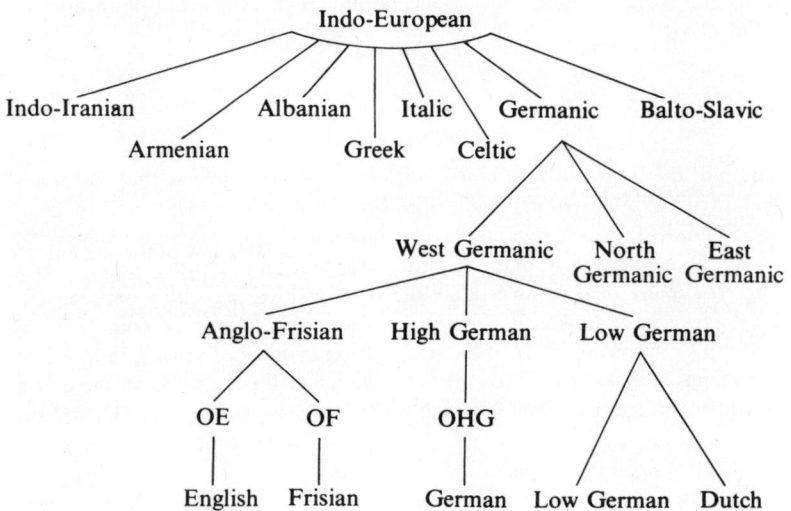

Schleicher's work marks the end of the first phase of historical linguistics, which can be characterized as follows:

(i) Language is seen as a biological entity. Language change is considered a natural development.

(ii) The tasks of linguistics were to prove the relationships between languages by establishing exact correspondences between comparable items and, based on this, the reconstruction of the common Indo-European language.

(iii) Studies of the old stages of the languages examined predominate over the investigation of the modern stages.

(iv) One of the original aims, the investigation of the mind in language, recedes in favour of formal studies.

1.2.4 *The* Junggrammatiker

MORE RIGOROUS RULES. Alongside the words showing regular correspondences, there was always a large number of exceptions, words and morphemes
whose development could not be accounted for. For the linguists in the second
half of the century, who wanted to make their science as exact as the leading
natural sciences, this state of affairs was not satisfactory. By analogy with the
natural laws, which were then believed to be strict rules of causality, stricter
rules were demanded for the study of language as well.

This demand had become even more plausible as a result of various discoveries proving that explanations could be found even for exceptions which,
up to then, had been inexplicable. The most famous of them is Verner's Law.

One irregularity of the first sound-shift was that IE k/p/t in medial position
became h/f/θ in some words (see above), but g/b/d in others. Verner managed
to show that this was due to the position of the stress in Indo-European. If
the stress preceded k/p/t, these sounds became h/f/θ; if the syllable imme-
diately following was stressed, they became g/b/d. Verner concluded that the
first sound-shift did not allow a large number of exceptions. Seemingly irregular cases had been shown to be perfectly regular.

The desire to make linguistics an exact science modelled upon the natural
sciences and the justification for this desire found in discoveries such as
Verner's Law[15] caused various linguists to formulate the 'law of the exceptionless operation of the sound-laws'. It stated that sound-laws operate without
exceptions, unless counteracted by other sound-laws (for example, Grimm's
Law was counteracted by Verner's Law) or by analogy (the plural of MHG
man 'man' is *man* 'men', according to the sound-laws it should be NHG *Mann*,
but it is *Männer* after *Lamm/Lämmer*).

This is the central idea of a group of linguists referred to as *Junggrammatiker* – Neogrammarians – including the Indo-European scholars Osthoff and
Brugmann, the German scholar Hermann Paul and others. While this principle had also, at least implicitly, been the guideline for the work of Grimm
and his contemporaries,[16] most of the other principles of the *Junggrammatiker*
differ from the practice of the first half of the century.

OTHER PRINCIPLES. Many of the principles reveal the positivist outlook of
the *Junggrammatiker*. Positivism regards observable facts as the only secure
basis for science. It is no wonder, then, that the following principles are
found:

(i) The study of modern forms is to be preferred to the study of the old stages
of a language, and the study of changes to the attempt to reconstruct
stages of which no written records exist. This did not mean that such
work was thought to be useless. Linguistics remained a historical science.
But the data provided in old records were not considered secure enough
for an exact science, and reconstruction could only be attempted on the

basis of a deeper insight into the functioning of sound-changes, which had to be gained first by careful observation.

(ii) This is closely linked with the preference given to the spoken language. Grimm had talked of *Buchstabenvertauschung*, but meanwhile Raumer ('Aspiration', 1837) and Brücke (*Grundzüge*, 1856) had emphasized the physiological aspect in the production of language, and Verner's discovery had shown the necessity of taking phonetic criteria into account.

(iii) The individual's use of language is the only secure basis for the study of language. This principle was directed against the biological view. The *Junggrammatiker* were certain that language did not have an autonomous existence.

(iv) The study of meaning is not the central task of linguistics. The *Junggrammatiker* thought that semantics did not lend itself to objective investigation.[17]

(v) Linguistics is in principle a historical science (Paul, *Prinzipien*, [5]1920: 20). This principle links the *Junggrammatiker* with the linguists of the first part of the century and distinguishes them from modern linguists.

CRITICISM: THE EXCEPTIONLESS OPERATION OF THE SOUND-LAWS. Unlike principles (i)–(v), which were generally accepted, the formula of the exceptionless operation of the sound-laws met with considerable criticism. This is mainly due to the fact that Osthoff and Brugmann in 1878 claimed for it the status of a natural law.[18]

It could easily be shown that sound-laws were different: they did not operate everywhere and at all times in the same way and did not allow predictions to be made (see also 1.3.3).

These and other arguments soon led to a revision of the formula. It now read: 'Die Lautgesetze, welche wir aufstellen, sind wie sich gezeigt hat, nichts anderes als Gleichmässigkeiten, welche in einer gewissen Sprache und Zeit auftreten, und nur für diese Gültigkeit haben.' (The sound-laws, which we establish, are – as has been shown – nothing else but regularities which are found and are valid only in a certain language and at a certain time.) (Delbrück, *Sprachstudium*, 1884: 128.) The formula retained its value as a methodological rule: before assigning the status of an analogy to an apparently irregular sound-change, every attempt should be made to see whether it could not be explained by a sound-law.

CRITICISM: CAUSES OF SOUND-CHANGE. As long as sound-changes had been considered part of the biological development of language or as a natural law, the question of how they were caused had not arisen. Therefore it is not surprising that the discussion focused on the causes of sound-changes, after the former ideas had been rejected. A prominent place in this discussion was occupied by the question of whether the individual speaker was aware of sound-changes or not, and whether he played an active part in them.

For the *Junggrammatiker* sound-change was an essentially unconscious process. The astonishing regularity could not be explained other than by assuming a physiological principle affecting all members of a language community in the same way at the same time. Their opponents emphasized that language was a social phenomenon and, consequently, that the change might well start in a small part of the community, and, by way of imitation, spread over the rest. (See, for example, Schuchardt, *Lautgesetze*, 1885.) Further causes were mentioned: incorrect imitation in language acquisition (Paul, [5]1920); incorrect imitation on a large scale, for example when a language is imposed on a people by conquerors (Ascoli, *Briefe*, 1887); the wish to use as little energy as possible in speaking counteracted by the wish to speak intelligibly (Jespersen, 'Lautgesetzfrage', 1886).[19]

The question of how and why sound-changes take place is still a matter of discussion. It has proved helpful to distinguish between the origin of the change and its spread. A further important distinction is the one between internal and external causes of sound-change, that is for example, causes to be sought in the structure of a language on the one hand and social change on the other.[20]

EVALUATION. Summing up one can say that many of the principles of the *Junggrammatiker* mark an important step towards twentieth-century linguistics. Their rejection of indefinable terms and the rigorous methods of investigation served as a model for later linguists.[21] The rejection of the biological view of language and the incorporation of physiological and psychological factors into its investigation is a further achievement of the *Junggrammatiker*, and their conviction that the study of language must be based on the spoken language is a universal principle for contemporary linguists.

On the other hand, the *Junggrammatiker* failed to deal with some important aspects of language. It was, however, not the neglect of syntax or of the problems of communication that aroused the first criticisms but their failure to provide a comprehensive theory of language, taking account of the links between language and the mind and language and society which had played such an important part at the beginning of the century (see 1.2.2). In the first third of the twentieth century these questions were discussed from several points of view by the psychologist W. Wundt, the Romance scholar K. Vossler, the founder of the *geistesgeschichtliche* school of linguistics, the dialectologists and the *Wörter und Sachen* movement.

1.3 The beginning of the twentieth century: language and culture

1.3.1 *Völkerpsychologie*

Wundt (*Völkerpsychologie*, 1900) revived some of Humboldt's ideas conceiving language as the creation of a language community. He tried to break down terms such as 'the mind in language' by relating linguistic items to particular modes of association in the mind of the speakers.[22] Language, according to Wundt, has to be studied in a general theory of expression, which in turn he saw as part of *Völkerpsychologie* also comprising other 'achievements' of communities, for example religion and customs.

1.3.2 *Geistesgeschichtliche Schule*
Humboldt's ideas also influenced Vossler. He regarded the development of language in the course of history as dependent on the development of the mind. However, unlike Wundt, he rejected the idea of language as a creation of the community. Instead, he emphasized the creative power of the individual, which brought linguistics very close to the study of literature.[23] Later, Spitzer, who was influenced by Vossler, was to claim that the difference between the creative power shown in literature and in everyday language was only a matter of degree, not of quality. Vossler himself would not go as far as that. Still, he regarded aesthetics as the proper place for the study of language.[24]

Although approving of Vossler's ideas on mind and language in general, most linguists would not agree with their practical application as presented in Vossler's *Frankreichs Kultur im Spiegel seiner Sprachentwicklung* (1921), where he tried to explain linguistic changes by changes in the *Zeitgeist*.[25] Similarly, the notion of linguistics as part of aesthetics met with criticism, as it disregards the differences between language as an element of art and everyday language (see Iordan and Orr, *Romance Linguistics*, 1970: 121).

1.3.3 *Dialectology*
Whereas Wundt and Vossler, following Humboldt, regarded the connection between language and culture as one of the given facts on which they based their studies, the dialectologists were compelled to take account of cultural development only by the results of their work. G. Wenker began his work for the *Deutsche Sprachatlas* on a strictly Neogrammarian basis. In fact he started collecting data from the German dialects in order to prove the exceptionless operation of the sound-laws. But instead of finding homogeneous dialectal areas as he had expected, he was forced to recognize that, apart from central areas in which all words were affected by a certain sound-law, there were fringe areas in which the sound-law affected fewer and fewer words. Thus, almost every word appeared to have its own area of validity.

This not only showed the exceptionless-sound-law thesis to be in need of modification (see note 16), but also contradicted the romantic concept of dialectal areas reflecting the settlement of the old German tribes. Other geographical and cultural factors had to be found in order to explain the regional distribution of the linguistic phenomena. The name G. Frings may be regarded as representative of this work. Early in the 1920s he managed to show the importance of the medieval territorial boundaries for the development of the Rhenish dialects. The idea that cultural centres and their spheres of influence were the primary cause of linguistic unity replaced the older concept. For Frings and his school dialectology meant the investigation of the spreading of linguistic items and the changes in their regional distribution as well as the cultural reasons for these changes.[26]

1.3.4 Wörter und Sachen

Due to the Neogrammarian influence dialectology focused for a long time on the study of sounds and morphemes. As the study of words gained importance, cultural factors became still more important. It is a well-known fact that words travel with the objects they denote (cf old Latin loan-words in English and German: street Strasse (via) strata; Fenster fenestra). On the other hand, cultural history can provide interesting explanations in etymology: the relationship between Wand (wall) and winden (to wind) could be accounted for by referring to the material once used for wall-building – wattle (Meringer, 'Etymologien', 1898). To promote studies of this kind Meringer and others founded the periodical Wörter und Sachen in 1909 as an organ for the joint investigation of folklore and language.

This short survey of the linguistic movements at the beginning of our century shows that their main concern was the study of language in a cultural framework. In pursuing this aim, the real objective – the study of language – was sometimes in danger of being neglected, as for instance later volumes of Wörter und Sachen prove.

On the other hand, in Germany more than elsewhere, the Junggrammatiker continued to hold a dominant position. But their principles, which had been stimulating at the beginning, threatened to become dogmas which were to hamper later development. Probably due to their influence, books dealing with essential problems of language met with no response when first published: Wegener (Untersuchungen, 1885), who investigated the question of what happens in communication, did not find proper recognition until the 1930s, when many of his ideas were taken up by Bühler (see Chapters 3 and 5), Gardiner (Theory, 1932) and Firth ('Ethnographic analysis', 1968, see also Chapter 5). Ries (Syntax, 1894) clearly points to the twentieth century.

Under these circumstances the new impulses had to come from abroad. They came in the form of de Saussure's Cours de linguistique général (1916). Here, language was regarded as a system of signs, the emphasis was put on internal linguistics (as against the language and culture movements) and especially on the synchronic approach to the study of language, ie the study of language at a certain period of time (as opposed to the diachronic approach – the study of the historical development of language). All the schools which follow can rightly be called Post-Saussurean, in that they apply some of his essential ideas.

Recommended further reading

Further information about all the topics dealt with in this chapter can be found in Robins (*History*, 1967), where they are integrated into a comprehensive history of linguistics from classical times to the twentieth century. A useful reader to go with this book is Arens (*Sprachwissenschaft*, 1969). The specifically German question of the rise of New High German is treated in Eggers (*Sprachgeschichte*, 1969) up to Schottel. For the time after up to Adelung and for the history of the writing of German grammars, Jellinek (*Geschichte I*, 1913) is still the standard work. A detailed introduction to the methods of historical linguistics has been given by Lehmann (*Linguistics*, 1964). For the counter-movements of 1.3, Helbig (*Geschichte*, 1974) can be recommended as a concise introduction with references to further literature.

Chapter 2

Content-oriented grammar

2.1 General remarks on inhaltbezogene Grammatik

We have seen that in the nineteenth century German linguists were mainly concerned with the historical analysis of language and that they concentrated on its formal aspects, *ie* the establishing of sound-laws, the diachronic description of inflexion systems, etc. In the late twenties and early thirties of this century we observe the beginnings of a counter-movement: the main impetus for the revival of the study of the content side of language came from Leo Weisgerber, who – inspired by the works of Cassirer, Porzig, and later Trier (see 2.3), and also by de Saussure's view of the linguistic sign as a combination of *signifiant* and *signifié* (Saussure, *Cours*, 1916) – outlined the basic principles of the so-called *inhaltbezogene Grammatik* (content-oriented grammar).

Weisgerber rejects the bias towards form in the approaches taken by Bopp and Grimm and goes back to von Humboldt's discussion of linguistic questions, which – in his view – opens much wider perspectives than the work of the German linguists working after Humboldt. As we shall see, it is Humboldt's concept of the *innere Sprachform* (see 2.2.2) which is the starting-point for Weisgerber's own considerations.

The development of *inhaltbezogene Grammatik* out of the Humboldtian tradition, which brought members of this school the name Neo-Humboldtians, may explain why Weisgerber's theory is more a philosophy of language than a theory of grammar. This is also reflected in the terminology he introduces and in the style in which his books are written; they are rather metaphorical in character and sometimes quite difficult for the modern reader. Of course, one must take account of the fact that Weisgerber developed most of his theory some fifty years ago, although his main work *Von den Kräften der deutschen Sprache* was published shortly after the Second World War and has subsequently been re-edited and modified.

The work of the *inhaltbezogene Grammatiker* is remarkable in so far as they clearly demonstrated that the content side of language has to be integrated into linguistic description – a parallel perhaps to the revival of the interest in semantics in generative transformationalist linguistics in the late sixties. In this chapter, we shall give a brief outline of Weisgerber's work and of the work of other grammarians in this tradition; this will also involve a short discussion of the Duden (*Grammatik*) which is widely recognized as the standard grammar of German.

2.2 The idea of an intermediate linguistic world

2.2.1 *Content structure*

Although Weisgerber does not deny the need for an analysis of linguistic forms (he calls this the *laut- oder gestaltbezogene Analyse*), he is mainly concerned with the analysis of the content structure of a language (*inhaltbezogene Analyse*). And here his main contention is that there is no direct 1:1 correspondence between linguistic forms and the objects of the real world they refer to. To illustrate this point, Weisgerber (*Grundzüge*, 1962: 57) takes an example from biology. From a scientific point of view there is no reason why one should distinguish vegetables[1] from fruit. If we make such a distinction in English (or in German), this does not reflect natural characteristics of the objects themselves, but is a distinction imposed on nature by (the view of the world of) a language community, which regards apples as 'fruit' and tomatoes as 'vegetables'.

These considerations have led Weisgerber (*Weltbild*, 1950: 18) to claim the existence of a *sprachliche Zwischenwelt* (an intermediate linguistic world), in which objects of the outer world are transformed into objects of the human mind:[2]

... ist die Sprache selbst der Ort, an dem sich der Aufbau der gedanklichen Zwischenwelt vollzieht, der Weg, auf dem die Welt des Seins in eine solche des Bewusst-Seins übergeführt wird.
(The language itself is where the development of the intermediate conceptual world is carried out, it is the process by which the world of being is transferred into one of conscious realization.)

The existence of an intermediate linguistic world is also one of the central issues of Humboldt's language philosophy (see Weisgerber, *Zweimal Sprache*, 1973: 112):

... dass die Sprache nicht bloss ein Austauschungsmittel zu gegenseitigem Verständnis, sondern eine wahre Welt ist, welche der Geist zwischen sich und die Gegenstände durch die innere Arbeit seiner Kraft setzen muss ...[3]
(Language is not merely a means of communication serving the needs of mutual understanding, but it is a real world which the mind must place between itself and objects by means of the inner workings of its force.)

It follows from this that the main task of an *inhaltbezogene Grammatik*, namely the study of the content structure of a language, has to be the analysis of the *sprachliche Zwischenwelt*.[4]

2.2.2 *The differences between languages*

If we compare some aspects of the vocabulary of different languages, the colour terms for example, we find that a term in the one language will not always correspond to only one term in the other language. Welsh, for instance, has only the three words *gwyrdd, glas* and *llwyd* for the same range of colours covered by *green, blue, grey* and *brown* in English (see Robins, *Linguistics,* 1964: 72). This means that different languages can impose quite different structures on reality.

There are a large number of such differences (although perhaps not quite such significant ones) between English and German. The following example from Leisi (*Wortinhalt,* [4]1971 : 67)[5] illustrates how the same processes are realized by different linguistic forms in the two languages:

	FOR LIQUIDS	FOR BOTH	FOR SOLIDS
small amounts	*spritzen*	*sprinkle*	*streuen*
larger amounts	*giessen*	*pour* *schütten*	

Each language creates its own *sprachliche Zwischenwelt* and it is the character of this *Zwischenwelt* which determines the *Weltansicht der Sprachgemeinschaft* (view of the world taken by the language community).[6] It is very important to note that Weisgerber does not try to find linguistic universals; on the contrary, he (Weisgerber, *Zweimal Sprache,* 1973: 70) agrees with Humboldt who characterizes the differences between languages as a 'Verschiedenheit der Weltansichten selbst' (a difference in the views of the world) and talks of a 'Selbstverwirklichung der Sprachgemeinschaften in der Muttersprache' (self-realization of the language community through its mother tongue) (1973: 188). The connection between the language and culture of a language community is one of the most important aspects of Weisgerber's theory (see especially *Muttersprache,* [2]1957, and *Kraft,* [2]1959).

2.2.3 *The wording of the world*

We have seen in the previous section that language structures the objects of the 'outer' world and that it builds up an intermediate linguistic world (*sprachliche Zwischenwelt*). Weisgerber has called this the *wording of the world* (*Worten der Welt*). It is a dynamic process, which Weisgerber (*Grundzüge,* 1962: 234) calls *Leistung*.[7] As, for Weisgerber, this is one of the central questions of linguistics, a *leistungbezogene Analyse* is also part of a comprehensive theory of language. Weisgerber (*Gestaltung*, 1962: 10) sees it as

> ... die eigentliche Aufgabe der Sprachwissenschaft, die Sprache in iher geistesgestaltenden 'Wirklichkeit' aufzusuchen, ... in den Vollzug ihrer welterschliessenden Kraft hinein zu verfolgen.
> (... the real task of linguistics to grasp language in its mind-shaping reality ... to pursue it to the completion of its world-view shaping force.)

The *wording of the world* is the main *Leistung* of a language: it is the process by which the *sprachliche Zwischenwelt* is built up. According to Weisgerber, the content structure of a language largely determines the world view and behaviour of a native speaker. The acquisition of his mother tongue by an individual is seen by Weisgerber (*Inhaltbezogene Grammatik*, 1953: 20) as 'das Lebendigwerden des muttersprachlichen Weltbildes im Sprachbesitz des einzelnen' (the coming alive of the mother-tongue world view in the language of the individual).[8] This aspect of a language, its influence on the thought and behaviour of the individual, is termed *Wirkung*.

However, Weisgerber does not claim that human thought is entirely governed by the given content structure of the language (*Muttersprache*), because the wording of the world can operate in two directions:[9]

(i) It can give structure to the 'outer' world which is present before language
(ii) But language can also create a new 'inner' world in that it coins new terms, etc.

2.2.4 *The dynamic nature of language*
The analysis of both the *Leistung* and *Wirkung* of a language show that language is dynamic in character. Weisgerber (*Grundzüge*, 1962: 30–6) adopts Humboldt's distinction between *ergon* (state) and *energeia* (process) and stresses the fact that language is *energeia* and that the dynamic analysis must be superior to the stative analysis, as language is a living phenomenon. Weisgerber (*4 Stufen*, 1963) draws up the following four levels of analysis:[10]

(i) *gestaltbezogen* (form-oriented)   ⎫   language as
(ii) *inhaltbezogen* (content-oriented)   ⎭   *ergon* (state)
(iii) *leistungbezogen* (power-oriented) ⎱   language as
(iv) *wirkungbezogen* (effect-oriented)   ⎰   *energeia* (process)

Although he stresses the importance of the *energeia* approach, it is at the second level of analysis that the *inhaltbezogene Grammatik* has provided most satisfactory results. In the next sections, after the discussion of the word field, we shall illustrate some content-oriented approaches to the word and the sentence.

2.3 The linguistic field

We have seen that for Weisgerber the system or what Humboldt called the *Articulation* of language is, as a fundamental principle, also applicable to the *sprachliche Zwischenwelt* (see 2.2.1). It is then logical for him to assume that this intermediate linguistic world is accessible to the investigating linguist. After Trier had defined and elaborated the term *sprachliches Zeichenfeld* (linguistic field), which others had used before him,[11] Weisgerber and his followers used it as a tool with which to tackle the problem of exposing the structure of the intermediate linguistic world.[12] Trier (*Wortschatz*, 1931: 11) recognized a strong debt to de Saussure, though he later denied that his own work on word fields had been inspired other than by practical considerations.[13] Following de Saussure Trier accepted the 'Ideen der Ganzheit, der Gliederung und des Gefüges' (1931: 25) as the principles of linguistic investigation. He saw the total vocabulary of a language as comprising a number of 'conceptual fields', words of similar meaning making up a word field which divided the 'conceptual field' into parts in such a way that the individual word acquired its meaning solely from its opposition to the others in the field. In 1931 Trier assumed that the 'conceptual fields' existed without gaps and also that they joined together to form higher-order structures. His work has also been criticized since because he seems to suggest that the word fields are discrete entities with rigid internal divisions.[14]

Trier, like de Saussure, distinguished the language system (*langue*) and the use of the system (*parole*), maintaining that words are elements of *langue* since the relations holding between them within the fields – and hence their meanings – are not established through the use of the system, but precede their use. Weisgerber points out the inadequacies, for his purposes, of both semasiology, which investigates the meaning of linguistic form, and onomasiology, which examines how things and concepts, *ie* reality, are referred to by linguistic form. He suggests that by being able to choose the 'right' word for a context from amongst a number of words of similar meaning the speaker of a language demonstrates the existence of word fields.[15]

We have discussed the fundamentals of Weisgerber's theory of language and have shown how this view of language was complemented by Trier's work. Although he adopted Trier's word field approach, Weisgerber did not neglect other forms of determination (*Bestimmtheit des Inhalts*).[16] The real importance of the word field becomes apparent in the attempts made by Weisgerber and others to apply it to the investigation of syntax.

2.4 The field approach and syntax

2.4.1 *Some general remarks*

For Weisgerber the basic sentence is one important indication of how a language community 'orders' its experience of the world, and many linguists who

can be loosely described as followers of Weisgerber and Trier have devoted
a great deal of research to the identification and analysis of sentence patterns.
Schwarz (Gipper and Schwarz, *Handbuch*, 1962, LXIII *passim*) claims that
wherever the linguist attempts content-structuring (*inhaltliche Gliederung*)
the field approach will be applicable.

2.4.2 *Brinkmann: sentence patterns and classes*
Brinkmann, whose grammar of German *Die deutsche Sprache* is subtitled *Gestalt und Leistung*, identifies four sentence models, each embodying a different
basic way of viewing situation, states and events. Brinkmann (*Deutsche
Sprache*, [2]1971: 522) describes these *Auffassungsweisen* (views of reality) as
follows:

> Ein Sachverhalt wird grammatisch und inhaltlich verschieden gefasst, wenn
> zum Aufschluss verschiedene Wortarten eingesetzt werden ... Mit diesen
> grammatischen Änderungen verbindet sich eine Änderung der Auffassungs-
> weise. Mit diesem Wechsel des Satzmodells wechselt zugleich (auch bei
> gleichbleibendem Wortbestand) der Sinn der Mitteilung für die Kom-
> munikation.
> (A state of affairs is conceived, both grammatically and semantically, in
> different ways according to the different word classes which appear in the
> predicate. These grammatical changes are accompanied by a change in the
> view of reality. When the sentence model changes, the meaning of the
> utterance for communication changes at the same time (even if the same
> words are used).)

He does not follow the same basic principles as the valency grammarians
(see Chapter 4) nor does he attempt to link his four patterns and the four
traditional sentence types (declarative, interrogative, imperative and exclama-
tive), since his patterns are derived from the word classes appearing in the
predicate, not from the basic functions of sentences in discourse (see Brinkmann, [2]1971: XVII and 522). To illustrate Brinkmann's approach we have
taken his own examples ([2]1971: 525).

(i) *Ich lese.*   einseitiger Verbalsatz (one-element verb sentence)
(ii) *Ich habe das Buch gelesen.*   zweiseitiger Verbalsatz (two-element verb
    sentence)
(iii) *Das Buch ist lesenswert.*   Adjektivsatz (adjective sentence)
(iv) *Das Buch ist ein Gesellschaftsroman.*   Substantivsatz (noun sentence).

To each sentence pattern Brinkmann ascribes discrete and complementary
meanings which derive from the class meaning of the word classes which
appear in the predicate. Brinkmann hints at a possible fifth type – the preposition sentence, for example

Das Konzert ist aus.

since although prepositions do not change their form, they do affect changes in nouns and adjectives.[17]

2.4.3 *Erben and syntax*

According to Erben (*Deutsche Grammatik*, 1968: 39) the word classes have complementary functions in discourse, being distinguished both by their syntactic possibilities and their morphological shapes. In addition members of different word classes contribute different 'contents' to a stretch of language: so *Fieber* (fever) is a 'thing' (*Ding*), *fiebern* (to be feverish) an activity (*Tätigkeit*) and *fieberig* (feverish) a quality (*Eigenschaft*) or condition (*Zustand*). Erben illustrates the arbitrariness of the ascription of 'events', 'states' and 'things' to the various word classes by comparing colour words in German, which are largely adjectives, with light-reflection words, which are largely verbs. So we find

Das Wasser ist blau, grün, etc

but

Das Wasser glänzt, leuchtet, etc

although in both cases we are 'describing' what is, objectively speaking, the reflection of light from an object. Erben (1968: 40) refers to *Farbträger* (colour-carriers) and *Glanzsender* (reflection-emitters).

Erben (1968: 115) adopts the definition of sentence plans given by Weisgerber (*Vier Stufen*, 1963: 138): 'die muttersprachlich gegebene Interpretationsrichtung für Erlebnisse und Ausbaurichtung für Gedanken' (the interpretation matrix for experiences and the direction of development for thoughts imposed by the mother tongue), but unlike Brinkmann, Erben (1968: 116–120) incorporates such decisions as declarative or non-declarative sentences, etc in his syntactic programme. Despite the importance which Erben ascribes to the categorial uniqueness of the three major word classes, it is the verb that determines the perspective (*Sichtweise*) of his eleven sentence types.[18] Erben prefers the terms *Satzmuster* (sentence patterns) or *syntaktisches Programm* (syntactic programme) to Weisgerber's *Satzbauplan* (sentence plan) since, in his opinion, it has not been shown that the sentence plans are the basic units of content structure at sentence level (*cf* Erben, *Abriss*,[11] 1972: 266, and Weisgerber, *Ganzheitliche Behandlung*, 1962).

2.5 Other content-oriented linguists

2.5.1 *Glinz*

Of the group of linguists commonly referred to as content-oriented grammarians Glinz is perhaps the one who has shown most interest in the pedagogic application of linguists' grammars. In his early work Glinz criticized the traditional approach to the analysis of the sentence and its constituent parts and regretted the neglect of this area of grammatical description.[19] *Die innere Form des Deutschen* (1952) is Glinz's contribution to a more 'scientific' description of German grammar. It is not, however, a pedagogic grammar, and Glinz's frequent recourses to neologism to avoid using terms with established meanings created confusion when the book first appeared in 1951.[20] In *Ansätze zu einer Sprachtheorie* (1962) Glinz discusses the way in which contents are realized in a language.[21] He attacks etymology for assuming that words (*Wortkörper*) have an original or basic meaning from which other meanings develop or derive, and opposes dictionary-making.[22] Similarly he sees no justification for believing that the phonological shape of a word is in any way a guarantee of its meaning.[23]

2.5.2 *The Duden grammar (Gipper and Grebe)*

In German-speaking countries the *Duden* (*Grammatik*, 1959, [2]1966, [3]1973) is widely regarded as the standard grammar and is appealed to as the arbiter in cases of dispute or doubt. For this reason the editor, Grebe, and the other contributors bear the heavy responsibility of producing a grammar that aims to satisfy the requirements of the layman while taking into account the linguists' insight into the structure of German.

A comparison of the prefaces of the first and third editions reveals a shift in emphasis. In 1959 the grammar was clearly influenced by content-oriented linguistics whereas this is no longer the case in 1973.[24] If we consider Gipper's contribution 'Der Inhalt des Wortes und die Gliederung des Wortschatzes' two differences strike us. Firstly, while still using content-oriented terminology Gipper concedes, in 1973, that any attempt to account for the facts of language must be based upon a grammar which also examines the process of first-language learning. He is willing to accept a broadly transformational approach to language acquisition – he is interested in language as a dynamic force growing in the child (see 2.2.4). Secondly, despite his acquiescence with regard to the transformational approach when it is applied to first-language learning, Gipper rejects the 'feature' approach to semantics ([3]1973: 465–9). We shall have more to say about semantic features in a later chapter.

2.6 Final remarks

If we have given the impression that content-oriented linguistics is more than an attitude to the study of language, this impression must be corrected now. The linguists whose work we have discussed accept the main principles of Weisgerber's and Trier's work but cannot be described as their disciples. Gipper and Schwarz (*Bibliographisches Handbuch*, 1962–6) emphasize the catholicity of the content-oriented approach, which is attested to by many references to the work of earlier scholars and to scholars representative of different theoretical positions.[25]

Since 1963 Weisgerber has added nothing to his theory of language. He has either defended it against attacks or has himself criticized others. He treats transformational-generative linguistics with at times cynical disapproval (see *Zweimal Sprache*, 1973). He does, however, intimate in the same work that his own approach and transformational linguistics are not mutually exclusive since he regards Chomsky as a potential Neo-Humboldtian.[26]

The last ten years have seen declining interest in the content-oriented approach, although the semantics revival in the early seventies has brought content-oriented concepts such as the word field back into focus. The linguistic theories which are the subjects of Chapters 4 to 7 have all gained ground at the expense of content-oriented linguistics, especially amongst younger scholars.

Chapter 3

The functional approach

3.1 General remarks on functional grammar

3.1.1 *Karl Bühler's use of the term function*

In this chapter, we shall present a linguistic theory which views language in a quite different way from *inhaltbezogene Grammatik*. This already becomes apparent if one considers how these linguists approach language. Within a functional model, a sentence like

[1] Würdest du bitte das Fenster aufmachen?

would be analysed in the light of the fact that it is the speaker's aim to direct the action of his interlocutor. If we take vocatives, such as *Brigitte*, it is considered important that they are used to address somebody. Functional grammar looks at sentences in respect of their main purpose, or function, and our examples could be said to function as appeals to somebody else. This is, of course, necessary if any communication is to take place.

But if sentence [1] expressed only this appeal, communication could hardly be successful as the hearer would not be able to tell what was expected of him.[1] And indeed, the utterance goes further than addressing the interlocutor, it contains a number of references to the real world, *das Fenster*, for example, referring to a window in the room the speakers are in, *aufmachen* to a process, etc. It follows from this that another important function of language is to name things and describe processes in the outer world, and also to express certain concepts or ideas present in the speaker's mind. This function is particularly prominent in certain types of statements, especially descriptions and definitions:

[2] In der Fränkischen Schweiz gibt es viele zackige Kalkfelsen.

[3] Unter einem Phonem versteht man die kleinste bedeutungsdifferenzierende Einheit einer Sprache.

A third function of language will have to be introduced if we compare the following sentences:

[1] Würdest du bitte das Fenster aufmachen?
[4] Würde es Ihnen etwas ausmachen, das Fenster zu öffnen?
[5] Mach' doch endlich das Fenster auf!

There is no essential difference in the basic meaning, or purpose, of these sentences – in each case somebody wants a window to be opened – but [1] is a polite request, which (because of the *du*) reflects some kind of familiarity between speaker and hearer, whereas [4] could be regarded as being extremely formal; [5], on the other hand, reveals a rather impatient and demanding attitude on the part of the speaker. Stylistic variations like these reveal some aspects of the situation in which the utterance is made and tell us something about the relationship between speaker and hearer,[2] but they also convey the mood of the speaker and his attitude towards what he is saying. The expression of the speaker's state of mind could be regarded as a further function of utterances.

Similar considerations led K. Bühler (*Sprachtheorie*, 1965: 25–33) to distinguish three basic functions of linguistic signs (*Sprachzeichen*): In his view, they fulfil

(i) A representational function (*Darstellungs- oder Symbolfunktion*) in that they refer to objects and facts of the real world
(ii) A conative function (*Appell- oder Signalfunktion*) in that they appeal to the hearer and determine his behaviour
(iii) An expressive function (*Ausdrucks- oder Symptomfunktion*) in that they express the inner state of the speaker.[3]

It is obvious that these functions never appear alone in an utterance, although one function can be more prominent than the others, as is the case with the conative function in vocatives like *Brigitte* or with the representational function in examples [2] and [3]. But even there the other functions

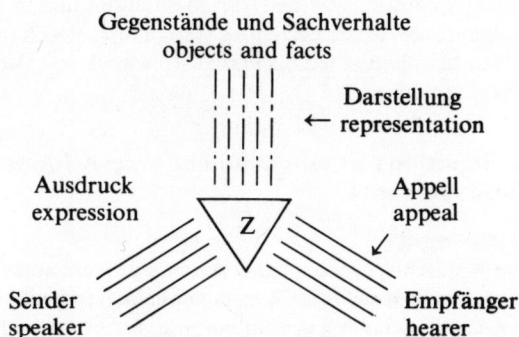

Gegenstände und Sachverhalte
objects and facts

Darstellung
← representation

Ausdruck
expression

Appell
appeal

Z

Sender
speaker

Empfänger
hearer

are also present: the three functions usually appear in combination with each other.[4]

This view of the three functions of the linguistic sign enabled Bühler (1965: 28) to draw the diagram on *p* 25 which he called *Organonmodell*, to show its relation to three non-linguistic components, namely the speaker and the hearer as well as objects and facts of the real world.

3.1.2 *Further developments since Bühler*

These ideas were developed by Bühler in his *Sprachtheorie* of 1934, but it was not until the late fifties that attempts were made to consider language mainly in terms of its functions.[5] This revival of interest in the functional approach in Germany can perhaps be ascribed to a widespread belief at this time that the study of grammar was in a state of crisis. The two schools of linguistics which had set out to overcome the well-known inadequacies of traditional grammar, namely the purely structuralist school and the followers of the early *inhaltbezogene Grammatik*, were not considered to have provided generally satisfying results.[6] The need for new developments in linguistics became particularly apparent in school-teaching, where pre-war grammar books – reintroduced after 1945 – were still being used.

Whilst some linguists, especially content-oriented grammarians, tried to elaborate the models they were using, others saw the necessity of taking a completely different view of language. Making function the central issue of a grammar, so they hoped, would help scholars to see linguistic phenomena in a new light and lead to a theory which could also provide the basis for new methods in German mother-tongue teaching.

In East Germany, one of these theories, the model of functional grammar developed by W. Schmidt, has since achieved considerable importance: W. Schmidt's *Grundfragen der deutschen Grammatik* (1965) has been given the status of an official school book in the German Democratic Republic. For this reason, we will concentrate on Schmidt's work and related approaches in this chapter. It is obvious, however, that the term function has not only been used by those linguists whose work we shall discuss as being representative of functional grammar.[7] We also wish to point out that in Germany this term is often used to characterize a school of linguistics which treats function in the mathematical or logical sense and that their work will also be excluded from the following discussion.[8]

3.2 Macro-functions of language and micro-functions of linguistic elements

3.2.1 *Communicative effect*

One of the basic questions functional grammarians were concerned with in the early sixties was how the process of communication could be described. If a speaker wants to achieve a certain purpose, for example if he wants to direct somebody's behaviour, he has to use a certain MEDIUM[9] (code), a *medium* which in the case of language is the spoken (or written) FORM (form) of an utterance, such as

[1] Würdest du bitte das Fenster aufmachen?
or
[6] Wären Sie so nett, mit dem Rauchen aufzuhören?

Communication could be considered successful if the person addressed acted accordingly, *ie* opened the window or stopped smoking.[10] G. F. Meier (*Zero-Problem*, 1961: 40) has coined the term KOMMUNIKATIVER EFFEKT (communicative effect)[11] for this, a term which is intended to designate any response a form could produce, such as arousing certain emotions, suggesting thoughts or concepts, provoking verbal or non-verbal actions.[12] Meier (1961: 40) then introduces FUNKTION (function) and defines it as 'die beabsichtigte (aus Erfahrung zu erwartende) und normalerweise erzielte kommunikative Leistung (Effekt)', *ie* the communicative effect to be achieved by a certain form.[13]

3.2.2 *The distinction between meaning and function*
So far, we have said that if a speaker wants to achieve a certain communicative effect, he has to use a linguistic form. But communication still could not take place if the speaker and the hearer did not associate the same ideas with that particular form, *ie* if the form did not have a common meaning. We have not yet considered meaning, but it now becomes necessary to draw a clearer distinction between meaning and function.

The two terms can easily be distinguished from each other by regarding form and meaning as essential components of the linguistic sign, whereas function is not a linguistic but an extralinguistic value. This is the way in which Schmidt introduces these terms in his 1969 model, where he adopts de Saussure's 'classic' dichotomy of FORM (*signifiant*) and MEANING (*signifié*) to characterize the linguistic sign: the term form embraces all linguistic phenomena which serve to produce communicative effects[14] and meaning is an abstracted property closely connected to the form in the consciousness of all members of the speech community.[15]

Function, the intended (and in most cases achieved) response by the hearer – the communicative effect – presupposes the meaning of linguistic elements, and is an extralinguistic phenomenon in so far as it is not regarded as part of the linguistic sign; it is a property of the fixed combination of form and meaning.

Taking our example [1], we can use this terminology and distinguish between the form of the utterance, which is the phonetic representation of *Würdest du bitte das Fenster aufmachen?* and the meaning of this utterance, which can be understood by all speakers of German. In a certain situation, the function of an utterance like [1] would be that the speaker makes the hearer understand that he wants the window to be opened, *ie* that he transfers his meaning to him.

This is not much more than saying that the function of the utterance is communication and indeed W. Schmidt ('Theorie', 1969: 149) talks of a *kommunikative Funktion* (communicative function) of the system of language as a whole, which he characterizes as follows: 'Die Funktion des sprachlichen Systems ist es, der Gesellschaft als Mittel der Verständigung und des Gedankenaustausches zu dienen.' (The function of the language system is to serve society as a means of communication and for the exchange of ideas.)

This communicative function is determined by linguistic and extralinguistic factors,[16] namely, on the one hand, by the meaning of the linguistic signs (*semantische Bedingtheit*) and the different structural relations holding between them (*strukturelle Bedingtheit*) and, on the other hand, by the sociological and psychological aspects of the relation between the linguistic signs and the members of the speech community (*pragmatische Bedingtheit*).[17]

The general function of language – to serve communication – can be divided into several subfunctions of linguistic signs (*sprachliche Zeichen*), namely the representational, the conative and the expressive.[18] These, too, are extralinguistic functions and, as in Bühler's model of communication, they only appear in combination with each other. It is important to note that in W. Schmidt's 1969 version function is used to refer to a clearly extralinguistic value, namely the communicative effect, whereas form and meaning are intralinguistic properties. This we can illustrate in the following way:[19]

INTRALINGUISTIC FACTS | EXTRALINGUISTIC EFFECTS

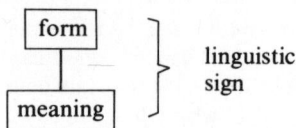

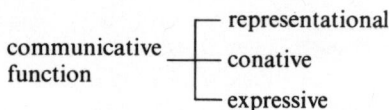

3.2.3 *Extension of the term function*

Communicative function has been defined as the extralinguistic effect to be achieved by a linguistic sign. The question to be considered in this section is whether all linguistic signs are able to carry function. The communicative function of our example

[1] Würdest du bitte das Fenster aufmachen?

is beyond doubt, but would a word like *Fenster* alone also fulfil this function? Certainly not, as if somebody just said *Fenster* his interlocutor would hardly be able to tell what the speaker's intention was; in other words, no communicative effect would be achieved.[20] In W. Schmidt's ('Kategorien', 1969: 522) opinion, communicative functions cannot be attributed to linguistic signs below the level of sentence: 'Sie allein lösen noch keinen Verständigungseffekt im Sinne der gesellschaftlichen Normen aus.'[21] (They do not, on their own, produce a communicative effect in the sense of social norms.)

On the other hand, it might be argued that in this particular sentence, *Fenster* has a function in that it expresses a certain meaning and so helps to create the meaning of the complete sentence, which, again, is necessary for the communicative effect of the utterance. This is quite a different sort of function. In order to avoid any terminological confusion, we introduce our own distinction between MICRO-FUNCTION, to refer to the function of a linguistic element in the creation of more complex linguistic units, and MACRO-FUNCTION, used to characterize Schmidt's communicative function (and its three subfunctions), because these are functions of utterances in an extralinguistic sense. Whereas Schmidt uses (*kommunikative*) *Funktion* only to refer to macro-functions, the use of the term function to refer to both types of function we have distinguished can be found in *Der deutsche Sprachbau* by W. Admoni (*Sprachbau*, ³1970: 4–7).

3.2.4 *Micro-functions*
Micro-functions are fulfilled by words and morphemes, and indeed both by lexical and grammatical morphemes, a distinction which Admoni adopts from traditional grammar. The function of lexical morphemes is to express meaning, whereas grammatical morphemes can have different functions,[22] as the following example may illustrate:

[7] Brigitte hat, obwohl es ihr selbst schon fast zu kalt war, dem Linguisten zuliebe doch das Fenster aufgemacht.

According to Admoni (*Sprachbau*, ³1970: 4), grammatical morphemes fulfil two functions:

(i) A semantic function in that they express a generalized meaning content (*abstrahierten Bedeutungsgehalt*): for example the notion of 'beneficiary' is expressed by the dative (*dem Linguisten*) and the time relation is made clear by the tense.
(ii) A structural function: the discontinuous morpheme of the present perfect tense (*hat* + participle auf*gemacht*) holds the whole sentence together.

3.3 The tasks of a functional grammar

Our outline of the theories of Schmidt and Admoni has shown that the term function can be used either in the sense of what we have called micro-functions, namely the function of a linguistic element within a structure, or to denote macro-functions, *ie* the extralinguistic functions of the language system as a whole.[23] The use of function in the first sense is quite common in linguistics and investigation of both micro- and macro-functions has not only been undertaken by W. Schmidt and Admoni, indeed it was the Prague School which gave considerable impetus to the functional approach towards language.

When discussing 'the achievements and merits of the Early Prague School',

J. Vachek ('Prague School', 1972: 12–14) refers to 'the most essential of all (which is) ... the emphasis put on the function performed by the language in the given speech community ... This approach visualizes language as a tool performing a number of essential functions or tasks in the community using it. The most outstanding (and the most obvious) among these tasks is obviously the communicative function, serving the needs and wants of the mutual understanding of individual members of the given language community.'

Function is here used in a sense similar to that used by W. Schmidt and G. F. Meier, and the early Prague linguists[24] also certainly represented an attitude to linguistics quite different from the rigorously distributional approach of Bloomfieldian structuralism. This understanding of linguistics as a science within the orbit of the social sciences is still strong among the younger generation of Czech linguists and in the more recent work of Halliday and his co-workers. Like the early Prague linguists, Halliday has used Bühler's model as a basis for the differentiation of the functions (macro-functions) of speech utterances.[25] The link with the social sciences is revealed by Halliday's ('Functional basis' 1973: 23) fundamental concern: 'Is the social functioning of language reflected in linguistic structure – that is, in the internal organization of language as a system?'.

Following up Halliday's question means applying the knowledge of the macro-functions of language to the analysis of linguistic structure with respect to the context of situation. This indeed seems to be the most important task of functional grammar, but it must be said that the works of W. Schmidt and Admoni have contributed very little to this discussion. Schmidt's theoretical considerations in his *Grundfragen der deutschen Grammatik* stand quite apart from his actual treatment of grammatical problems, which is not fundamentally different from the work done by other grammarians, for example Brinkmann or Admoni.[26]

Admoni, who demands a polydimensional approach to language, is aware of the necessity of considering extralinguistic factors in the description of linguistic structure. 'Die kommunikative Funktion der Rede verlangt, dass Klarheit und Gliederung des Satzaufbaus sich mit Biegsamkeit und beträchtlicher Beweglichkeit verbinden.' ('The communicative function of discourse requires that the clarity and the structuring of the sentence be contrived with flexibility and considerable mobility.')[27] At various points in his grammar, Admoni attempts to integrate the influence of these extralinguistic factors without having demonstrated in what way the structure of an utterance is determined by its discourse function.[28]

It must be admitted that so far no grammar has been written which has consistently applied the principles of the functional approach to the description of a language.[29] Nevertheless the theoretical ground for such a grammar has been prepared: its task would be to show how the function of an utterance and the context of situation in which it is used determine the structure of that utterance, in other words, to explain why people say what they say in the form in which they say it.[30] The work of G. F. Meier, W. Schmidt and Admoni, and perhaps even more so, the work of Halliday,[31] have made it clear that such a functional theory of language falls within the scope both of a theory of meaning and of a theory of sociolinguistics.

Chapter 4

Valency and sentence patterns in dependency grammar

4.1 General remarks on dependency grammar

The basic principle of dependency grammar is the view that a sentence does not merely consist of the semantic information of its lexical items and their linear order, but that another important constitutive feature has to be incorporated into the theory of syntax: it is assumed that the elements of a sentence stand in certain dependency relations to each other, which are part of an underlying hierarchical structure.[1] In 4.4.1 we shall show that these dependencies can be looked upon as co-occurrence relations, because the occurrence of one element is dependent on (or presupposes) the occurrence of another element. Formally, these dependencies or interdependencies between the different elements are often represented in so-called stemmas:[2]

[1] Ute trinkt gerne einen erlesenen Cognac.

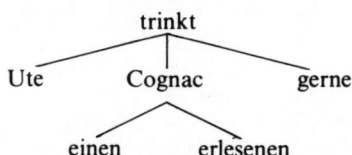

trinkt
Ute   Cognac   gerne
einen   erlesenen

This stemma shows that some elements are to be taken as being dependent on others. So *trinkt* is the governing element (or REGENS) of *Ute, einen erlesenen Cognac* and *gerne*, which are DEPENDENTES, but *Cognac* also governs *einen* and *erlesenen*. These structural relations, as well as the semantic content of the different elements, make up sentence [1].

An important difference from transformational grammar, where the initial symbol of the tree is S (sentence), is that in most cases dependency grammar takes the finite verb as the highest unit of the hierarchy. This has also been done in predicate logic[3] and there are good linguistic reasons for doing so as the verb occurs in a relatively restricted number of syntactic positions and plays a central role in the sentence, but to some extent the choice of the initial symbol is arbitrary.[4] The same is true of the character of the assumed dependency relations, where, as will be seen later, interdependencies and pure dependencies between elements must be distinguished.

It is important to note, however, that the traditional distinction between subject and predicate (which entails a distinction between subject and object) has been rejected by dependency grammar partly because this distinction is considered to be based on a principle imported into linguistics from formal logic, but also for linguistic reasons: thus, for example, a special rank for the subject among the dependents hides the principle of the conversion mechanism of active into passive sentences and vice versa. It has also been realized that some sentences need, in addition to subject and verb, other elements (traditionally called objects and adverbs) in order to be complete; this is a further argument for the abolition of the subject–object distinction. (Compare Heringer, *Theorie*, 1970: 18, Stötzel, *Verhältnis*, 1970: 119, and Brinker, *Modelle*, 1977: 79–80, 98–9).

The idea of dependency grammar has been strongly influenced by the French structuralist L. Tesnière, who started working in this field in 1934 and whose *Éléments de syntaxe structurale* (published posthumously in 1959) provides a comprehensive analysis of French and German within the framework of a dependency model. It seems worth mentioning, however, that the central ideas of dependency grammar – taking the verb as the structural centre of the sentence and assuming dependency relations between the elements – had been put forward before Tesnière by Meiner in the eighteenth century and later by Behaghel, Bühler, Neumann and others (see Engelen, *Untersuchungen*, 1975: 37). But Tesnière's influence should not be underestimated as he was the first to provide a technical apparatus for dependency grammar, the critical discussion of which has given new impetus to the work of many other linguists. This chapter is intended to give a short survey of work done using the framework of dependency grammar, concentrating on the theories of valency and sentence patterns developed in Germany.

4.2 Valency theory

4.2.1 *The notion of valency*
The prominent position of the verb in many dependency models can be justified by the fact that it largely determines the structure of the whole sentence, as the following considerations show:

[2] Ute schläft.
[3] Ute besucht den Linguisten.
[4] Der Linguist gewöhnt Ute das Rauchen ab.

None of the parts of these sentences can be deleted:

[2]a *schläft.
[3]a *Ute besucht.
[4]a *Der Linguist gewöhnt Ute ab.
[4]b *Der Linguist gewöhnt ab.

Although [2] to [4] each represent a structural minimum, between one and three dependents are needed to form a complete sentence. We may regard it as a property of the verb to require a number of syntactic positions in a sentence. This feature has become known under the name of VALENCY.

The idea is already present in Bühler's (*Sprachtheorie*, 1965: 173) writings, when he says: '... dass die Wörter einer Wortklasse eine oder mehrere Leerstellen um sich eröffnen, die durch Wörter anderer Wortklassen ausgefüllt werden müssen.' ('... that the words of a word class open up one or several positions in their syntactic environment, which have to be filled by words of other word classes.') The term valency was introduced into linguistic theory by Tesnière, who took it from chemistry, and it is used widely today, but in some cases without being defined exactly.[5]

Brinkmann has used VALENZ to describe the character of verbs in relation to other parts of the sentence, classifying German verbs into eight classes, which are determined by the way the syntactic positions are occupied.[6] Whereas Tesnière and Brinkmann talked of valency, Erben has coined the term WERTIGKEIT to refer to the structural relations of the verb. He distinguishes monovalent, divalent, trivalent and tetravalent verbs and takes this theory as the basis of a distinction of four different basic types of sentence patterns in German.[7]

Usually valency is regarded as a verb-specific property, but some linguists prefer to attribute it to all word classes, *eg*. Admoni with his FÜGUNGSPO-TENZEN.[8] Very often valency is used in the rather vague sense in which it has so far been introduced, but it is obvious that for a serious treatment of the problem the term must be further elaborated.

4.2.2 *Different kinds of valency*

We must now consider whether the necessity of completion is a structural, semantic or communicative one.

[5] Ute kennt ihn.   [6] Ute freut sich.
[5]a *Ute kennt.   [6]a *Ute freut.

Despite the similarity between [5] and [6], there is an important difference between the elements *sich* and *ihn*, as can be seen from [5]a and [6]a. [6]a is ungrammatical, but the semantic information is obvious: the *sich* has to be added for purely syntactical reasons and is predictable, whereas [5]a is incomplete both on the levels of structure and content; we could also find:

[5]b Ute kennt sie/den Professor/etc.

These considerations lead to the distinction between valency on the structural or syntactic level and valency on the semantic level.

The STRUCTURAL VALENCY (SYNTAKTISCHE VALENZ) of a verb determines the number of complements it requires to form a grammatical sentence. So verbs like *schlafen* could be described as monovalent; *besuchen, freuen* and *kennen* are syntactically divalent and *abgewöhnen* is an example of a trivalent verb.

The SEMANTIC VALENCY (INHALTLICHE VALENZ) refers to the necessity of completion on the level of content. It is made up by the possibility of opposition and is determinable by questions:[9]

[5]c Wer kennt ihn?	[6]c Wer freut sich?
[5]d Wen kennt Ute?	[6]d *Wen freut Ute?

With many verbs there is no difference between structural and semantic valency, but with some reflexive verbs (the so-called implicit reflexives like *sich freuen* and *sich begnügen*)[10] the semantic valency is less than the structural. A problem is presented by the so-called impersonal verbs like *es regnet*, where the semantic valency is definitely 0, but it can be argued that they are either syntactically monovalent or avalent, because the syntactic position is always occupied by the same element *es*.[11] Whereas with Tesnière it is unclear whether he is concerned with structural or semantic valency, this distinction has been made more explicitly in most of the more recent treatments of the question, especially by Helbig and Heringer.

A different definition of valency has been attempted by applying methods of relational logic and defining a LOGICAL VALENCY. This approach, however, does not play a great part in the linguistic analysis of individual languages, but some linguists have argued that logical valency may be found fruitful for the comparison of languages on a universal basis.[12]

4.2.3 *The character of the dependents*
This section will be mainly concerned with the further analysis of structural valency, in particular with the character of the dependents. Most theories of grammar have recognized that not all dependent elements have the same function or status in a sentence:

[7]   Ute besucht den Linguisten morgen in London.
[7]a Ute besucht den Linguisten morgen.
[7]b Ute besucht den Linguisten in London.
[7]c Ute besucht den Linguisten.
[7]d *Ute besucht morgen in London.
[7]e *besucht den Linguisten morgen in London.

The dependents show a different degree of cohesiveness to the verb: the deletion of *morgen* and *in London* does not affect the grammaticality of the sentence, whereas *Ute* and *den Linguisten* are essential. The latter will (using

Tesnière's terms) be called ACTANTS, the former CIRCONSTANTS. Note that this distinction is based on structural necessity and that *morgen* and *in London* can be essential elements from a communicative point of view in certain contexts.[13]

The problem we are confronted with is that of finding exact criteria by which to distinguish *actants* and *circonstants*. Tesnière characterizes *actants* as being directly involved in the action described by the verb. Syntactically, their number is determined by the valency of the governing verb and (in French) they can be realized as subjects, accusative or dative objects. For him all other constituents are accounted *circonstants*, which give the circumstances under which an action takes place and there are no restrictions on their occurrence. Helbig has shown, however, that when a distinction between *actants* and *circonstants* is made according to purely structural criteria, it becomes necessary to include also other constituents in the list of possible *actants*: prepositional cases (Ute schreibt *auf der Schreibmaschine*), predicatives, some necessary adverbials, subordinate clauses and infinitive constructions.[14]

But the setting up of precise structural criteria presents considerable difficulty.[15] Potential deletability is insufficient as a characterization of *circonstants*, since in sentences like

[8] Ute trinkt gerne Frankenwein

both *gerne* and *Frankenwein* are deletable, although *gerne* is definitely less closely related to the verb than is *Frankenwein*, which is part of the structural plan of *trinken*. Heringer treats these cases – his own example is *Emil singt* (*ein Lied*) – as ellipses and suggests characterizing *circonstants* as constituents that can be added to any sentence of a language (provided they are compatible with its general semantic structure), while *actants* can only co-occur with a very limited number of verbs and therefore are not freely addable (*frei hinzufügbar*):[16]

[2]*b* Ute schläft gerne/in London/...
[2]*c* *Ute schläft Frankenwein/den Linguisten/...

Following Helbig's terminology, we can now distinguish between

(i)   OBLIGATORY ACTANTS, which cannot be deleted (in our examples: *Ute, den Linguisten*),
(ii) OPTIONAL ACTANTS, which can be deleted, but not easily added to other sentences (*Frankenwein, ein Lied*) and
(iii) CIRCONSTANTS, which can be deleted and added (*gerne, morgen, in London*).[17]

4.2.4 *Valency dictionaries*

If the valency theory is to supply an apparatus of rules for generating all the correct sentences of a language (and if it is to supply useful information for the foreign learner of a language), it not only has to state the number of obligatory and optional *actants* a verb can take, but also to describe them – either morphologically or semantically. The first attempt at this was the *Wörterbuch zur Valenz und Distribution deutscher Verben* by Helbig and Schenkel in Leipzig, which appeared in 1968. In 1975, Engelen published his *Untersuchungen zu Satzbauplan und Wortfeld* and in the following year Engel and Schumacher presented their *Kleines Valenzlexikon deutscher Verben*, which is the first of a series of valency dictionaries to be provided by the Mannheim school.[18] (See 4.2.5.)

Helbig and Schenkel distinguish three stages of description: stage I is concerned with the number of *actants* a verb takes, stage II with their cases and stage III with the semantic features of the *actants*. Stage I simply gives the valency of the verb, listing the number of obligatory and optional *actants* separately. Stage II describes the syntactic quality of the *actants* in purely formal (or morphological) terms like Sn, Sa, Sd, Sg ('Substantiv im Nominativ, Akkusativ, Dativ, Genitiv', noun in the nominative, etc), pS ('präpositionales Substantiv', prepositional noun), NS ('Nebensatz', subordinate clause), I (infinitive without *zu*), Inf (infinitive with *zu*), Adj (adjective), etc. The semantic specification of these *actants* is provided in stage III, where Helbig and Schenkel (*Wörterbuch*, 1968: 125) make use of such features as Hum (human), Anim (animate).[19] As an illustration of this we will take the verb *trinken*:

I trinken $_{I} + (_I) = 2$
II trinken → Sn, (Sa/pS)
III Sn → Hum (*Der Verunglückte* trinkt.)
Sa → – Anim (flüssig) (Er trinkt *Milch*.)
p = von
pSd → Anim (Er trinkt *von der Milch*.)

As the valency dictionary lists the distribution of 500 German verbs, it is an important aid to research into the German verb system, especially into problems of homonymy and synonymy, where the distribution of the verbs is of great interest. Helbig points out that it can also be usefully applied in teaching German as a foreign language, as much interference occurs in the field of verb valency.[20]

4.2.5 *A theory of sentence patterns*
Valency theory considers an adequate description of the simple sentence to be the first and necessary step towards a more comprehensive theory of syntax, which will, in its turn, provide the basis for the study of the meaning of sentences. The same assumptions were made at about the same time both by Helbig and Heringer, who were independently of each other elaborating the notion of valency, and by Engel working at the *Institut für deutsche Sprache*

in Mannheim. Engel's approach had a slightly different emphasis, his aim being to establish basic sentence patterns for German.[21]

Engel's analysis of the different sentence elements (*Satzglieder*)[22] also leads to the distinction between *actants* (*Ergänzungen*) and *circonstants* (*Angaben*). As the *circonstants* are not necessary for the grammaticality of the sentence, only the *actants* occur in the basic sentence patterns, because they have sentence-constitutive character. For the establishment of sentence patterns it is necessary, however, to distinguish between different kinds of *actants* and the following classification can be set up:[23]

0	nominative object (subject)	5	stative adverbial
1	accusative object	6	directional adverbial
2	genitive object		
3	dative object	7	identifying complement
4	prepositional object	8	attributive complement

Although elements 5 and 6 are specified semantically and 7 and 8 are characterized by referential identity (*Ute ist eine nette Studentin. Ute fühlt sich müde.*), the classification has been made on purely syntactic grounds. The syntactic behaviour of these elements has been analysed following a number of syntactic transformation tests devised by Engelen (*Untersuchungen*, 1975: 90). Quite simple criteria can be found to distinguish elements 0 to 6 from each other, namely tests using question elements or pro-forms:[24]

Question element	*Pro-form*
1 wer/was	pronouns in the nominative
2 wen/was	pronouns in the accusative
3 wessen	pronouns in the genitive
4 wem	pronouns in the dative
5 wo(r) + preposition	da(r) + preposition (*eg: darauf*)
6 wo, wie lange, wann	da/dort, so lange, dann
wohin	dahin/dorthin

These tests reveal the different character of the elements *in Nürnberg* and *nach Nürnberg* as stative or directional adverbials in:

[9]   Ute wohnt *in Nürnberg*.   [10]   Ute fährt *nach Nürnberg*.
[9]a *Wo* wohnt Ute?   [10]a *Wo* fährt Ute?[25]
[9]b *Wohin* wohnt Ute?   [10]b *Wohin* fährt Ute?
[9]c Ute wohnt *dort*.   [10]c *Ute fährt *dort*.
[9]d *Ute wohnt *dorthin*.   [10]d Ute fährt *dorthin*.

This syntactic classification of the *actants* enables Engel to represent sentence patterns (*Satzbaupläne*) in the form of code numbers, which consist of the numbers of all constitutive elements. Both obligatory and optional *actants* are listed, but optional *actants* are put in brackets. So our sentence

[11]   Der Linguist gewöhnt Ute hoffentlich das Rauchen ab.

belongs to the sentence pattern with the code number 013, as it contains a nominative object (0: *Der Linguist*), a dative object (3: *Ute*), an accusative object (1: *das Rauchen*), and a *circonstant* (*hoffentlich*), which does not influence the sentence pattern. Our other examples are given the following numbers:[26]

0   Ute schläft.
01   Ute besucht den Linguisten morgen in London. Ute kennt ihn.
0(1) Ute trinkt gerne einen erlesenen Cognac.
013 Der Linguist gewöhnt Ute hoffentlich das Rauchen ab.
0(4) Ute schreibt auf der Schreibmaschine.
05   Ute wohnt in Nürnberg.
06   Ute fährt nach Nürnberg.
07   Ute ist eine nette Studentin.
08   Ute fühlt sich müde.

A comprehensive list provides about thirty different sentence patterns for German. The number of elements has been restricted to three in the simple sentence as more complex sentences can easily be derived from the basic patterns. The so-called *Ausbaupläne* (extension plans) account for cases where the place of an *actant* is taken by a clause,[27] as in

[12] Der Linguist weiss nicht, ob er Ute das Rauchen abgewöhnen kann.

So far the theory of sentence patterns provides a technical way of stating the valency of a verb and the syntactic function of its *actants* (0–8), but as in the valency theory syntactically relevant semantic features can be incorporated in the theory.[28]

The fact that all the sentences of a language can be derived from a number of basic sentence patterns must not lead us to forget that the sentence pattern itself is a purely abstract concept in so far as it is a result of the idealization of data. It does not give any information about word order, the mood of a sentence (declarative, interrogative etc), or variation of conjugation. So all of the following belong to the sentence pattern 01 (see also 15.3):

[7]   Ute besucht den Linguisten morgen in London.
[7]*f* Besucht Ute den Linguisten?
[7]*g* Ute hat den Linguisten besucht.

4.2.6 *Sentence patterns and valency theory*

We have seen that the theory of sentence patterns and the valency theory choose the same approach towards the description of language. Their structural analysis of the simple sentence starts with the verb and leads to a distinction of obligatory and optional *actants*, which are closely related to the verb, and *circonstants*, which are not constitutive elements of the sentence. Both theories then realize the need to take account of semantic features. As there is no great difference in the principles they adopt nor in the results they achieve, the models of valency and sentence patterns can be treated as compatible theories and indeed Heringer ('Wertigkeiten', 1967 and 'Analyse', 1970) has indicated how a valency theory can be expanded into a theory of sentence patterns.

The differences between the two models are mainly terminological. Helbig classifies *schlafen* as a monovalent verb, which demands a noun in the nominative (Sn), whereas Engel would say that it can occur in sentence pattern 0. Combining both terminologies, we will describe verbs like *schlafen* as V_0, *besuchen* as V_{01}, *trinken* as $V_{0(1)}$, etc. It will be the concern of the next section to outline a comprehensive theory of syntax along the same lines as the theories of valency and sentence patterns.

4.3 A model of dependency grammar

4.3.1 *Valency as a dependency relation*
We now ought to consider the character of the classification of verbs we set up in the previous section. Saying that a verb belongs to the V_{01} class means that whenever this verb occurs, a nominative *actant* (*Ergänzung* E_0) and an accusative *actant* (E_1) will occur as well.[29] Therefore statements about the valency of a verb are statements about the co-occurrence relations of this verb with certain types of *actants*. We state if-then relations: if V_0 (*schlafen*) occurs, E_0 must occur as well (for instance, *Ute*); if V_{01} occurs, then E_0 and E_1 must occur. These co-occurrence relations are called DEPENDENCIES.[30]

The valency and sentence pattern theories are mainly concerned with the verb and its complements, but DEPENDENCY GRAMMAR – a grammar which makes dependency one of the principles of structural description – must also account for the relations between other linguistic elements, for instance, between adjectives and nouns.[31] But for which linguistic elements can dependency relations be claimed?

The collocations between particular lexical items, as well as idiomatic phrases are not relevant to a theory of syntax, they belong to the field of semantics. Dependency grammar deals with the relations between different syntactic categories. A stemma like

schläft

|

Ute

does not mean that the lexical item *Ute* presupposes the lexical item *schläft*, but that both words stand as examples of syntactic categories. The stemma could also be written as:

V_0

|

E_0

The syntactic categories between which such dependencies are assumed must always be of the same level. So we can state dependency relations between morphemes, or between words, or classes or strings of such elements.

This is the view of dependency that has been adopted by Heringer (*Theorie*, 1970; *Syntax*, 1970) and Engel ('Bemerkungen', 1972) and in the following discussion the term will be used in this sense, namely to denote a co-occurrence relation between linguistic elements of the same level.

4.3.2 Different kinds of dependency

The dependency relations between different syntactic categories may differ in character, as is illustrated by the following example: A V_0 verb (*schlafen*) demands the occurrence of a nominative *actant* (E_0) (*Ute*), but not vice versa, as the nominative *actant* can also co-occur with other classes of verbs, *eg* V_{01} verbs (*Ute besucht den Linguisten*). An attempt to formalize these differences has been made by Engel (1972: 142–4), who suggests the following symbolism:[32]

$A \rightarrow B$: A occurs only in the presence of B, but B can also co-occur with other elements. This is the relationship between V_0 and E_0, which has been described above:

$$V_0$$
$$\downarrow$$
$$E_0$$

A noun and its morpheme for case and number are another example of this relation. The nominative morpheme n_0 demands a noun N, whereas N can also co-occur with other case morphemes, such as n_1 (accusative).

$$n_0$$
$$\downarrow$$
$$N$$

$A \leftarrow B$: B can only occur if A appears, but does not necessarily occur at all. This type of dependency represents the relation between article and noun: the article can never occur without a noun, but the noun does not always occur with the article.[33]

$$N$$
$$\uparrow$$
$$Art$$

This example shows the arbitrariness of the direction of the arrows, because instead of saying that the noun is a necessary condition for the article, we could also say that the article was a sufficient condition for the occurrence of the noun and state the following dependency:[34]

Art
↓
N

A↔B: A and B only occur together. This relation is called INTERDEPEN-
DENCY. This is the relation between the morphemes of case and
number with the finite verb and the 'subject':

[13]a   *Der* Linguist forsch*t*.
[13]b   *Die* Linguist*en* forsch*en*.
[13]c   **Die* Linguist*en* forsch*t*.

A→ B: The occurrence of A permits the occurrence of B, but does not demand
it. B can also occur in other contexts. The verb takes this relation to
all optional elements, *circonstants (Angaben* like *gerne)* and optional
actants:

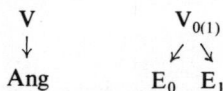

V $V_{0(1)}$
↓   ↙ ↘
Ang E_0 E_1

4.3.3 *A model of dependency grammar*

The discussion of the Helbig and Schenkel valency dictionary and Engelen's
sentence patterns has already shown that a purely structural analysis is not
sufficient. This has also been taken account of by Engel (1972), who incorporates syntactically relevant semantic features in his stemmas:

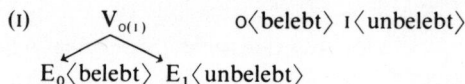

(1) $V_{0(1)}$ o⟨belebt⟩ 1⟨unbelebt⟩
        E_0⟨belebt⟩ E_1⟨unbelebt⟩

The above stemma could be taken as a representation of sentences like

[14] Ute trinkt Frankenwein/einen Cognac/etc.
[15] Die Studentinnen essen Äpfel/eine grosse Mahlzeit/etc.[35]

The place of an *actant* could also be taken by a subordinate clause, for
example (compare Engelen's extension plans in 4.2.5):

[16] Wer guten Wein schätzt, trinkt Frankenwein.

Stemma (1) provides a structural description on the level of sentence elements (*Satzglieder*), but it is also possible, on a deeper level of analysis, to
draw a diagram of the dependencies of the different morphemes of sentence
[14]. We then have to introduce the following categories:

As in transformational grammar, an auxiliary complex (aux) is necessary
to contain the tense, person and number morphemes of the verb V.[36] In
example [14] *Ute trinkt einen Cognac* the auxiliary complex carries present

tense and singular numbers, which in the case of *trinken* are realized by the addition of a *t* to the stem.[37]

The aux presupposes a verb V (V←aux), but in order to make clear that its occurrence is not restricted to $V_{o(1)}$ verbs, a relational indicator X has to be applied in our stemma:

$$V_{o(1)}$$
$$\uparrow$$
$$\ast$$
$$\text{aux}$$

The nominative *actant* E_0 is *Ute*, which consists of the nominative singular morpheme n_0 of the noun and the stem of the noun N.[38]

$$n_0$$
$$E_0 = \downarrow$$
$$N$$

Accordingly, E_1 in our example (*einen Cognac*) represents a complex of four morphemes: n_1 (the accusative singular morpheme of the noun), N (the stem of the noun), art_1 (the accusative morpheme of the article), and Art (the article). As art_1 and Art are related in the same way as n_1 and N are, and the occurrence of the article morpheme (*art*) is only possible in the presence of a morpheme *n*, the dependency relations between the four morphemes are as follows:[39]

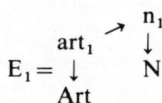

$$\begin{array}{ccc} & & n_1 \\ & art_1 \nearrow & \downarrow \\ E_1 = & \downarrow & N \\ & Art & \end{array}$$

These changes enable us to draw the more detailed stemma (II) for the sentence

[14] Ute trinkt einen Cognac.

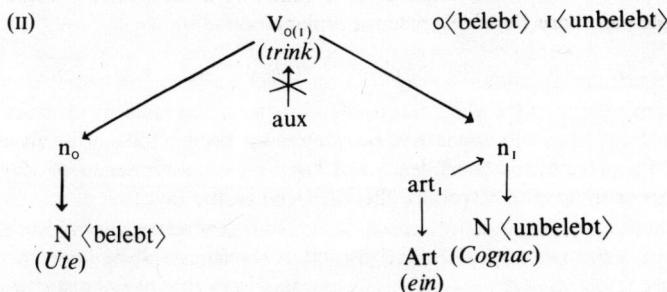

(II) $V_{o(1)}$ o⟨belebt⟩ 1⟨unbelebt⟩
                         (*trink*)
                         $\ast$
                         aux

       n_0 n_1
       $\downarrow$ $art_1 \nearrow$ $\downarrow$

    N ⟨belebt⟩ $\downarrow$ N ⟨unbelebt⟩
     (*Ute*)   Art (*Cognac*)
                                           (*ein*)

A stemma of this kind is a way of demonstrating the dependencies between the morphemes of a sentence and it establishes a hierarchy of the elements, in which the verb is the governing element.[40] Dependency relations have thus been made the basic principle of a structural description of syntax. The position of a dependent element in the stemma not only shows its relation to other elements, but also allows statements to be made about its syntactic function: E_0 is the 'subject', etc.

If a structural description of this kind is to be regarded as the base component of a transformational grammar, it has to produce linear chains. This Engel's model does by the application of projection rules.

$$N + n_0 \quad + \quad V_{o(1)} \; + \; aux \; + \; Art + art_1 \; + \; N + n_1$$
$$\text{Ute} \quad / \quad \text{trink} \quad \text{t} \quad / \quad \text{ein} \quad \text{en} \; / \; \text{Cognac}$$

This chain resembles the surface structure of the actual sentence, but nevertheless the introduction of transformational rules will be needed for the generation of more complex sentences.[41]

4.4 The role of dependency grammar in present-day linguistics

The illustration of Engel's model has shown that dependency can be made the basic principle of a theory of syntax which is able to satisfy several important demands made of a grammar: it provides structural descriptions of sentences, states syntactic functions and produces linear chains. A dependency grammar does not, however, have to take the form of Engel's model. Since Tesnière, various attempts have been made to follow up his ideas and to overcome the inadequacies of his *Eléments de syntaxe structurale*. In America, Gaifman and Hays[42] have discussed dependency as a principle of linguistic description, but it was probably Heringer's clear definition of the term dependency as a co-occurrence relation which provided the basis for further investigation in this field (the elaboration of Engel's model for example). Engel (1972: 115) describes dependency grammar as a '... Sprachtheorie, die darauf beruht, Kategorien gleichen Ranges in spezifischen Relationen darzustellen.' ('linguistic theory which is based on the principle of representing categories of the same level in specific relations.') In Engel's view dependency is one way of attributing structural descriptions to sentences, but not the only possible way. He prefers it to other principles because of the great explanatory value of dependency grammar in revealing relations between the actual elements of a sentence.

However, although dependency has received growing attention in recent years, the principle of dependency had long been ignored by many linguists of other schools. The reason for this may well be the fact that even amongst the adherents of dependency schools there is no general agreement about the place of dependency relations in a grammar. Heringer and Baumgärtner, for instance, look upon dependency as an essential principle of linguistic description, but hold that it is, in itself, insufficient.[43] They claim that a dependency system has to be supported by a constituency system and that phrase structure grammar and dependency grammar are complementary components of a grammar and not, as Engel would say, alternative ways of describing syntax. Both Heringer and Baumgärtner have developed their own theories of grammar, which, however, differ considerably.[44]

This is perhaps the great weakness of dependency schools. All proposals for the integration of dependency in a comprehensive theory of syntax have been made rather tentatively and none of them has been widely accepted as a standard theory, as Chomsky's version of TG was in the late sixties. More recent work that has been published is mainly concerned with the question of how to make dependency relations part of an underlying structure in trans-formational grammar. Here the work of Robinson and Vater is worth men-tioning; they have tried to establish a valency-based deep structure, which shows some similarities to Fillmore's case grammar. But again, these should be treated as tentative proposals rather than as self-contained theories. It must also be noted that there is some controversy amongst adherents of dependency grammar as to whether dependency is a useful principle for the representation of the deep structure of a transformational grammar or whether dependency grammar as such presents an alternative to transformational grammar. This is the view advocated by Hudson (*Arguments*, 1976), who has further de-veloped the dependency approach in his model of daughter-dependency grammar.[45]

The only part of dependency grammar which has so far been successfully applied to linguistic description and used as a research tool is the valency theory. Here, the approaches of Helbig and Heringer and the large-scale pro-jects of the Mannheim school (Engel and Schumacher) can be regarded as a generally accepted model which has provided the basis for work in pedagogic grammar and foreign language pedagogy (compare 4.2.4), as well as for theoretical research, which may indeed lead to the establishment of a standard valency theory.

Recommended further reading

Tesnière's work has only been outlined in so far as his ideas have influenced linguistic theories of interest for our subject. Critical introductions to his theory can be found in most of the works on valency quoted, but see especially Heringer (*Theorie*, 1970 and 'Analyse', 1970), Stötzel (*Verhältnis*, 1970), Engelen (*Untersuchungen*, 1975) and Brinker (*Modelle*, 1977). The most de-tailed explanation of Tesnière's notions of *connexion*, *junction* and *translation* is in Baumgärtner ('Spracherklärung', 1965).

Valency theory. For a discussion of the methodological questions we recom-mend the articles by Heringer. In 'Wertigkeiten' (1967) he discusses the prob-lem of logical valency, which he thinks important for linguistic research in

the fields of meaning description, translation and onomasiology. Helbig has
published many articles on valency (most of them in the journal *Deutsch als
Fremdsprache*), but a good summary of his ideas is to be found in the preface
of Helbig and Schenkel (*Wörterbuch*, 1968). For a treatment of special problems of valency theory see the articles in Helbig (ed, *Beiträge*, 1971) and Schumacher (ed, *Untersuchungen*, 1976). The work of the Mannheim school of
linguists is best represented by the works by Engel and Schumacher. For possible applications of the valency theory in teaching German as a foreign language, see especially Heringer ('Analyse', 1970) and Helbig and Schenkel
(*Wörterbuch*, 1968: 76).

Engelen (*Untersuchungen*, 1975) is a very interesting contribution to the
analysis of the German verb system. As an introduction to dependency
grammar we recommend Engel ('Bemerkungen', 1972), where he discusses
Baumgärtner and Heringer and suggests his own alternative. Baumgärtner
('Konstituenz', 1970) is a theoretical discussion of the principles of constituency and dependency (see also Brinker, *Modelle*, 1977). Heringer (*Theorie*,
1970) presents a very complicated model of syntax, which consists of a dependency component and a constituency component as well as an *Inhaltssyntax*.
Even if one does not adopt his formalization, it is worthwhile reading his discussion of the grammatical categories of German. The problem of TG and
its relation to dependency grammar is treated in Vater 'Model', 1973; in
greater detail, *Subjekt- und Objektsätze*, 1973) and also by Helbig ('Valenz',
1969).

Maas ('Dependenztheorie', 1974) presents a critical discussion of various
approaches of dependency grammar, not only concentrating on German contributions.

American and British linguists have dealt with problems similar to valency,
see especially Fillmore ('Case', 1968), Halliday ('Language Structure', 1970)
and Hudson (*Arguments*, 1976). Compare also the approach taken in the *Dictionary of Contemporary English* (ed P. Proctor, Longman, 1978).

Chapter 5

Pragmalinguistics

5.1 General remarks on pragmalinguistics

5.1.1 *The pragmatic aspect of linguistic analysis*

Most theories of language which we have discussed so far, including the *inhaltbezogene Grammatik* and the *Dependenzgrammatik*, are either theories of SEMANTICS, of SYNTAX, or a combination of both. The dependency model has clearly illustrated that a comprehensive treatment of syntax will also involve considering semantic factors. However, if we consider linguistics to be one branch of SEMIOTICS, *ie* the general theory of signs, then the analysis of the linguistic sign cannot be restricted to SYNTAX and SEMANTICS. The standard semiotic theories of Morris (*Foundations*, 1938) and Carnap (*Introduction*, 1942), for instance, suggest a threefold division of the analysis of the sign into SYNTAX, SEMANTICS, and PRAGMATICS. Brekle (*Semantik*, 1972: 23) adopts this distinction and applies it to the analysis of the linguistic sign, describing the three aspects as follows:

 (i) SYNTAX is mainly concerned with the coordination and linear ordering of different signs, *ie* it investigates the relation of a sign to other signs in an utterance.

 (ii) SEMANTICS studies the meaning of a sign, *ie* the relation between the sign and those objects, processes, etc of the real world that the sign can refer to.

 (iii) PRAGMATICS analyses the relation which holds between speakers and hearers (or the speech community) on the one hand and a sign (or a chain of signs) on the other.

The diagram on *p* 48 may illustrate this[1] (see also 3.1.1):

The pragmatic aspect of language analysis has received very little attention in most theories of language, but according to Wunderlich ('Pragmatik', 1971: 153) the description of the COMPETENCE of a speaker/hearer must not restrict

other linguistic signs

SYNTAX

linguistic
sign

SEMANTICS   PRAGMATICS

objects,   speakers/
processes,   hearers
etc

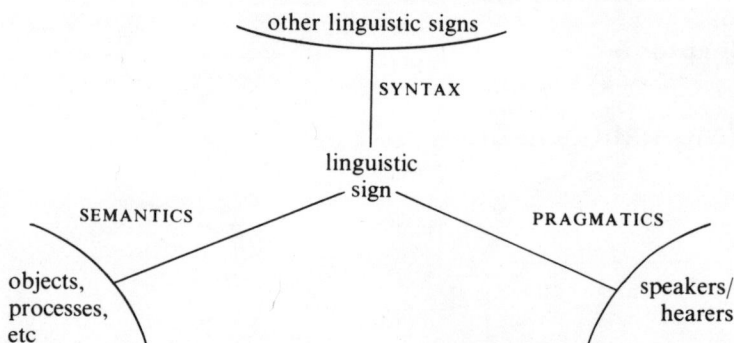

itself to statements about the conditions making for syntactic and semantic
well-formedness. It should, furthermore, include certain conditions of ade-
quacy a sign has to fulfil if it is to be communicatively adequate. To take an
example: a sentence like *Schau mal, jetzt regnet es* only makes sense if both
speaker and hearer are in a situation where they can actually realize that it
has started raining. The utterance would be regarded as meaningless or non-
sensical if it were made in a lecture room without windows where one can
neither see nor hear the rain. This example illustrates that the situation of
utterance is relevant to judging its meaningfulness and appropriateness.

Within linguistic description, it is for a theory of PERFORMANCE that pragmatic factors are most relevant (see Wunderlich, *Tempus*, 1970: 80), but since
as yet no such theory exists, pragmalinguists have been concerned with the
setting up of a theory of COMPETENCE. However, the term COMPETENCE is
here used in a much wider sense than by most transformational grammarians,
who apply it only to the grammatical correctness of sentences. This pragmalinguistic COMPETENCE is often referred to as COMMUNICATIVE COMPETENCE
(see Hymes, 1972; and also Habermas, 'Kompetenz', 1971, or Hüllen,
Linguistik, 1976); Wunderlich ('Pragmatik', 1971: 175) describes it as follows:

> Kompetenz ... bedeutet das Vermögen von Sprechern und Hörern, sich
> in (idealisiert gedachten) Sprechsituationen verständlich zu artikulieren
> bzw. das Artikulierte zu verstehen.
> (Competence is the ability of both speakers and hearers to make themselves
> understood and to understand what is said to them in (ideal) situations of
> utterance.)

The analysis of COMMUNICATIVE COMPETENCE means that the object of
investigation cannot be the isolated sentence (as is the case in dependency and
transformational grammar), but that whole UTTERANCES will have to be considered.

5.1.2 *The school of pragmalinguistics*
In that pragmalinguistics is concerned with the analysis of utterances in given

situations it is apparent that the task of the pragmalinguist is quite different
from that of the linguist working within the theoretical framework of *inhaltbezogene Grammatik* or *Dependenzgrammatik*. The relationship between pragmalinguistics and *funktionale Grammatik* is different in that the intended communicative effect of an utterance – the main issue of functional grammar (see
3.2.1) – falls, in fact, within the scope of pragmatics. It is true that both theories
are concerned with the same problem, namely in what way the structure of
an utterance and the situation in which it is made are linked, but their
approaches differ from each other since pragmalinguistics does not place the
same emphasis on function, but stresses that the study of language, or of linguistic behaviour, is only part of a comprehensive analysis of human actions
(*Handlungstheorie*) (see Wunderlich, *Sprechakttheorie*, 1976: 30–50: compare
also 3.3).

Pragmalinguistics in West Germany is a relatively new development in linguistics. The interest in pragmalinguistic studies emerged in the late sixties,
when Wunderlich – who, while also working in text grammar, has remained
the main representative of the discipline – turned his attention to pragmalinguistics. The discussion of his suggestions will show that pragmalinguistic theory
has been greatly influenced by British and American speech act philosophy,
the best-known representatives of which are Austin and Searle (see Maas and
Wunderlich, *Pragmatik*, 1972: 71–80; compare Chapter 3). This connection
with philosophy may explain the interest some German philosophers
(Habermas, Savigny) have taken in this particular linguistic model.[2]

In 5.4, we will demonstrate how pragmatic factors can be integrated into
a semantically-based model of syntax and give a brief outline of the approach
Burgschmidt and Götz (*Kontrastive Linguistik*, 1974) have developed to contrast English and German. It is interesting to see how quickly the ideas discussed in pragmalinguistics have influenced language teaching in the schools.
For this reason, we exemplify, in the final section of this chapter, one possible
application of the pragmalinguistic approach using a proposed curriculum for
the teaching of English.

5.2 The context of situation

5.2.1 *Speaker and hearer*

[1] Tschüss, Brigitte!
[2] ?Tschüss, Herr Professor!
[3] Auf Wiedersehen, Brigitte/Herr Professor!

Whereas the rather casual *tschüss* is quite common as a greeting formula
amongst students or friends, it could hardly be used by a student to greet a
professor without his breaking social rules.[3] Greeting formulae can be
regarded as typical examples of pragmatic relations (see Brekle, 1972: 24),
because they illustrate how the form of an utterance can be dependent on the

social relations holding between speaker and hearer. Of course, there are other examples of this, the use of polite plurals in some languages (*Sie* in German, *vous* in French), for instance (see also 3.1.1).

The structure of an utterance, however, is not only determined by the relationship between speaker and hearer, it also depends on the speaker's assumptions about the hearer's standard of education, his knowledge of a certain subject, the speed with which he will react, etc (see Wunderlich, *Tempus*, 1970: 80). Compare the following sentences, for example:

[4] Im phonetischen Teil des Fremdsprachenunterrichts ist auch die allophonische Ebene von gewisser Relevanz.

[5] Im Fremdsprachenunterricht sollte man auch solche Auspracheunterschiede berücksichtigen, durch die keine Verständnisfehler im eigentlichen Sinn entstehen können.

Both sentences could be spoken by a lecturer in linguistics discussing the teaching of pronunciation. If he were speaking to linguists or students with a knowledge of linguistics, he might employ the terminology of sentence [4], which he might well avoid if his audience consisted of a group of conservative school-teachers, listening with hostile scepticism, and he did not wish to strengthen their prejudices against modern linguistics. In this case he might make himself understood better if he said something like [5].[4]

5.2.2 *Deictic elements in language*

In 5.1.1 we said that it was one of the tasks of a pragmalinguistic model to establish situation-oriented criteria for the meaningful use of linguistic utterances. This is necessary because some utterances cannot be said to be meaningful if taken out of context. Take the following examples, for instance:

[6] Brigitte hat jetzt Hunger.

[7] Die Linguistikvorlesung findet gleich in diesem Hörsaal statt.

Utterance [6] only makes sense if it is clear which person is meant by the word *Brigitte*, and, of course, the *jetzt* refers to the time of speaking, which we have to know in order to understand the meaning of the sentence (see Savigny, *Philosophie*, 1974: 68). Or, to take another example, [7] can only be used in a situation in which it is obvious which lecture is being referred to and in which speaker and hearer can actually see the lecture room – otherwise the element *in diesem Hörsaal* would not make sense. Compare, however:

[8] Im Frühjahr 1976 trafen Bundeskanzler Helmut Schmidt und Premierminister Harold Wilson in Rom zusammen.

[9] Vorlesungen finden in Hörsälen statt.

Sentences [8] and [9] do not require a particular context to be meaningful,[5] a general truth value can be attributed to them, *ie* they are either true or false. This is different in the case of [6] and [7], whose truth value according to Wunderlich ('Pragmatik', 1971: 156) depends on *when, where* and *by whom* the utterance is made. This can be explained by the fact that [6] and [7] contain DEICTIC ELEMENTS, which make reference to certain features of the situation.[6]

Such deictic elements can refer to TIME (tenses, adverbs of time like *jetzt* or *gleich*), to PLACE (demonstratives: *der, das, dieser*, or adverbs of place like *hier*), and also to PEOPLE, or more specifically, to the participants in the speech act (personal pronouns) (see Leech, *Semantics*, 1974: 350). Wunderlich ('Rolle', 1970: 25) exemplifies the deictic character of personal pronouns using *hier* and *dort*:

[10]*a* Ich bin jetzt hier in Nürnberg.
[10]*b* *Ich bin jetzt dort in Nürnberg.
[11]*a* Du bist jetzt hier in Nürnberg.
[11]*b* Du bist jetzt dort in Nürnberg.
[12]*a* Er/Sie ist jetzt hier in Nürnberg.
[12]*b* Er/Sie ist jetzt dort in Nürnberg.

[10]*b* is ungrammatical because *dort* is not compatible with *ich*, which implies *hier*. This also explains why [11]*b* and [12]*b* are grammatical, but can only be used if the speaker himself is not in Nürnberg at the time of speaking. These examples show why the location of the speaker is also relevant to a pragmalinguistic description.[7]

5.2.3 *Meaning in context*
We have seen that there are utterances which are meaningful independent of any context – they can be attributed a general truth value. Other types of utterances, namely those containing deictic elements, can only be considered to have meaning in specific situations. Wunderlich ('Pragmatik', 1971: 154) gives another example of the relationship between meaning and context:

[13] Brigitte, entweder du gehst oder du gehst nicht.

This can either be read as a tautology, or as an expression of indifference on the part of the speaker, but it could also be a rather impatient hint that Brigitte ought to make up her mind whether she intends to leave or not. In a given situation, however, the meaning of the speaker will be quite clear.

The pragmalinguists' theory will have to take account of all the relevant features of context which determine the structure of an utterance. While they deserve recognition for attempting the systematic integration of these factors into modern linguistic models, it must be said that, as such, the concepts underlying their approach are not new, but go back to the British contextualist school. Both the anthropologist Malinowski, who studied the influence of cultural factors on language, and J. R. Firth, the first Professor of General Linguistics of Great Britain, dealt with language in terms of CONTEXT OF SITUATION. Firth ('Ethnographic analysis', 1968: 154–5) described his own approach in the following way:[8]

The linguist sets up interior relations of three main kinds:

(i) The interior relations of elements of structure, words or other bits and pieces of the text;
(ii) the interior relations of systems set up to give values to elements of structure and the bits and pieces;
(iii) the interior relations of contexts of situation.

The interior relations of the context of situation may be summarized as follows ...:

a: The relevant features of participants: persons, personalities.

1 the verbal action of the participants.
2 the non-verbal action of the participants.

b: The relevant objects.
c: The effect of the verbal action.

It is only a small step from the view that language must be regarded within the context of situation or culture to the view that it is best considered as one form of human action.[9] This is the basis of speech act philosophy – the discussion of which will reveal other linguistic elements referring to the situation of utterance.

5.3 Utterances seen as illocutionary acts

5.3.1 Speech act philosophy

The basic principles of speech act philosophy were developed by the Oxford philosopher J. L. Austin, who examined sentences like the following:

[14] I name this ship *Queen Elizabeth*,

or, taking an example from German,

[15] Ich verspreche, Brigitte das Rauchen abzugewöhnen.

Making an utterance like [14] or [15], Austin (*Things*, 1962: 5) argues, is not so much describing an action, but rather performing an action. The promise is made in that the speaker says *Ich verspreche* ..., and there is no other way of promising.[10] Austin calls verbs like *name* or *promise* (*versprechen*) PERFORMATIVES, whereas the making of the promise (*ie* the utterance) is called an ILLOCUTIONARY ACT.[11]

Let us consider the following example

[16] Da geht es steil hinunter!

If Brigitte and her boy-friend were walking along a Cornish coastal path, and she suddenly cried out *Da geht es steil hinunter* because her friend was walking dangerously close to the edge of the cliff, then the utterance would have the same meaning as [17] or [18]:

[17] Vorsicht, da geht es steil hinunter!
[18] Ich warne dich, da geht es steil hinunter!

In this case, utterance [16] would have to be taken as a warning, we could also say that Brigitte had performed the ILLOCUTIONARY ACT of warning. However, [16] need not necessarily be regarded as warning: for instance, Brigitte might be at home showing her slides of Cornwall to some friends and say *Da geht es steil hinunter*, just to describe the beauty of the scenery, more in the sense of

[19] Schaut mal, wie steil es da hinunter geht.

Whether [16] is the illocutionary act of warning or the illocutionary act of making a statement will, in the context of situation, be quite apparent. It is also indicated by linguistic features such as intonation.

5.3.2 *The double structure of utterances*
Let us now consider the following utterances:

[18] Ich warne dich, da geht es steil hinunter.
[19] Schaut mal, da geht es steil hinunter!
[20] Findest du, dass es da steil hinunter geht?

In these utterances, the illocutionary acts of warning, making a statement and asking a question are indicated by the introductory clauses *Ich warne dich*, *schaut mal*, and *findest du*. The utterance as a whole not only expresses the illocutionary act, but also conveys other information: information concerning the object under discussion. This we call the PROPOSITION of an utterance,[12] which in the case of [18–20] is *Da geht es steil hinunter*. The governing clauses *Ich warne dich*, etc serve to establish a relation between speaker and hearer and fix the pragmatic meaning (*den pragmatischen Verwendungssinn*) of the proposition.

These considerations have led Habermas ('Kompetenz', 1971: 210) to claim a double structure for communication: in his view, an utterance serves communication on two different levels, namely

(i) on a level of intersubjectivity, on which speaker and hearer communicate *with* one another, and
(ii) on a level of objects, processes, etc *about* which speaker and hearer communicate.[13]

An utterance then consists of two parts, namely the performing of an ILLOCUTIONARY ACT and the making of a PROPOSITION. In [18] *Ich warne dich, da geht es steil hinunter*, the illocutionary act is realized by a PERFORMATIVE VERB, however it need not necessarily be overtly expressed in the structure of the utterance, as is illustrated by our example [16] *Da geht es steil hinunter*, where the illocutionary 'act' is made clear by the context. Even if it is not overtly expressed, the illocutionary act is always implied in the utterance and therefore must appear in its deep structure[14] (see Habermas, 1971 : 209).

This brings us back to our model of pragmalinguistics. The INTENTION of the speaker[15] – whether he wants an utterance to be a warning, a promise, a statement, or a question, etc – is most certainly an important factor to consider in the analysis of pragmatic relations. It is through the illocutionary force of an utterance that a hearer knows whether to take the proposition as a warning, a description, and so on. This is why the ILLOCUTIONARY FORCE in some way governs the PROPOSITION (see 5.4.2).

5.4 A pragmalinguistic approach to syntax

5.4.1 *The situation of utterance*
The aim of a pragmalinguistic model as outlined in 5.1.1 is to describe the situation in which an utterance can (meaningfully) take place. Summarizing the points made in 5.2 and 5.3, we can say that the situation of utterance includes:

  (i) the utterance itself, where one can distinguish between its phonological-syntactic properties and its meaning-content,
 (ii) the speaker of the utterance,
(iii) the hearer of the utterance.

(ii) and (iii) will also have to cover the social relations normally holding between speaker and hearer, the special relationship established between them by the utterance (*Sprecher-Hörer-Konstellation*) as well as the knowledge and abilities of speaker and hearer.

 (iv) the place of the utterance (*Ort und Wahrnehmungsraum*),
  (v) the time of the utterance,
 (vi) the illocutionary act, which includes the intention of the speaker.

This catalogue of aspects determining the situation of utterance has been suggested by Wunderlich ('Pragmatik', 1971 : 178), and in a rather similar form also by Leech (*Semantics*, 1974: 350) and Van Dijk (*Text*, 1977: 195). (See also Admoni (*Sprachbau*, ³1970: 230–56) and 3.3.)

5.4.2 *A semantically-based deep structure*
How can these factors be made part of a general theory of syntax? Pragmalinguists have been influenced by the generative semantics model (Lakoff, McCawley) and predicate logic. Ross ('Sentences', 1970) and Wunderlich (*Tempus*, 1970) have made different proposals for including the situation of utterance in the generative transformational model.[16] A quite different approach to the problem has been taken by Burgschmidt and Götz (1974)

for the purpose of a contrastive analysis of English and German. They regard their model as a tentative proposal as to how situational components could be integrated into a theory of syntax rather than as the final model itself.

Burgschmidt and Götz (1974: 36) use the common distinction between the SURFACE STRUCTURE of an utterance and its DEEP STRUCTURE (see also Burgschmidt *et al*, *Zielsprache*, 1975: 31). The term SURFACE STRUCTURE is used to refer to the actual form of the utterance, the form it takes in speech, whereas by DEEP STRUCTURE Burgschmidt and Götz mean a hypothetical underlying structure, ordering the meaning-content and the factors of the situation of the utterance. Their deep structure is semantically based, *ie* it is a hierarchy of the *signifiés* of linguistic signs.[17] The deep structure is converted into the surface structure by application of a series of transformations.

The deep structure suggested by Burgschmidt and Götz (1974: 43) contains a PROPOSITION (see 5.3.2) and several other components which dominate the proposition and most of which are determined by the context of situation. It takes the following form:

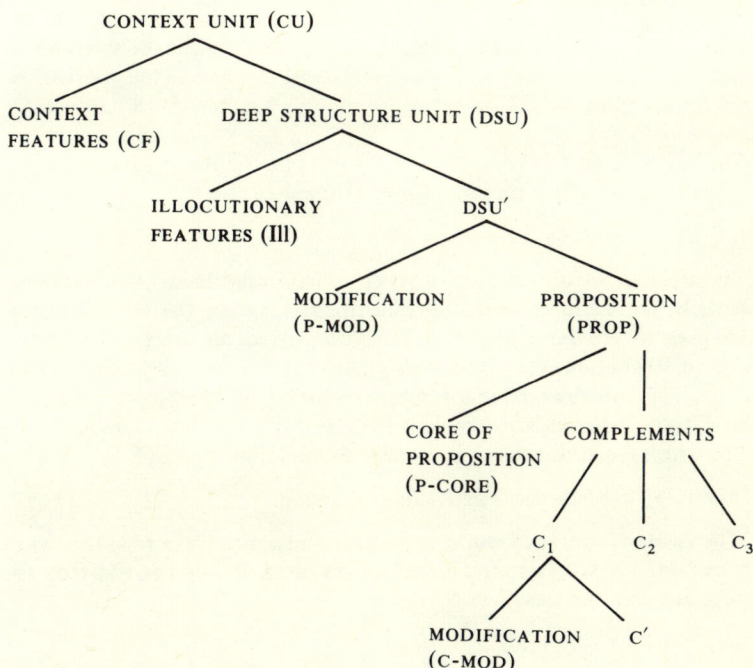

The CONTEXT UNIT is the highest element in the deep structure hierarchy. Thus the analysis goes beyond the isolated sentence and includes the context.

The CONTEXT UNIT (CU) is divided into CONTEXT FEATURES (CF) and the
DEEP STRUCTURE UNIT (DSU):

[i] $CU \rightarrow CF + DSU$

General context features include all relevant aspects of the linguistic and
situational context, such as the relationship between speaker and hearer, or
general relations of time and aspect, which are relevant within a larger context.
Often these CONTEXT FEATURES have to be realized on the surface, for instance, number and tense are obligatory elements in each sentence.

More specific CONTEXT FEATURES concern the linking of several deep-
structure units. They are relevant for topicalization (which, in German, can
be expressed by word order), linkings of time, place and cause as well as pronominalization. Pro-forms are only possible if it is clear from the context who
or what a pronoun refers to (see also 5.2.2).

The DEEP-STRUCTURE UNIT (DSU) consists of ILLOCUTIONARY FEATURES
(Ill) and the DSU-REMAINDER (DSU'):[18]

[ii] $DSU \rightarrow Ill + DSU'$

ILLOCUTIONARY FEATURES concern the illocutionary act the utterance is
intended to perform (*Sprechhandlungsfunktion*); *ie* whether the speaker intends his utterance to be a statement, a question, a command, etc (see Burgschmidt and Götz, 1974: 39).

The DSU-REMAINDER (DSU') can be divided into the PROPOSITION (PROP)
and the MODIFICATION OF THE PROPOSITION (P-MOD):

[iii] $DSU' \rightarrow P\text{-}MOD + PROP$

The MODIFICATION OF THE PROPOSITION includes basic time relations,
especially the relation between the time of speaking and the time an action
takes place (*Sprechzeit/Handlungszeit-Verhältnis*) (see also 12.1). The view of
the action by the speaker (*Aspekt*) also falls under P-MOD. *Modality* includes
those *signifiés* which express possibility, probability or necessity of a proposition. Finally, *negation* is also regarded as a MODIFICATION OF THE PROPOSI-
TION, which could then be characterized in the following way:

$P\text{-}MOD \rightarrow Time + Aspect + Modality \pm Negation$

The PROPOSITION itself contains the real communicative core of the DEEP-
STRUCTURE UNIT.[19] It is subdivided into the CORE OF THE PROPOSITION (P-
CORE) and its COMPLEMENTS (C):

[iv] $PROP \rightarrow P\text{-}CORE + C_1 (+ C_2)(+ C_3)$

The P-CORE is a verbal *signifié* with semantic valencies (see also 4.2.2), *ie*
it has to be completed on the level of content by the COMPLEMENTS. A verb
like *trinken*, for instance, needs an *agens* (somebody who drinks) and can have
a *patiens* (something which is drunk). The place of one of these COMPLEMENTS

can either be taken by another DEEP-STRUCTURE UNIT[20] or by a nominal *signifié*, which can be split up into

[v] C→C-MOD+C′

The MODIFICATION OF THE COMPLEMENT (C-MOD) does not affect the whole of the proposition, but only one complement. This category includes number, definiteness, or indefiniteness respectively. On the surface, this is realized by the definite or indefinite article, etc.

In order to derive the surface structure from the deep structure, a number of transformations will have to be applied.

We take the following extract from *The Lover* by H. Pinter to demonstrate the practical analysis of a sentence with this model:

RICHARD: What about this afternoon? Pleasant afternoon?
SARAH: Oh yes. Quite marvellous.
RICHARD: Your lover came, did he?
SARAH: Mmnn. Oh yes.
RICHARD: Did you show him the hollyhocks?
         Slight pause.
SARAH: The hollyhocks?
RICHARD: Yes.
SARAH: No, I didn't.
RICHARD: Oh.
SARAH: Should I have done?
RICHARD: No, no. It's simply that I seem to remember your saying he was interested in gardening.
SARAH: Mmnn, yes, he is.

        [*The Collection and The Lover*, 1963, Eyre Methuen, *p* 51]

The DEEP STRUCTURE of *Should I have done?* could be represented in the way shown on *p* 58.

The previous mention of *show the lover the hollyhocks* causes replacement of this phrase by *do*, Ill is realized in word order and in intonation, and C-MOD is realized by the introduction of *should* (modality) and the insertion of *have+en* (to indicate time and aspect).

5.4.3 *The value of this model*

It is obvious that the approach taken by Burgschmidt and Götz (1974) must not be regarded as a fully elaborated model of syntax. Its great weakness is that it does not provide a mechanism for the generation of sentences, since it fails to specify the character of the transformations which derive the surface structure of an utterance from its deep structure. This criticism, however, also seems to apply to other models of syntax which have tried to account for pragmatic factors.[21]

On the other hand, Burgschmidt and Götz's model has great explanatory

CU

CF: married couple, informal

type of text: dialogue

previous mention of *lover, show the lover the hollyhocks*

DSU

Ill: question

DSU$'$

C-MOD: time: past
aspect: action completed
modality: necessity, obligation

PROP

P-CORE: *show*

C_1: agens

C_2: patients

C_3: beneficiary

C-MOD	C$'$	C-MOD	C$'$	C-MOD	C$'$
sing def	*I*	pl def	*holly-hock*	sing def	*lover*

value with regard to the ordering of the different factors of the situation of utterance. It considers different kinds of contextual aspects (CF) which are relevant to a pragmalinguistic description, and it clearly illustrates that factors like the intention of the speaker (Ill), or the view the speaker takes of the proposition (P-MOD) play a major role in determining the structure of an utterance.

5.5 The role of pragmalinguistics in present-day German linguistics

5.5.1 *The application of pragmalinguistic ideas to language teaching*

Although it is obvious that a theoretical model like the one suggested by Burgschmidt and Götz cannot be directly applied to language teaching, the new insights into the functioning of language which have been revealed by pragmalinguistic analysis have also been adopted both in German mother-tongue teaching (see, for instance, Kochan and Wallrabenstein, *Aussichten*, 1974[22]) and in the teaching of foreign languages in Germany (Hüllen, *Linguistik*, 1976). In foreign language teaching, where traditionally most weight had been put on grammatical correctness, the didactic aim has now become COMMUNICATIVE COMPETENCE in the foreign language: the learner is to acquire a command of a certain stylistic register so that he will be able to express himself appropriately in given situations, and he is to be taught how to perform illocutionary acts in the foreign language, *ie* he has to learn how to make requests, demands, etc. In pragmalinguistic teaching, these factors range above pure grammatical correctness.[23]

In order to illustrate how pragmalinguistic insights can actually be applied to language teaching, we shall discuss a curriculum proposed for the second year of English at Bavarian grammar schools. It sets up nine different communicative skills (*kommunikative Fähigkeiten*), such as expressing one's own emotions, attitudes, or coming into contact with other people (Institut für Schulpädagogik, 1975: 30–4), which are subdivided into certain situations of utterance (*Sprechanlässe*).[24] The expression of doubt, questioning of what has been said, etc is illustrated in the way shown on *p* 60.

5.5.2 *The importance of the pragmalinguistic approach*

The teaching of COMMUNICATIVE COMPETENCE may be considered a rather idealistic aim as it presupposes GRAMMATICAL COMPETENCE, but it is certainly adequate to approach language teaching with the emphasis on communicative aspects.[25]

We have seen that an adequate description of syntax must go beyond the limits of the isolated sentence and take account of such factors as the intentions of the speaker, linguistic and situational context. These determine the stylistic level of the utterance, but also influence the choice of pro-forms, of the tense and other deictic elements. It is the merit of pragmalinguistics not only to have drawn attention to these factors but also to have made valuable suggestions for the integration of these aspects into a formalized model of syntax.

Thus the pragmalinguistic approach provides more satisfactory results than *funktionale Grammatik* (compare 3.3), although it must be admitted that as is the case in dependency grammar (see 4.4) none of the models put forward within the school of pragmalinguistics has achieved the status of a generally recognized standard theory. We shall see in the next chapter that the insights

LERNZIELE	LERNINHALTE	
KOMMUNIKATIVE FÄHIGKEITEN	SPRECHANLÄSSE (*Vorschläge*)	SPRACHLICHE MITTEL (*Beispiele*)
– Zweifel anmelden, Unsicherheit ausdrücken, infragestellen;	Der Sprecher ist mit dem Gesagten nicht ganz einverstanden, ist unsicher oder will (um höflich, kooperativ zu sein) nicht widersprechen.	(A) – It's a beautiful day, isn't it? (A) – *Well, yes, but isn't it a bit too hot?* (A) – The Germans are a very hard-working people. (A) – *Well, I don't know.* (Some of them are, I suppose.) – Television is bad for children. (A) – *Some programmes certainly are, but on the whole, I don't know.* (A) – Mary is rather selfish. (A) – *Perhaps you are right./Do you really think so?* – Monkeys are stupid animals. – *Why (do you say that)?* – Look at them. (All they do is hop up and down.)
– nicht akzeptieren, widersprechen, ablehnen.	Der Sprecher ist mit dem Gesagten nicht einverstanden, ist anderer Meinung.	(– Have a banana.) – No thanks.) – Don't you like fruit? – *Well, I like fruit, but no bananas.* (A) – Mr Grundy is an old bore. – *No, he isn't.*/(A) – *I don't think he is.* – That hotel is much too expensive. We can't stay there. – *Of course we can.* (It only looks so grand.)

of pragmalinguistics play an important role in another branch of linguistics, namely in text linguistics.

Recommended further reading

A very comprehensive introduction to the basic ideas of the pragmalinguistic approach can be found in Wunderlich ('Pragmatik', 1971), where he is mainly concerned with deictic elements and different approaches to the integration of the factors of situation of utterance into the generative transformational model. The same ideas are outlined in much greater detail with special consideration of the tenses in Wunderlich (*Tempus*, 1970). Also very useful as an introduction is the book by Maas and Wunderlich (*Pragmatik*, 1972).

The didactic application of pragmalinguistics has been discussed by Hüllen

(*Linguistik*, 1976), who also includes a very useful introduction to the basic principles of pragmalinguistic theory (*pp* 1–70). The book by Burgschmidt and Götz (*Kontrastive Linguistik*, 1974) may be of great use to those readers who are interested in a contrastive analysis of English and German.

German discussions of speech act philosophy can be found in Savigny (*Philosophie*, 1974), Schnelle (*Sprachphilosophie*, 1973), and Dittmann (*Sprechhandlungstheorie*, 1976). These books also contain interesting contributions to the philosophy of language. For pragmalinguistics as part of a general *Handlungstheorie* see Wunderlich (*Sprechakttheorie*, 1976) and Heringer (*Praktische Semantik*, 1974). Wunderlich (*Sprechakttheorie*, 1976) is a very comprehensive outline of speech act theory and pragmalinguistics.

Chapter 6

Text linguistics

6.1 General remarks on text linguistics

In Chapters 1 to 5 we have shown that the scope of linguistic analysis has widened in our century: from a largely diachronic to a synchronic approach, from the analysis of lower-order elements of structure to higher-order elements (sentence patterns, verbs and their valencies) and, more recently, increasing attention has been paid to the social context of language use.

When discussing dependency grammar we saw that the linguistic context can influence the choice of which *actants* are included within a sentence (see Chapter 4, note 19). Pragmalinguists and functional linguists were also shown to have taken the linguistic context into account in their work. Pragmalinguists especially are interested in the mutual interdependence of language and action (*Sprache als Handlung*), and such features as deixis and communicative intention also lead them to consider the extralinguistic context. Functional linguists have examined both the micro-function (text-constituting function) and the macro-function (communicative function) of language (see Chapter 3).

The sentence is then no longer generally regarded as the highest unit of description. Pragmalinguists, for example, talk of utterances (*Äusserungen*): a linguistics comprising the context of utterance cannot limit itself to the abstract unit of description, the sentence. Apart from Wunderlich (see Chapter 5), Hartmann was one of the first German linguists to recognize that the text should be taken as the prime unit of description, thus shifting emphasis from the sentence to the utterance/text – an object of potentially greater complexity. Language is, after all, used primarily and almost exclusively in TEXTS.[1]

Two questions about texts need to be asked: firstly, what distinguishes a text from a random sequence of sentences? Secondly, is there an identifiable number of text types? We shall look first at some of those features of texts which help to constitute their textuality and will then consider the question of text types.[2]

6.2 The text

6.2.1 *Three levels of analysis*

Every text is intended to have a communicative effect: we can demonstrate this using an utterance from 5.3.1, *Da geht es steil hinunter*. Within a linguistic text (taking into account the situation of utterance) this could function as a warning, a comment, a directive, etc. How it is interpreted would have to be explained by a theory of the rules of action (*Handlungsregeln*).[3]

We shall now examine a text using it to illustrate one model of text analysis. The text is taken from Wolfgang Hildesheimer's *Zeiten in Cornwall* (1971: 77–80). [Frankfurt: Suhrkamp.]

[1] Kein Hindernis kommt mir entgegen, niemand überholt mich, wohl aber bewegt sich plötzlich vor mir in meiner Richtung, schnell anwachsend, ein schwarzer Reiter, ein eleganter Herr in Reitbreeches und Reitstiefeln, mit steifem Hut, die Gerte waagrecht zwischen den Handschuhen über dem Sattel haltend, dem Alltag hoch enthoben auf seinem glänzenden Pferd, dessen gelockerten Trab er in einem leicht schleudernden Rhythmus mitvollzieht und damit um ein geringes übertreibt: eine Art doppelte Übertragung nach oben, als müsse er einem Spalier von kritischen Beschauern dartun, dass er, wenn auch nicht mehr ganz leicht an Gewicht, doch leicht im Sattel sitze. Vorsichtig überhole ich ihn, spüre dabei im Rücken seinen Blick von oben auf mich herab, bin sicher, dass dieser Blick, selbst wenn der Herr in Gesellschaft wäre, niemanden etwas verraten würde, auch ihm selbst nicht, er ist ein Herr bis in die letzten Blickwinkel, auch ohne Zeugen. (I am not approaching any obstacle, no one is overtaking me, yet suddenly in front of me and moving in my direction there is a rider dressed in black who is rapidly increasing in size – an elegant gentleman in riding breeches and boots, wearing a bowler, the riding crop held between his gloves, horizontal to the saddle. On his shining horse, whose relaxed trot he parallels with a slightly pitching rhythm, in this way exaggerating it somewhat, he is far removed from everyday concerns. He is, as it were, doubly transposed to a higher level as if obliged to demonstrate to rows of critical observers that if no longer exactly a light-weight he can still carry himself lightly in the saddle. Overtaking him carefully I sense, while doing so, his eyes looking at my back from on high: I am sure that even if the gentleman were in company this look would give nothing away either to anyone else or to the rider himself – he is a gentleman down to the last detail, even without witnesses.)

It is clear from *Reitbreeches*, *Reitstiefeln*, *Sattel*, etc that, in this text, *Reiter* is to be understood as being animate, it is not denoting an object found in offices (an alphabetical marker used in card indexes). Similarly *im Sattel sitzen* is used in the literal sense, although a metaphorical interpretation (in the sense of *to be firmly established in life*) is not wholly excluded. Weinrich (*Sprache*,

1976: 13) refers to this way in which words create contexts for each other, and are thus disambiguated, as DETERMINATION. In interpreting utterances we rely not only on our textual competence but also on our knowledge of the socio-cultural context. A text is full of directives (*Anweisungen*) to the hearer/reader to refer to his model of reality. Since in the language-code many text constituents are polysemic, it is the task of the speaker/writer to give unambiguous REFERENCE DIRECTIVES. Only in texts can monosemy be established.[4]

We can now say that it is not only necessary to analyse the extralinguistic context because of the influence of the speaker's intention on the structure of an utterance, but also because the extralinguistic context provides the key to the way the reader decodes an utterance. But, of course, reference to the socio-cultural context does not provide all the clues for the understanding of a message, as is clearly illustrated by the following example:

[2]*a* Brigitte liebt Hermann.
[2]*b* Hermann liebt Brigitte.

In both sentences, the same directives to the socio-cultural context are being used (*Brigitte* and *Hermann*), but there is a – perhaps determining – difference in the meaning of the two sentences, which is made clear by the position of the constituents in the sentence. Such features as the position of constituents and congruence between them (nouns and verbs) show how the elements of the text are linked with each other or with the situation; they can therefore be called CONNECTION DIRECTIVES.

In text linguistics, all these factors will have to be considered. The model of textual analysis proposed by Kallmeyer *et al* (*Textlinguistik I*, 1974) distinguishes the following levels of analysis:

(i) The level of intended effect (*Ebene der Konsequenz*)
(ii) The level of reference to the model of reality (*Ebene der Referenz*)
(iii) The level of connection directives (*Ebene der Konnexion*).[5]

It is important to note that connection directives play an important part in the establishment of textual coherence, which is a prerequisite for the establishment of textual meaning (level ii) and communicative effect (level i). Thus coherence is one of the central issues in the creation of a text and we shall therefore focus our attention on textual cohesion in the next section or two.[6]

6.2.2 *Cohesion and the function of pronouns*

If one took the sentence *Vorsichtig überhole ich ihn* without the established context of passage [1], it would hardly make sense. Within the frame of text [1], however, the reader can identify *ich* and *ihn*: *ich* substitutes for the narrator and *ihn* for *ein schwarzer Reiter*. Thus we can see that pronouns are significant and frequent indicators of TEXTUAL COHERENCE, they also belong to the connection directives. Further on in the second sentence *der Herr*, although not a pronoun but itself a nominal group, is also used as a substitute for *ein schwarzer Reiter*. It is also by such substitutions that coherence is established in a text.[7]

Let us now consider what a pronoun actually substitutes for in a text. The first *er* in our text replaces *ein schwarzer Reiter* and, at least potentially, everything predicated of the horseman – his dress, his bearing, his style of riding; the last *er* in the text can conjure up an even more detailed picture.[8] Referential identity is, however, not a necessary precondition for the establishment of a cohesive relation. For example:

[3] Gestern habe ich mir ein neues Auto gekauft. Heute früh gingen die Bremsen kaputt.

Here there is coherence, though not referential identity – *Auto* and *Bremsen* cohere. We also find cohesive relations established on a level of abstraction, in this example:

[4] Täglich fahren Tausende von Autos an unserer Wohnung vorbei. Der Lärm macht mich krank.

The reader's knowledge of the world – his model of reality – helps him to equate cars (*Autos*) and noise (*Lärm*).[9] It is clear that substitution elements make a major contribution to the creation of textual coherence.

6.2.3 *The function of articles*

A further class of words which help to create coherence are the articles. Articles are not scattered randomly throughout texts; the indefinite article is frequently found to precede the definite article. In text [1] we find *ein schwarzer Reiter*, *ein eleganter Herr* and further on *der Herr*. The indefinite article can generally be said to point forward, to have a CATAPHORIC function, whereas the definite article frequently points back, it has an ANAPHORIC function.

If in text [1] we found *der schwarze Reiter* rather than *ein schwarzer Reiter*, the definite article would be a directive to the reader to identify a horseman already mentioned in the text. Since none has yet been mentioned, this backward directive might well leave the reader unable to identify the horseman. In text [1] we do, however, find nominals – for example *die Gerte, den Handschuhen, dem Sattel* – used with a definite article, although the nominal has not been previously mentioned in the text. Weinrich (1976: 197) accounts for this use of the definite article by appealing to the SEMANTIC FRAME (*Regel des Rahmens*).[10] The semantic frame for the above nouns is *Reiter*; this relationship is sometimes referred to as semantic anaphora.

In the case of such utterances as, for example,

[5] Der Mensch ist ein Säugetier

where no particular person is meant, Weinrich (1976: 169) argues that the information pointed to by the article *der* cannot be retrieved anaphorically but appeals to the hearer/reader's cultural knowledge.[11]

Other closed-class items which also modify nouns – possessives, demonstratives and interrogatives – have functions which complement those of the articles.[12]

We hope to have shown that there is sufficient complexity in the syntactic and semantic relations holding between the elements of texts to justify an analysis within a framework such as that proposed by Kallmeyer *et al* (*Textlinguistik I*, 1974).

6.3 Text types

6.3.1 *Text structure*

We have seen that coherence is a necessary condition for the creation of texts, but is it a sufficient criterion? Let us consider the following short texts:

[6]*a* Hier ist Bayern drei, die Servicewelle von Radio München. Autobahn München–Nürnberg.

[6]*b* Hier ist Bayern drei, die Servicewelle von Radio München. Autobahn München–Nürnberg. Drei Kilometer Rückstau zwischen den Anschlussstellen Feucht und Nürnberg–Mögeldorf wegen einer Baustelle.

(This is Bayern 3, the service-frequency of Radio Munich. Motorway München–Nürnberg. Traffic held up along three kilometres of motorway between exits Feucht and Nürnberg–Mögeldorf because of road works.)

Although both [6]*a* and [6]*b* are coherent, [6]*a* would not be considered a text since it is incomplete. COMPLETION should not be confused with length, as proverbs or even a one-word utterance such as *help!* can constitute a text. Completion is the requirement that the intital theme or topic of the text should be developed and brought to an acceptable conclusion. So both coherence and completion can be said to be the necessary conditions for the creation of texts.[13]

6.3.2 *An attempt to classify texts*

In Chapters 2 and 4 we described attempts to classify sentences according to basic sentence patterns and valency patterns. We now turn to the second of the questions raised at the beginning of this chapter: can texts also be classified and categorized? Let us consider the following text, text [7], and compare it with texts [1] and [6]. The passage is taken from an issue of *Der Spiegel* published at a time when the magazine was under attack for having drawn attention to a case of 'bugging' (*Der Spiegel*, 21 March 1977: 22):

[7] Die Presse ist schuld, Funk und Fernsehen sind schuld, das versteht sich in allen Staaten, in denen es eine halbwegs freie Pressemeinung gibt, beinahe von selbst.

Wenn der Kanzler nicht weiss, was sein Kanzleramtsvorsteher Schüler antwortet; wenn der Kanzleramtsvorsteher Schüler nicht weiss, was aufgrund seiner Anordnungen geschieht, namentlich nicht, dass aufgrund seiner Anordnungen die Gesetze gebrochen werden: Die Presse ist schuld...

(The press is responsible, radio and TV are responsible, this almost goes without saying in every country in which the press is more or less free to say what it likes.

When the Chancellor doesn't know what the Head of the Chancellor's Office says in reply to a question, when the Head of the Chancellor's Office doesn't know what happens as a result of his instructions – that is to say when he does not know that as a result of his instructions the laws are broken: it is the fault of the press.)

One important difference between text [7] and text [6]*b* is that whereas [6]*b* is an objective report, [7] is argumentative in character. (The fact that one is a spoken and the other a written text is irrelevant for our purpose, the spoken text will, as a radio news-flash, probably have been written in the first place anyway.)

Werlich (*Text Grammar*, 1976) distinguishes five basic TEXT TYPES which, according to him, correspond to five innate ways of viewing reality – description, narration, exposition, argumentation and instruction.[14]

If we compare [6]*b* and [1] we shall find a further criterion for the classification of texts, the distinction between fictional texts [1] and non-fictional texts [6]*b*. Werlich refers to these as the two TEXT GROUPS.[15]

Text [7] can be classified as an example of the text type *argumentation*, more specifically it is a comment on a state of affairs. Comment is not the only possible manifestation of this text type, it is one of the conventional manifestations of a text type which Werlich (1976: 46) refers to as TEXT FORMS.[16]

6.3.3 *Text production and text analysis*

We have seen that both coherence and completion are necessary conditions for the creation of texts. We shall take as an example the single sentence text

[8] He who makes no mistakes makes nothing.

This contains both a theme (Werlich uses the term *thematic text base unit*) and its completion or rheme. Since the text has coherence and sequence forms which ensure termination, it is complete. Werlich argues that this is true of all texts, however long or short, and he posits a rank-scale of text units.[17]

6.3.4 *Pedagogical implications of textual analysis*

This theoretical model of text analysis has been used by Werlich to develop new methods in foreign language teaching. The aim is *textformspezifische Strukturvermittlung*, ie Werlich (*Stories*, 1975: 5–8) believes that structures should be taught in relation to the text forms in which they are commonly used. The learner must recognize the differences between the various text forms, both on the levels of structure and style; Werlich's exercises aim then at such skills as developing a logical argument, the use of connection directives and the establishment of a theme/rheme structure.

Werlich's analysis of the text form *story*, for instance, involves the discussion of temporal text structuring. (A story usually starts with what Werlich calls a time span indicator (*last year*, etc) and is continued with a number of temporal sequence signals (adverbials of time, verbal groups in the past tense, etc) and is finally completed by a temporal terminator (such as *at last*).) Werlich (1975: 21) uses the following example:

He [Daniel Webster] was an influential member of Congress *in the first half of the nineteenth century.*	A TIME SPAN INDICATOR (a *time adverbial*)
When Daniel Webster was a boy in the district school in New Hampshire,	A TEMPORAL SEQUENCE SIGNAL (a *temporal clause*)
he *was* not famous for cleanliness.	A TEMPORAL SEQUENCE SIGNAL (a *verbal group* in the Past Tense)
Finally the teacher, in despair, told him if he appeared again with such dirty hands she would beat him.	A TEMPORAL TERMINATOR (a *time adverb*)

This can, of course, give only a very superficial impression of the application of theoretical text analysis to foreign language teaching. It is important to note, however, that text linguistics has influenced curricula,[18] especially since in West Germany text-based comprehension tests are gaining wide acceptance as the standard test form for the foreign language examinations taken in the *Gymnasium* (equivalent of British grammar school). Werlich's theory in particular has had great influence on a report of the interstate commissions set up to make proposals for a greater level of standardization in the *Abitur* examinations. As such, Werlich's text grammar can be expected to achieve an importance far beyond its value as an original contribution to the growing literature within the field of text grammar.[19]

6.4 Final comments

If much of the descriptive work we have reviewed in this chapter does not make a radical break with established linguistic procedures, this should not surprise us. Literary criticism, textual criticism, philology and linguistics have all taken an interest in texts, indeed many of the findings of text linguists are little more than a rigorous restatement of already established facts of language use. Again, the text linguist does not and cannot work autonomously: pragmatics, semantics, sociology and literary disciplines impinge on and contribute to the work of the text linguist. However, text linguistics is not old wine in new bottles. The attempt to account for the text as a whole, however inadequate descriptions may have proved so far, is a step towards a wider linguistics, and the determination of many linguists to integrate non-linguistic features of utterances into descriptions has uncovered a host of problems for which satisfactory answers still have to be found.

Even the definition of the text is still a matter of controversy but we can hardly expect this to be otherwise: no possible text grammar can ever fully account for the most creative and personal use of language – literature. And the biggest question still remains: how do all these factors influencing language use actually bear upon the individual speaker's choice of what to say and how to say it?

Recommended further reading

Dressler (*Einführung*, 1971) is a brief but informative introduction to the many questions asked by text linguists. This handbook is very much a conscious attempt to launch supra-sentential linguistics. Dressler and S. J. Schmidt (*Bibliographie*, 1973) provide short resumés of part of the growing literature of text linguistics. Here, as in Dressler (*Einführung*, 1971) text linguistics is understood to embrace a large number of other subdisciplines of linguistics. P. Hartmann ('Texte', 1971) discusses some of the theoretical implications of the discipline. Kallmeyer *et al* (*Textlinguistik I*, 1974), Werlich (*Text Grammar*, 1976) and Weinrich (*Sprache*, 1976) all deserve close reading. The need for textual analysis has already been pointed out by Weinrich in his remarkable philosophical essay *Linguistik der Lüge. Kann Sprache die Gedanken verbergen?* (1964).

Chapter 7

Transformational generative grammar

7.1 Transformational grammar in Germany

Transformational generative grammar (TG) differs in one important respect from the other linguistic theories we have treated. Whereas linguists working within the theoretical framework of *inhaltbezogene Grammatik* or dependency grammar, for example, have worked in comparative isolation from non-German scholarship, TG is a model of language used throughout the world. It has been used to describe various languages and also makes strong universalist claims about the human *faculté de language*. The aims of this book preclude us from writing an introduction to TG, we shall only be able to discuss briefly some of the contributions made by German scholars to controversial areas of the theory, to consider the early application of TG to the description of German and to mention some of the criticisms made of the model.[1]

Although linguistic science has a long history and is a firmly established discipline in Germany, the linguistics boom of the early sixties was a transformationalist boom. Chomsky's work was welcomed by many young scholars for its break with the traditions of European structuralism and because it made far-reaching claims about the nature and structure of the human mind, thus seeming to place linguistics firmly amongst the sciences and apparently leading it away from the subjectivism of philology.[2] Many transformational linguists also identified their approach with progressive ideas and *Sprachwissenschaft* (linguistic science) with a conservative stance. In the late sixties TG was carried along on a surge of enthusiasm, which naturally enough aroused the antagonism of more traditional structuralists and philologists. Coseriu considers, for example, that arrogance, bad manners and a nonchalant disrespect for tradition characterize transformationalists in their academic dealings with others.[3]

7.2 The application of TG to the description of German

7.2.1 *Syntactic description*

As we have indicated, Chomsky claims that TG is a model of language applicable to all languages. Can the model, however, serve for the description of German although developed using data from English? Bierwisch (*Grammatik*, 1963: 30) points out that word order is one area of syntax in which German differs greatly from English.[4] For reasons of economy – in order to reduce the number of rules required – Bierwisch (1963: 31–6) adopts clause-final position as the primary position of the finite verb in an underlying structure.[5] Although the position of the German finite verb can differ, both in main and dependent clauses, from the position of the corresponding English finite verb, Chomsky's 1957 model allows for these differences; so although the facts of German syntax do not concur with English, the descriptive linguist has no difficulty in accommodating them in his description. Similarly, Motsch (*Syntax*, 1964), discussing the syntax of the German adjective, supports Chomsky's claim that the predicative use of the adjective is the primary use.[6]

These two contributions to the *Studia Grammatica* series reflect clearly the early enthusiasm aroused by Chomsky's 1957 model. Although later adaptations which resulted in the Standard Theory of 1965 were considered in revised editions of these monographs, it is evident reading them today that they are interesting mainly in so far as they document attempts made to apply TG to the description of German despite the inadequacies of the model.

7.2.2 *Semantics and generative grammar: interpretive semantics*

In the 1960s interest moved away from the description of discrete areas of syntax to questions of potentially greater theoretical importance. In the United States and elsewhere the discussion provoked by Chomsky's 1957 model crystallized into a dispute between linguists on the relationship between syntax and semantics.[7]

Baumgärtner ('Struktur', 1967) sees in componential analysis and the interpretive semantics model of Katz and Fodor ('Structure', 1963) a way of overcoming the dichotomy between Trier's paradigmatic meaning fields and Porzig's syntagmatic relations. Baumgärtner (1967: 166) suggests that the concepts of field meaning (*Bedeutungsfeld*) and sentence meaning (*Satzbedeutung*) are the main and complementary elements of any semantic analysis and further that this division can be overcome using selection restrictions.[8] Porzig's syntactic relations will now be considered in terms of selectional rules which will, for example, reject [2] as ungrammatical

[1] Der Mann schneidet das Haar mit der Schere
[2] *Der Mann mäht das Haar mit dem Messer

because of the incompatibility between verb and object, ie *Haar* (hair) does not collocate with *mähen* (mow), and between verb and instrumental, ie *mähen* and *Messer* (knife) (*cf* Baumgärtner, 1967: 168).

In this model the term field will be restricted to lower-order lexematic classes, which will not be arrived at by considering the complete meaning of lexemes but by reducing them to their semantic components.[9] This componential analysis is also required so that the context restrictions can be formally stated; in our example above the verb *mähen* will be specified as appearing in the context of such lexemes as *Gras* (grass), *Getreide* (corn), etc, but not of other lexemes such as *Papier* (paper), *Tuch* (cloth), etc which also have the feature '+cuttable'. The analysis must however only be concerned with linguistic facts, a semantic analysis does not aim to set up biological or philosophical taxonomies.[10]

7.2.3 *Semantics and generative grammar: generative semantics*
One would also want the grammar to account for the relations holding between such synonymous sentences as

[3] Ute gefällt dem Linguisten
[4] Der Linguist mag Ute.

Rohrer (*Funktionelle Sprachwissenschaft*, 1971) claims that a grammar which fails to derive two such sentences from the same underlying semantic structure is failing to provide an adequate description of the language. Brekle (*Generattive Satzsemantik*, 1970: 50–1) argues that only non-configurational concepts such as those employed by Fillmore can account for these relations.[11] The modalities – tense and aspect – can also be separated from the proposition, which consists of a verb and a number of case-relations (compare Chapter 5). The formalization of these insights is a problem to which symbolic logic seems to offer a solution.[12]

Rohrer makes three main criticisms of interpretive semantics. Firstly, it does not distinguish between meaning (*Bedeutung*) and reference (*Bezeichnung*), since while *Abendstern* and *Morgenstern*, for example, have the same referent they are different in meaning. Similarly *Das Glas ist halb voll* and *Das Glas ist halb leer*, although referentially identical, are rarely interchangeable in discourse. Secondly, transformations, both so-called stylistic transformations and such transformations as passivization, do, according to Rohrer, change meaning (*Bedeutung*). Thirdly, like Brekle, Rohrer insists that synonymous sentences must be derived from the same deep structure. The semantic base will not contain grammatical categories such as noun, verb, etc but predications (*cf* 8.4.2). Categorial meaning will be realized at a higher level particularly if the features of the semantic/logical base are regarded as universals.

Rohrer mentions two further aspects of meaning that must be taken into account: the level of the speaker perspective (*Ebene des Gesichtspunkts des Sprechers*) will allow speakers of German to realize the concepts underlying

[5] Ute gelang es, von ihrem Nachbarn abzuschreiben

only with the impersonal *es* or the successfully achieved goal as grammatical subject, whereas in English the one who successfully achieves his goal, is the grammatical subject if the goal is also mentioned. The second aspect is the level of information value (*Ebene des informativen Wertes*) which comprises theme and rheme choices and the relations holding between one sentence and another within the same text. Choices at this level are also determined by extralinguistic factors.[13]

7.2.4 *Semantic universals*

A central question within this discussion is whether there is a 'universal inventory of sense components' (Lyons, *Semantics II*, 1977: 44), since both models – interpretive semantics and generative semantics – use semantic components which are often claimed to be universals. We now turn to two monographs which discuss the universals question with reference to German.

Bierwisch ('Semantic universals', 1967: 35) presents a componential analysis of German adjectives of size and concludes that there are 'basic dimensions of the human apperceptive apparatus', which are identifiable in the semantics of these adjectives.

Bierwisch examines a number of antonym pairs, including *weit: nah*, *hoch: tief*, *lang: kurz*, *gross: klein*, and ascribes a feature 'polarity' ('+POL') to that adjective of each pair which can be used with a degree adverbial such as *doppelt so*, *halb so*, etc. With the pair *schnell: langsam* we find, according to Bierwisch (1967: 8).[14]

[6] Das Auto fährt halb so schnell wie die Eisenbahn

but not

[7] *Das Auto fährt doppelt so langsam wie die Eisenbahn

other antonym pairs, for example *gut: schlecht*, both admit the degree adverbial

[8] Ute strickt doppelt so gut wie Klaus
[9] Ute kocht halb so schlecht wie Klaus

Bierwisch elaborates his classification system and arrives at a number of features which he refers to as semantic primitives. One of these is 'dimension' which has three potential realizations according to the object described. So *Wagen* (car) can be described using all three dimension features, *1 lang*, *2 breit*, *3 hoch*, whereas for *Zigarette* we use only *1 lang* and as the second dimension *2 dick*. *Stange* (pole), depending upon how it is viewed by the observer, can be described using either *1 lang* or *1 hoch* and *2 dick*. Often all three dimensions can be subsumed under the cumulative *gross*. This is true of *Wagen*, whereas to *Stange* we can apply the adjective *gross* together with *dick*.

Stange shows that the position of the observer to the object is important; this Bierwisch calls the feature '+observer'. So we understand *tief* in connection with *Schublade* as referring to the horizontal axis going away from

the observer, whereas with *Meer* it refers to the vertical axis. The other semantic primitives which Bierwisch recognizes are the relationship of the object
to the ground and the observer's expectations of the minimum and maximum
dimensions of an object.

Bierwisch (1967: 34) concludes that these semantic primitives are not to
be confused with facts of geometry, physics or biology. Further, they are
features of whole structures such as spatiality and verticality and he suggests
that they may be structured in ways as yet unrecognized. Perhaps his most
important claim is that these features are part of a child's innate mental capacities, since a child is able to grasp these spatial and size relations through the
semantics of his language long before he has understood the complexities of
relative size, dimensions and observer position. Since these elements are combined according to general principles, they should not be treated as an unordered set, as a mere bundle of features. He claims that only the careful analysis of lexical items to uncover the underlying universal semantic markers can
be regarded as a successful analysis.

One of the areas which Bierwisch points out as a fruitful area of semantic
investigation is the linguistic realization of synaesthesia. Baumgärtner ('Synästhesie', 1969) suggests that syntagmas of the kind *hartes Licht, stumpfes Blau*
and *spitzer Schrei* are made up of elements which do not normally co-occur.
The adjective *hart*, for example, usually collocates with nouns denoting
objects. Baumgärtner (1969: 3) claims that adjectives are here not being used
metaphorically or in a non-literal sense since they can often neither be paraphrased nor replaced by other lexemes.[15] He suggests three levels of compatibility for the hundred or so adjectives that can be used in synaesthetic expressions. Normal compatibility (*helles Licht*), possible compatibility (*hartes
Licht*), where the adjective normally collocates with nouns denoting substance,
and non-compatibility (**lautes Licht*).

For each of the senses Baumgärtner identifies primary antonym pairs
amongst the adjectives which have normal compatibility with nouns denoting
an aspect of this sense. For sight we find *hell: dunkel*, for hearing *laut: leise*,
for taste *süss: sauer*, for the sense of touch *heiss: kalt* for temperature, *rauh:
glatt* for surface quality, *hart: weich* for consistency and *spitz: stumpf* for
shape. Baumgärtner (1969:13) maintains that only the sense of smell is always
dependent upon synaesthetic usage, for example *ein süsser Duft*.

Just as Bierwisch's interest is in discovering the patterning behind our use
of adjectives of size and dimension, so Baumgärtner working independently
asks whether there is any universality in the tendency to ascribe sense impres-
sions derived from one sense to another sense source. If we compare English
and German in this respect, we do find parallels: *soft light, weiches Licht, ein
süsser Geruch, a sweet smell*.

Since a purely syntactic analysis is not sufficient to describe the structure
of a language, semantic questions, especially questions of semantic compatibility, cannot be left out of the analysis. However these matters have also been

discussed by structural linguists such as Coseriu (see Chapter 8), who has attacked the assumptions about the nature of language underlying the TG approach. We now turn to Coseriu's critique and to another by a Marxist linguist, Motsch.

7.3 Criticism of TG

7.3.1 Coseriu's critique

Coseriu (*Leistung*, 1975) makes four main criticisms of TG. Firstly, TG neither considers nor discusses functions in individual languages. He says (93–6) that it is not enough to exclude as ungrammatical such sentences as

[10] *I writes
[11] *We was writing

for the linguist must also say something about the relative content (*Inhalt*) of grammatical utterances such as

[12] I have written a letter
[13] I wrote a letter.

Similarly Coseriu (1975: 95) argues that

[14] *This are a round square

is not ungrammatical because *this* and *are* cannot be combined but because the functions of singular and plural are not congruent, syntagmatic combinations being determined by functions and not vice versa.[16]

Secondly, TG fails to distinguish between what is linguistic and what is extralinguistic. Coseriu (1975: 26–8) mentions two far-reaching implications of the failure to distinguish MEANING (*Bedeutung*), REFERENCE (*Bezeichnung*) and SENSE (*Sinn*).[17] Firstly, if the linguist is not clear about how he is using the term meaning, he will not be clear about his objectives. Secondly, he will be unable to distinguish between ungrammatical utterances and nonsense. Coseriu (1975: 64–6) claims that of the three utterances

[15] *Ich begegnete ihn
[16] *Rainer ist neu
[17] *Wir kochen das Klavier

[15] is unacceptable for lexico-grammatical reasons, [16] for lexical reasons and [17] because it is nonsense (*ie* for extralinguistic reasons).[18] Reference is the province of universal grammar and meaning will be treated by the investigation of particular languages, while the text linguist will consider sense or textual meaning.

Thirdly, TG neglects the paradigmatic axis. Since the rules of TG and co-occurrence restrictions apply largely to syntagmatic relations, the contrasting functions of elements chosen from a paradigm are ignored. Speech is not a stringing together of elements, since at every point in the chain paradigmatic choices are made.[19] Equally, syntagmatic relations holding between elements in the chain are relations of co-determination in that each addition to a string affects not simply the adjacent elements but the whole string. It is not then the presence of a particular element in a chain nor the function of any one element that makes up the functions of the whole, as the example of word order shows. Functions are to be understood as properties of language, not as properties of individual elements. From this Coseriu (1975: 78) concludes that regarding such functions as negation, modality, imperative, etc as conjoined elements in a chain reveals a profound deficiency of TG.

Finally Coseriu attacks the arbitrary nature of the analytical procedures adopted by transformationalists. He rejects intuition – the alleged source of many transformational insights – and dismisses paraphrase as a heuristic principle in the investigation of *langue*, though not of *parole*. He accepts that a theory of language does not necessarily have to be based on facts of language use, but he denies that the insights of transformationalists correspond to the reality of language use.[20]

7.3.2 *Motsch's objections to the transformational approach*

Motsch (*Kritik*, 1974) criticizes structural linguistics from de Saussure to TG, seeing in TG a natural development from earlier structuralist models. While Coseriu would no doubt disagree with much of what Motsch has written, they agree in one respect – in their rejection of the degree of idealization transformationalists impose on their linguistic data by insisting on the ideal speaker/hearer. It is not necessary to share Motsch's philosophical position to appreciate the acuity and intellectual force of his arguments. He lays a philosophical foundation for the growing realization that language as action (pragmalinguistics) and language as a social phenomenon (sociolinguistics) cannot be regarded as only peripheral aspects of the theory of the linguistic sign. This is not, of course, to say that the pragmalinguist and the sociolinguist has to be a Marxist. It is, however, the case that in Germany dissatisfaction both with the descriptive power of TG and its theoretical preoccupations has motivated a growing interest in the relationship between language, society and the individual.

Motsch (1974: 123–4), whose early work was undertaken in an exclusively TG framework, emphasizes that the need to modify the theory is not in itself a sign of weakness, since the process of modification using examples and counter-examples adheres to a good dialectic principle. He nevertheless rejects TG as a useful heuristic instrument.[21]

We shall concentrate on three main criticisms, all of which can be subsumed under Chomsky's failure to see language in its social context: his acceptance of innate ideas, his lack of historical perspective and his principle of the ideal speaker/hearer. Motsch (1974: 132) criticizes the interest shown in such peripheral matters as the nature of semantic relations and universal features when the much larger question of the relationship between a natural language and society is excluded from the theory.[22] Motsch suggests that the Marxist theory of society, which emphasizes the determining function of social and economic factors, not only offers adequate explanations for many facts of language use but will act as a meta-theory enabling the linguist to discover which questions he ought to be asking.

Motsch does not deny that man's genetic make-up will predispose him to view the world in certain ways, but he rejects the conception of language development as the product of a genetic programme. Thought, philosophical categories and laws are, he argues, historically determined and reflect the growth of the human organism and the dialectical process of confronting and understanding the world. Nor does Motsch deny that there may well be semantic universals, but he would call universal those aspects of languages which must be present for them to function both as a means of communication and as a means of understanding the world.

According to Motsch, Chomsky's neglect of the dynamic historical function of language can lead him to assume that the relationship between universal grammar (the general human or universal aspects of language) and individual languages is an element–class relationship. Motsch (1974: 161) declares that it is rather a dialectical relationship between the general-human and the concrete-historical. Chomsky's assumptions about universal grammar and individual languages enable him to ignore those very factors which determine why the grammar of a particular language is as it is and which aspects of the language system, at a given time, provide the dynamism to change it in accordance with social pressures.

By analysing competence at the expense of performance, TG loses sight of the unity of the language system and actual communication using language – the two aspects of language being quite interdependent. Motsch accepts Chomsky's assumption that there is a system of rules underlying language use, and that these rules are 'known' despite lapses and slips of the tongue. He does not however accept the necessity to postulate an ideal speaker/hearer divorced from historical time, social links and communicative objectives. This shows, Motsch (1974: 77) argues, TG to be part of the tradition of structuralism with its preoccupation with language as a system.

7.4 Concluding remarks

The development of the theory of TG has not been greatly influenced by the work of German scholars (with the exception of Bierwisch) or by the facts of the German language. The contributions made to this discussion, which have concentrated on the place of semantics in generative grammar, are similar to those made elsewhere.

A separate matter is that of the status of TG in Germany. In recent years, enthusiasm for TG has waned amongst linguists because progress has been slow and because criticisms of the model have revealed some serious theoretical deficiencies. For many descriptive linguists too, TG has proved disappointing; no TG grammar of German has offered insights into the structures of the language which had not already been revealed by others. The often arrogant claims for TG's role in mother-tongue and foreign language teaching are now rarely heard. Too little heed has been paid in the past to those linguists and teachers who warned that, however adequate a model might be for the purposes of the theoretical linguist, it would not necessarily prove to be a good pedagogic tool.

At the time of writing eclecticism is the rule. Many alternative approaches – Engel's dependency grammar and Wunderlich's pragmalinguistic model, for example – include a transformational component. The *Duden* (*Grammatik*, ³1973) reflects this move away from single models: it now comprises contributions from scholars working in the theoretical framework of *inhaltbezogene Grammatik*, dependency grammar and TG.

Recommended further reading

Bechert, Clément, Thümmel and Wagner (*Einführung*, ²1971) is a widely used introduction to TG with many German examples. The early volumes of the *Studia Grammatica* series represent the most thorough attempt to apply TG to the description of German. Wunderlich (ed) (*Probleme*, 1971) and Wunderlich (*Tempus*, 1970) include significant contributions to the post-*Aspects* discussion. Coseriu (*Leistung*, 1975) and Motsch (*Kritik*, 1974) deserve to be read carefully for their close criticism of TG.

Chapter 8

Some issues in German semantic studies

8.1 General remarks on semantic analysis in Germany

In the early phase of German *Sprachwissenschaft* the study of meaning, especially the study of the changes in meanings, played a central part in linguistic
analysis, as we have shown in Chapter 1. Later, content-oriented grammarians
also gave a very prominent place to the study of meaning-factors in the description of language. Since then, however, most linguistic theories developed in
Germany have concentrated mainly on problems of syntax, or, in recent years,
on the analysis of pragmatic factors. This has meant that the systematic study
of semantics – which together with syntax and pragmatics constitutes the three
aspects of semiotic analysis[1] – has been comparatively neglected. This peripheral interest in semantic theory should not necessarily be taken to indicate
that these linguists consider semantics irrelevant; as our treatment of the development of dependency grammar in Chapter 4 has shown, syntacticians
came to realize that a purely syntactic analysis which does not allow for the
integration of semantic considerations must remain inadequate. Similarly, one
can hardly imagine a purely pragmatic analysis which does not in some way
or other presuppose or integrate semantics, especially as it is extremely difficult
to draw a clear dividing line between semantics and pragmatics (*cf* Lyons,
Semantics I, 1977: 114–19).[2]

Nevertheless, a shift of the focus of interest can be observed: the student
of syntax is not primarily interested in describing the meanings of lexical items
as such, what is of interest to him are those semantic features which determine
whether two lexical items can occur in a sentence or not, *ie* the problem of
what Chomsky has called selection restrictions. As we have seen in Chapter
4, semantic features are introduced into syntax to explain why a sentence like
*Der Armleuchter tanzt as opposed to Thea tanzt is unacceptable. As selection
restrictions are only one small area of semantics, it comes as no great surprise
to discover that the theoretical basis of semantics within such theories of

syntax is rather weak. Most linguists have adapted some version of componential analysis, because this semantic model is widely used in generative transformational grammar. (Some German linguists have developed this approach within a generative framework, mainly Bierwisch and Baumgärtner, as we have seen in Chapter 7.)[3]

Interestingly, some of the scholars who have been explicitly concerned with semantic theory (and who have not just seen it as a way of accounting for certain phenomena in syntax) have attempted to combine the theoretical framework of componential analysis and the study of lexical fields, which, since Trier and Porzig, has played an important role in German semantic theories. In addition, some of the work of West German structural semanticists seems to derive from the work of the French structuralist school – Greimas and Pottier may be mentioned as the most influential representatives – which may also explain why structural semantics in the Federal Republic has been largely developed by scholars of Romance languages (by Coseriu, Geckeler and Heger amongst others). Many East German linguists have different backgrounds: G. F. Meier, for example, whose work has already been referred to in Chapter 3, and Wotjak both have explicitly taken account of problems of translation theory (and possible developments in the field of machine translation) as the starting-point for their work in semantics.[4]

8.2 Meaning

8.2.1 *The linguistic sign*
In the course of this book we have repeatedly referred to the two components of the linguistic sign (morpheme, word, etc) as FORM and MEANING.[5] Whereas it is commonly accepted that the form of a linguistic sign can be described as a chain of phones (or, in the written medium, as a chain of graphemes), there is no common understanding amongst linguists on the status of meaning. We cannot outline here the philosophical controversy about the character of the meaning component of the linguistic sign (and the relation holding between meaning and form),[6] but must restrict ourselves to reminding the reader of properties of meaning already outlined in Chapter 2: there are good reasons for regarding meaning as a mental image of an object rather than as the object (referent) itself. The meaning of the linguistic form *Studentin*, for instance, is not a particular girl, but rather the ideational image in the mind of a speaker of a girl studying at university. It follows from this that only those features which are shared by all (or most) speakers of a language are relevant to a description of a particular linguistic form: in the case of *Studentin*, for example, one speaker might imagine a blonde girl, another a brunette, etc, but this merely shows that hair colour is not a relevant criterion for determining the meaning of *Studentin*. Wotjak (*Untersuchungen*, 1971: 32) defines meaning, for which he uses the term SEMEME (SEMEM), in the following way:

Dieses Semem ist als eine überindividuelle gesellschaftlich-kommunikative Norm zu verstehen, die, in der Kommunikation aus den mit den sprach-lichen Formativen im Bewusstsein der Sprachbenutzer gekoppelten indivi-duellen Abbildern heraus entstanden, als eine synchronisch weitgehend in-variante intersubjektive Grösse in sich Abbildfaktoren vereinigt, die den subjektiven Abbildern gemeinsam sind.

(This sememe is to be taken as a supra-individual social and communicative norm, which, having grown from the individual images linked with linguistic forms in the minds of speakers, is synchronically largely invariable and intersubjective in character and consists of those components of images which are common to the subjective images.)

If we accept this definition of meaning, the relation holding between lin-guistic forms and objects of the real world is not a direct one. It is often referred to as *Abbildungsbeziehung* (Brekle, *Semantik*, 1972: 30) in order to make it clear that the meaning connected with a linguistic form is the mental image (*Bewusstseinsinhalt*) of objects (states and situations) of the real world.[7]

8.2.2 *Meaning and the extralinguistic world*

In order to make this distinction clear, we can imagine a set of objects of the real world $\{x_1 \ldots x_n\}$ which can be seen as fulfilling certain conditions or pos-sessing certain distinct properties. For instance, it could be regarded as a pro-perty of the set of *Studenten* (in the German sense of the word) that they are registered at a university. This is one of the conditions one has to meet in order to be a student. We can thus establish a set of features $\{\alpha, \beta \ldots \varepsilon\}$ to be fulfilled by the objects $x_1 \ldots x_n$, in our case by all students.

The *Abbildungsbeziehung* now holds between the linguistic form *Student* (or /ʃtʊˈdɛnt/) and the set $\{x_1 \ldots x_n\}$, which in its turn is characterized by the set of features $\{\alpha, \beta \ldots \varepsilon\}$. According to Brekle (1972: 30-7), who develops these ideas in his discussion of the semiotic theory provided by Morris, the meaning of a linguistic sign (which he calls DESIGNATUM) stands for the class of objects of the real world, *ie* for the class of students, or, to express it differently, for the idea of student. The linguistic form *Student* can then be applied to all in-dividuals meeting these conditions.[8] Brekle (1972: 35) illustrates this 'semantical rule' in the following way:

This view of the *Abbildungsbeziehung* between the objects of the real world and a linguistic form *A* enables Brekle (1972: 36-7) to characterize *meaning* in the way shown on *p* 82.

Das Designatum (= Bedeutung) von *A* kann nun aufgefasst werden entweder als die Klasse der Gegenstände $x_1 \ldots x_n$ (die Aufzählung der Ele-mente einer solchen Klasse ist aber wegen der Weite der vorkommenden Gegenstandsbereiche faktisch nicht möglich), oder als die Intension (= Begriff) einer solchen Klasse, repräsentiert durch begriffliche Merkmale, die mit den auf die allgemeinste Form gebrachten Bedingungen der Zuordnung

Zeichenform linguistic form	*Student*	*bedeutet* means	*Designatum* meaning	{Student}

anwendbar auf / applicable to ↓

↑ *konstituiert* / constitutes

Gegenstände objects	$x_1 \ldots x_n$	*erfüllen* meet	*Merkmalsmenge oder Menge der Bedingungen* {*an einer Hochschule immatrikuliert* ...} set of features or conditions {matriculated at a university ...}

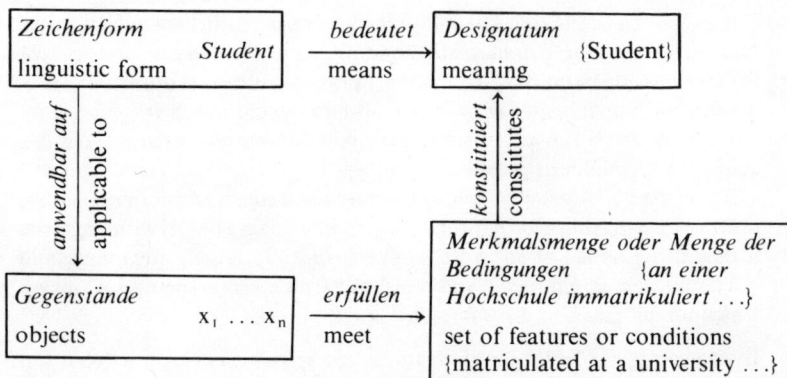

von *A* zu $x_1 \ldots x_n$ identisch sind.

(The meaning of a linguistic form *A* can now be taken as either the class of objects $x_1 \ldots x_n$ (due to the range of objects covered, listing the elements of such classes would seem impossible, however), or as the intension (*Begriff*, concept) of such a class, represented by ideational components, which are identical with the conditions of the relation of *A* to $x_1 \ldots x_n$ in their most general form.[9])

8.3 Componential analysis and the lexical field

8.3.1 *The analogy between semantics and phonology*

Whereas in the previous section we have been concerned with the problem of what we mean when we talk of the meaning of a lexical item, we shall now consider how the meanings of lexical items can best be described. In Chapter 2, we have discussed the importance of the concept of lexical fields within content-oriented grammar;[10] Trier's work may appear even more significant, however, when one considers that modern German structuralists also take the word field as the starting-point of their investigation of the structure of vocabulary.

Coseriu (*Probleme*, 1973: 53), for instance, analyses lexical field structures (*Wortfeldstrukturen*) as being made up of lexical items in direct opposition to each other and dividing amongst themselves a spectrum of meanings (*Bedeutungszone*), which is called a *lexical field*. Thus the German adjectives *alt, jung, neu* form a word field as do the verbs *rennen, laufen, schwimmen, tanzen.*[11]

But how can word fields be analysed? When looking for an answer to this question, one may be helped by remembering that semantic investigation and phonological analysis can be compared in a number of respects (the equivalent of lexical fields on the phonological level being provided by the two classes of vowels and consonants). According to Coseriu (1973: 58–72), the following parallels can be drawn.[12]

(i) Both on the levels of content and sound *oppositions* can be observed *between units that have some properties in common*: the phonemes /t/ and /d/ of the German consonant system, for instance, share the features 'plosive' and 'dental', but differ in that /t/ is 'voiceless', whereas /d/ is 'voiced'. Likewise *Professor* and *Student* both refer to people connected with a university, but with different functions within it. Coseriu's own example is that the verbs *stehen, sitzen, liegen* share the meaning of specifying position in relation to a horizontal plane but differ in the type of position they denote.

(ii) The concept of *neutralization* can be applied both to semantics and phonology: it is a well-known fact that in word-final position in German all plosives are 'voiceless', the /t/–/d/ opposition (as in *Rates–Rades*) being neutralized (both *Rat* and *Rad* are pronounced /raːt/). According to Coseriu (1973: 60) neutralization in semantics can be caused by the context in which an item appears: in the same way that *Professor* and *Student* suggest university level, *Lehrer* and *Schüler* would usually be used to refer to people working at school. This, however, need not necessarily be the case as it is possible to refer to *Professor Geckeler* as *Professor Coserius Schüler*. Other examples are the nouns *Mann* and *Frau*, both of which can be referred to by the unspecified (or neutralized) *Mensch*, or *Kuh*, which, despite the existence of *Bulle*, in most contexts is used to refer to both sexes of the species.

(iii) As in phonology, lexical units can be split up into *components*. In the same way that /p/, /t/, /k/ and /b/, /d/, /g/ are distinguished by the features 'voiceless' and 'voiced', lexical groups like *Student, Schüler, Lehrling, Auszubildender* can be contrasted with *Professor, Lehrer, Meister* and *Ausbilder*: a feature 'learn' can be attributed to the first set, whereas items of the second set share a feature 'teach'. Using the features 'stative' and 'intransitive', Coseriu (1973: 62) distinguishes the group *liegen, stehen, sitzen* from the group *legen, stellen, setzen*, which can be characterized as 'dynamic' and 'transitive'.

(iv) In phonology, distinctive features do not appear in one correlation only, but *the same oppositions apply recurrently*, ie the distinction between 'voiceless' and 'voiced' applies not only to /t/ and /d/ but to many consonants of German. This principle is also true of semantic features: the same components that distinguish *Student, Schüler, Lehrling* (or *liegen, stehen, sitzen*) must also be used to distinguish *Professor, Lehrer, Meister* (or *legen, stellen, setzen* respectively).

(v) Coseriu (1973: 64) holds that *the same types of oppositions* can be found in phonology and lexical field analysis:

    a: OPPOSITIONS OF DEGREE (*graduelle Oppositionen*) in phonology can be found in respect of the varying degree of openness or closeness of vowels. This type of opposition can also be found in vocabulary; it is presented by lexical fields such as *eisig, kalt, kühl, lau, warm, heiss*.

  b: EQUIPOLLENT OPPOSITONS (*äquipollente Oppositionen*) hold when all
  the terms comprising a field display an equal measure of opposition
  to the others. For instance, in phonology this relation holds between
  such features as 'bilabial' (/b/), 'dental' (/d/), 'velar' (/k/) etc; in
  semantics colour terms like *rot, gelb, grün, blau* can be taken as an
  example of equipollent oppositions.[13]

  c: PRIVATIVE OPPOSITIONS (*privative Oppositionen*) apply to pairs in
  which one element is determined by the presence of a particular feature
  (as /d/ is by the feature '+voice') which the other lacks (/t/ has
  '−voice'). It is not difficult to find this type of opposition in lexical
  structure: *fällen* and *fallen* (or *töten* and *sterben*) may serve as
  examples, as *fallen* lacks the feature '+cause' that *fällen* has.

These are only some of the analogies which can be drawn between phonology and semantics (see Wotjak, *Untersuchungen*, 1971: 67–78). They seem
to suggest certain similarities between the phonological and semantic
structures of languages, although important differences between the two levels
must not be obscured, as Coseriu points out. These similarities can be used
as arguments in favour of adopting the same approach to the analysis of
semantic structure as the one that has been applied to the investigation of
sound-structure. Such an investigation would then attempt to describe the
meanings of lexical items or lexemes (for which some linguists use the term
sememes) by splitting them up into minimal distinctive features of meaning,
which are called SEMES (SEME).

8.3.2 *Lexical field analysis using semantic components*
According to Coseriu (1973: 54–5) *semes* can be arrived at by lexical field
analysis. We shall now try to illustrate how this can be done and compare
some verbs belonging to the field of motion: if we take *rennen* and *schleichen*,
for instance, the obvious distinguishing feature is (relative) speed, *ie rennen*
can be marked '+ *Geschwindigkeit*', whereas *schleichen* must be characterized
as '− *Geschwindigkeit*'. Other verbs of motion, however, do not seem to indicate whether the movement involved is fast or slow; *reiten*, for example, refers
to both walk and canter, *ie* the feature *Geschwindigkeit* is irrelevant to the
description of the meaning of *reiten*, which we will show by a feature '± *Geschwindigkeit*'.

A further difference between *reiten* and *rennen* is that the activity *reiten* involves a means of transport (*eg* a horse), whereas *rennen* does not. On the
other hand, *reiten* and *rennen* can be distinguished from *schwimmen* by a
feature characterizing the medium, which in the case of *schwimmen* is '+
Wasser', in the case of *reiten* and *rennen* '+ *Erde*'. In this way semes can be
established which finally enable us to distinguish the verbs in this lexical field.

It is obvious that the verbs of motion all share the feature 'movement', which
can be referred to as '+ *dynamisch*' and is very similar to a feature '+ *delokal*'.

Coseriu has called this an *Archilexem*[14] because it characterizes the whole of the lexical field. In some very special uses, however, verbs may not show these features. *Thea bummelt*, for instance, could mean that she is rather slow at work, which would not involve '+ *dynamisch*'. (See 8.3.4.)

8.3.3 *Classemes*

The preceding examples may suffice to explain the basic principle of establishing semes (distinctive features of meaning) through lexical field analysis. The fact remains, however, that even if the meanings of all the items in a lexical field can be sufficiently distinguished from one another in this way, they have still not yet been adequately described (*cf* Wotjak, *Untersuchungen*, 1971: 187–188), because we cannot account for the fact that both *Thea kommt* and *Der Armleuchter kommt* are acceptable sentences in German, as is *Thea tanzt*, whereas **Der Armleuchter tanzt* is not.[15]

We thus come to the problem of which words can occur together in a sentence, a question which has been treated under different labels in various theories: Porzig referred to this kind of relation between two lexical items as *wesenhafte Bedeutungsbeziehungen* (see Lyons, *Semantics I*, 1977: 261–6), whereas modern linguists often talk of SELECTION RESTRICTIONS or CO-OCCURRENCE RESTRICTIONS in this context (*cf* Leech, *Semantics*, 1974: 141–6). As we have seen in Chapter 4, these features are relevant to syntax and one could ask whether we are justified in treating them as part of semantics at all. But although the fact that *tanzen* can only be applied to humans and trained animals is not a property of the activity itself, it can hardly be denied that it is a feature of the meaning of the verb and thus must be taken account of in a theory of meaning. (This view is supported by Leech, 1974: 142, and by Palmer, *Semantics*, 1976: 101.)

It is important, however, to remember that this kind of feature is not revealed by field analysis. This fact has been used by Coseriu (1973: 77–8) to draw a terminological distinction between SEMES ('minimal distinctive features of meaning that are operative within a single lexical field')[16] and CLASSEMES ('very general sense components that are common to lexemes belonging to several different lexical fields'. Lyons, *I*, 1977: 326). Classematic differences are manifested in the different ways in which lexical items combine with other lexical items.

Features like 'human' or 'animate' are considered to be classemes as they are common to nouns such as *Thea, Linguist, Kind, Leiche*, which belong to different lexical fields. However, the classeme 'human' attributed to these nouns is in some respects different from the feature 'applicable to human nouns' which we attributed to the verb *tanzen* and which can also be used to characterize adjectives like *jung* or *blond*. This means that we have to distinguish between classemes which are determining in character in that they denote a certain property (PRIMARY CLASSEMES) and classemes which are determined in that they can only be applied to items specified by a primary classeme (these

Verbs of human motion	ARGUMENT (SUBJEKT)			Muskelkraft Extremitäten		PREDICATE (AKTTYP)			Umgebungsbedingt Medium					
	Belebt	Mensch	Aktor	Arme	Beine	Dynamisch	Schnell	Vertikal Max	Erde	Wasser	Luft	Mittel	Standardsprache	Emotion
bummeln	Zug +[−]	+	+	−	bei der +[−] Arbeit	bei der +[−] Arbeit	−	−	+	−	−	−	+	+
kommen	+[−]	+[−]	Auto +[−]	⊦	Auto +[−]	+	+	−	+	+	+	−[+]	+	−
laufen	+[−]	+[−]	+	−	+	+	±	−	+	−	−	−	+	−
reiten	+	+	−	−	−	+	±	−	+	−	−	+	+	−
rennen	Zeit +[−]	+[−]	+	−	+	+	+	−	+	−	−	−	+	(−)
schleichen	Zeit +[−]	−[+]	+	−	+	+	−	−	+	−	−	−	+	+
tanzen	Kreisel +[−]	+	+	−	+	+	±	−	+	−	−	−	+	+
schwimmen	+[−]	−[−]	+	+	+	+	±	−	−	+	−	−	+	−
unsicher sein	+	+	−			−		−	−	−	−	−	−	+
Zustand (z.B. Fett)	−	−	−	−	−	−	−	−	−	+	−	−	+	−

could then be referred to as SECONDARY CLASSEMES. Coseriu, 1973: 82).[17]

Very similar ideas have been put forward by Leisi – his *Wortinhalt* (1971: 71) first appeared in 1952 – who remarks that while nouns classify the object they refer to, verbs of motion, for instance, not only classify the type of action but also the object in motion. The fact that the categorizations provided by noun and verb must not clash with each other has been referred to by Leisi as SEMANTIC CONGRUENCE. The categorization made by the verb must either be identical with that of the noun (*Die Flüssigkeit fliesst*) or more embracing (*Wasser fliesst*).

In our example *Der Armleuchter tanzt* we clearly observe a violation of the principle of semantic congruence in that *tanzen*, specified by a secondary classeme 'applicable to human nouns' co-occurs with a noun that lacks the feature 'human'. In certain contexts, however, such violations are permissible and we shall refer to this usage as metaphorical.[18] If Thea were taken to a ball, for instance, but only had eyes for somebody else, for a blond linguist, who perhaps asked her for a dance, then Thea's companion might very well say *Der Armleuchter tanzt auch noch mit ihr*! Apart from stylistic values, this sentence would be synonymous with *Der blonde Linguist tanzt mit Thea*. A similar example is provided by the phrase *Der Kongress tanzt*, which was originally meant as a complaint about the idle life of the participants of the 1815 Congress in Vienna. Again, we have a violation of the principle of semantic congruence which is explicable in terms of metaphorical use.

8.3.4 *The lexical field of verbs of human motion*
In 8.3.2 we have shown how semes distinguishing various verbs of motion can be arrived at and have demonstrated the need to integrate some more general semantic components such as 'human' into the description.[19] As the usefulness of the distinction between semes and classemes can easily be questioned, we shall not retain it for the purposes of practical analysis. What is important, however, is that both types of semantic features are taken into account, *ie* that features denoting properties of the verb (*Akttyp*) as well as features of the subject carrying out the action are included. This has been done by Wotjak (*Untersuchungen*, 1971) in his large-scale analysis of verbs of human motion. Wotjak also includes features referring to the linguistic level (standard language) and to the emotional impact of some verbs.[20] In some cases, Wotjak's table also shows some special meanings of the verbs under analysis, for example, *Der Zug bummelt*.

Although we cannot give an adequate description of the theoretical basis of Wotjak's work,[21] which is largely based on intuition (1971: 180–5), his analysis may serve as an example of how componential analysis can be applied to the description of lexical fields. The table opposite presents only part of his analysis of verbs of human motion in German.

8.4 The interlingual approach to meaning

8.4.1 *The character of the distinctive features of meaning*

Wotjak's attempt to describe a lexical field by means of componential analysis[22] has shown that the theoretical basis of field theory has been improved by the application of this formalism. Whereas in the previous section we have been concerned with the ways in which componential analysis could be used to describe the lexical structure of a language, here we shall deal in brief with a more theoretical problem concerning the status of the sense components. The question we are to be concerned with is whether the analogy with phonological analysis can be expanded to enable us to reduce semantic description to a small and universal set of distinctive features as has been done successfully in phonology.

This leads us back to the question of the nature of semes, which have been defined as distinctive features of meaning that are operative within a lexical field. This implies, however, not only that semes are applicable to a specific language but that they cannot be established for the whole language, having seme status only within one particular word field. Even if the semes arrived at by the analysis of a particular lexical field can be used in the componential description of other lexical items, it is by no means certain that they still maintain their distinctive character and do not merely function as additional components of meaning. This objection to seme analysis has been raised by Heger (*Monem*, [2]1976: 41–5), who, on the basis of this argument, denies that semes can be regarded as universals.

The approach advocated by Heger is very similar to Meier's ('Noematische Analyse', 1966). Meier takes an interlingual approach to the description of meaning. His basic sense components, called NOEMES (NOEME) are defined by their place in an extralinguistic conceptual coordinate system. The inventory of such basic ideational elements must be large enough to allow for all the sememes (meanings) of any natural language to be made up of a combination of noemes.[23]

8.4.2 *Basic semantic relations*

According to Heger ([2]1976: 43) it is noematic analysis which provides the basis for a contrastive analysis of different languages, because, for example, noemes are not bound to any particular language and can thus be used for the description of any language.[24]

Heger adopts the same interlingual (*aussereinzelsprachlich*) approach to the description of more complex sense relations, namely relations holding between various items. Such relations have been taken account of by many grammarians, *eg* the case grammar approach is one that is well known. Other linguists have used the methods of logic and applied them to the description of language. In this context, so-called predication analysis is of special interest: the predication (*ie* the meaning of a sentence) is split up into relational terms, the predicates, and into the terms which are related, the arguments. Thus a simple sentence like *Thea liebt den Linguisten* may be seen as containing the two arguments *Thea* and *der Linguist*, which are related by the predicate *lieben* (compare Leech, 1974: 128–36, and Palmer 1976: 106–11).[25]

Heger ([2]1976: 105) takes a very similar approach in his attempt to establish general deep-structure representations of basic sense relations, except that his model not only involves two elements (argument and predicate), but comprises three components:

(i) An ACTANT A, the position of which can be taken by noemes,
(ii) A RELATOR R, the position of which can be taken by noemes, but which is also marked for semantic valency ($_1$R, $_2$R etc; compare 4.2.2.),[26]
(iii) A PREDICATOR P, which is bivalent and establishes the relation between the actant and the relator.[27]

An extremely simple relation between an actant and a simple monovalent relator could then be represented in the following way:

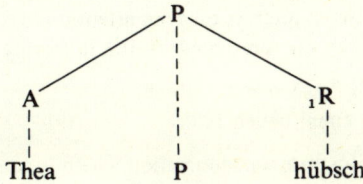

A model of this kind could be taken as a representation of linguistic forms like *Thea ist hübsch*, *Thea war hübsch* or *die hübsche Thea*, but, as A and $_1$R are specified by universal components of meaning (noemes), also *Thea is pretty* or *Thea est jolie*, etc (Heger, [2]1976: 115).

In the case of a bivalent relator, two actants A_1 and A_2 are also involved. They are subsumed under A*. We shall try to illustrate the relations 'bigger than' and 'as big as' which are three-dimensional relations (Q(3d)). This type of two-place relator can be split into the character of the dimension (in our case Q(3d)) and the two positions to which it refers (1/2). The symbolic representation would then look like this (compare Heger, [2]1976: 117):

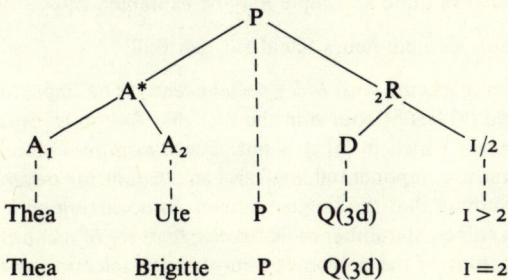

This model represents sentences like *Thea ist grösser als Ute*, which is indicated by $1 > 2$, whereas $1 = 2$ must be taken to mean *Thea ist ebenso gross wie Brigitte*.

We cannot elaborate Heger's model of actants any further, but hope to have illustrated the basic principles of his approach. The introduction of the relations of time, place, cause, inclusion and quantity enables him to propose models which could be seen as rather elaborated deep-structure representations of sentences of natural languages, taking account of theme/rheme structure, speech act classification and presuppositions. Heger ([2]1976: 5) himself is aware of one great weakness of his analysis resulting from the fact that he does not provide any formalism to demonstrate how his general deep-structure representations could be related to surface structures of natural languages.

8.5 Once again: context

8.5.1 *Polysemy*

In the final section of this chapter we turn our attention to some basic problems of semantics, such as the one presented by the following pair of sentences:

[1] Thea macht sich für den Ball hübsch.
[2] Thea kauft sich einen neuen Ball.

These two sentences illustrate a phenomenon which is commonly referred to as POLYSEMY, *ie* when one linguistic form has two or more different meanings. As in English, the word *Ball* in German can either refer to a round object used in games or denote a formal social event at which dancing takes place.[28] It is remarkable that despite the polysemy of *Ball* neither [1] nor [2] is ambiguous, *ie* the hearer/reader knows perfectly well which of the two meanings is intended in either case.

This is obviously due to the determining role of linguistic context. Within the framework of componential analysis this can be quite easily explained by selection restrictions which we have discussed in 8.3.3. The sememe 'play object' (if we may roughly paraphrase its meaning in this way) is incompatible with the meaning components of *hübsch machen für*, whereas in [2] the semantic features of *kaufen* rule out the reading 'social event'. That relations of this kind are not always quite so simple may be explained by

[3] Thea kauft sich ein neues Kleid für den Ball

in which *kaufen* co-occurs with *Ball* ('social event'). The important difference between [2] and [3] lies of course in the fact that *Ball* in [2] is the object (or *patiens*) of *kaufen*, which in [3] it is not. These examples seem to illustrate two points: firstly, componential analysis can account for disambiguation in context by assuming that the linguistic items co-occurring with a polysemic item provide a sufficient number of distinctive features of meaning to rule out all but one meaning of the polysemic item through selection restrictions (see

Heger, [2]1976: 54; Meier, 'Noematische Analyse', 1966: 126–7).[29] Secondly, these examples may provide further evidence for the contention that grammatical relations like those which determine the different meanings of *den Ball* in [2] and [3] cannot simply be treated as matters of syntax, but are highly relevant to the semantic interpretation of a sentence and thus must also be accounted for by selection restrictions.[30]

8.5.2 *Semantics and pragmatics*
There are, however, some cases in which linguistic context does not provide sufficient information to ensure a clear disambiguation of a polysemic item. Let us take

[4] Thea freut sich auf den Ball
[5] Thea findet den Ball schön

each of which allows for both meanings of *Ball*. In the one case, Thea could be imagined as a small girl thinking of a birthday present, whereas in the other reading she is likely to be somewhat older. This example shows that semantics and pragmatics cannot really be strictly separated from one another, but have to be combined.[31]

8.5.3 *Semantics and textual analysis*
The fact that the meaning of a lexical item is largely dependent on its conext is not only true of polysemic words, as can be seen by looking at some problems in translation theory (Neubert, 'Invarianz', 1973). If we take the following sentences,

[6] Thea traf den Linguisten auf dem Ball
[7] Thea traf sich mit dem Linguisten auf dem Ball

we find that they differ somewhat in meaning; [6] suggest that their meeting was accidental, whereas [7] refers to a planned meeting (*cf* Leisi, *Wortinhalt*, 1971: 106). These sentences could then perhaps be translated into English as follows:

[6'] Thea happened to meet the linguist at the ball
[7'] Thea had arranged to meet the linguist at the ball (and actually did so).

These translations suggest that while the actual representation of all the meaning components of the German sentences is possible in English, the translation will be rather clumsy if the distinction in meaning is not lexicalized. Now, if *treffen* or *sich treffen mit* appears later in the same text – in a sentence like *Der Linguist, mit dem sich Thea getroffen hatte, war ein bekannter Soziolinguist*, for example – it would hardly be necessary to provide the same precise (and clumsy) translation again, as the nature of their meeting has already been described. In this case then, the English verb *meet* would take over components of meaning mentioned earlier in the text. We have already drawn attention to this while discussing Kallmeyer's view of reference in 6.2.3. Thus sentences [6] and [7] have once again demonstrated that the meanings of lexical items must not be analysed in isolation: Wotjak ('Invarianz', 1973: 72–3) comes to the conclusion that a sememe consists of a number of sense components, but that not all of them need be actualized in a given context.[32]

A similar problem is raised by a lexical distinction such as that holding between *barrister* and *solicitor*, which is not just a distinction made in the language, but a distinction typical of the British legal system. In translation, one will have to consider whether the German reading public will be familiar with this distinction and whether it is relevant to the text, which again leads to pragmatics. In a legal text, the distinction must certainly be made clear by using paraphrases like *vor Gericht praktizierender Rechtsanwalt* (for barrister) or *Rechtsberater* (for solicitor), which, in the wider context of, say, a novel where someone's profession is just mentioned in passing, would seem hypercorrect and indeed textually inadequate. This in fact means that the translator is concerned not only with semantics but also with pragmatic and textual analysis (Neubert, 'Invarianz', 1973: 15–19).[33]

Our treatment of meaning in context has shown, we hope, that lexical meaning should not be treated as a strict and invariant property, but rather that allowance should be made for special meanings or meaning components if words are used in context. So perhaps after all, Humpty Dumpty was not too far from the truth when he said 'If I use a word, it means what I choose it to mean – neither more nor less', even if acknowledgement of it makes the task of the linguist more laborious.

8.6 Concluding remarks

Semantic studies in Germany have been largely determined by various versions of componential analysis. This is not only true of the linguists working within the framework of transformational grammar (whose views on semantics have been treated in Chapter 7), but also of the structural semanticists, who, as we hope to have shown, have successfully applied the componential approach to the analysis of lexical fields. This means that the influential ideas of Trier and Porzig have been taken account of in a formal representation of lexical structure.

The roots of componential analysis are much deeper. The idea of establishing a set of 'atomic' features of meaning can be traced back to the German philosopher Leibniz (see Land, *Signs*, 1974: 135–9). Tempting as such an idea may be, we have to realize that there is still some way to go before such an inventory of distinctive features of meaning – similar to the set of features used in phonology – can be established. This is mainly due to two problems of componential analysis which have as yet remained unsolved.

The first problem is posed by the question of the universal character of sense components. Wotjak (*Untersuchungen*, 1971: 45) assumes that the semes arrived at through lexical field analysis are at least partly universal entities and regards the sememes, the bundles of semes, as language-specific properties. As we have seen, this view has been attacked by Heger, who, like Meier, advocates the interlingual approach which leads to the establishment of the conceptual components referred to as noemes. However, the status of noemes has no theoretical foundation and in practical analysis seems to present just as many problems as seme analysis, so that it can be doubted whether there is really any essential difference between semes and noemes.[34]

Moreover, neither approach has been able to solve the second major problem of componential analysis, namely the question 'Where does the splitting up into components stop?', *ie* how do we know what an atomic concept of meaning is? At present, linguists are far from being able to give a satisfactory answer to this questions, as even Wotjak, if only in a footnote, has admitted (*Untersuchungen*, 1971: 45 note 170, and see also Baumgärtner, 'Struktur', 1967: 176).[35]

These problems of componential analysis are by no means limited to the work of German scholars adopting this approach, and indeed componential analysis has been severely attacked by some linguists in recent years (Palmer, 1976: 88–91, and Lyons, I, 1977: 331–5). Despite its obvious inadequacies, the merits of componential analysis could lead one to see in it a useful instrument for use within a larger theory of semantics (Leech, 1974: 125). As we have shown in 8.5, such a comprehensive theory of meaning will also have to cross boundaries and take account of problems which fall within the scope of the syntactic, pragmatic or textual theories which have been treated elsewhere in this book.

Recommended further reading

An extremely useful and very readable introduction to semantics is provided by Brekle (*Semantik*, 1972). Wotjak's *Untersuchungen zur Struktur der Bedeutung* (written in 1968 and first published in 1971) provides a very detailed outline of various approaches to semantics and thus illustrates the development of this branch of linguistics. For a practical study of the lexical system of English and German, see Leisi (*Wortinhalt*, 1971).

Chapter 9

Sociolinguistics

9.1 General remarks on sociolinguistics in Germany

Sociolinguistics can well be considered the best-known branch of linguistics in the Federal Republic. When linguistics is discussed in public, for example in the press or on television, the problems raised usually fall within the scope of sociolinguistics.

In order to understand how this state of affairs could arise, one has to recall the atmosphere of the late sixties and early seventies: the student rebellion and the formation of a social democrat/liberal coalition under Willy Brandt were indications of a widespread desire for reform. The determination to create greater social equality led to the demand for profound changes in the educational system: all children, irrespective of their social background, were to be given equal opportunities. In this context, two questions were raised: to what extent is a child's success at school determined by his use of language and could the fact that some working-class children do badly at school be related to their linguistic background and, if this was so, what conclusions are to be drawn?

It is not surprising that many left-wing scholars turned their attention to the work of the sociolinguists Bernstein (Great Britain) and Labov (United States), whose research seemed relevant to these questions.[1] Depending upon their political standpoints, linguists have drawn different conclusions from the research done in this field, some issues such as compensatory education have provoked bitter controversies amongst linguists and educationists. In this chapter we shall try to outline the main arguments developed in the course of this discussion, which centred on the nature of the link between social class and language, although in recent years interest in these matters has decreased. Our outline will involve examining the work of Ammon, Jäger and Oevermann, but it must be pointed out that the research carried out by these linguists (and many others whose work we cannot mention here) is so very complex that we can only discuss the basic arguments.

Soziolinguistik has established itself as one of the social sciences but the term *Soziolinguistik* is used in Germany in a more limited way than *sociolinguistics* is in English-speaking countries.[2] Sociolinguistics in Germany owes little to the firmly established linguistic discipline dialectology (*Mundartforschung*), which, although it has also examined some aspects of the relation of language and social class, has done so in a very haphazard way.[3] Regional dialects are, however, still being studied as is shown by the recent publication of a German dialect atlas, König (*dtv-Atlas*: 1978).

9.2 Types of variation in language

9.2.1 *Regional variation*

Like any other language, German must be regarded not as an unvarying entity but rather as an abstraction derived from various group languages. To recognize this, we need only compare the speech of people living in different areas. The differences in pronunciation are perhaps the most striking: someone living in Nuremberg pronounces *sie* and *sprechen* as [si:] and [ʃprɛçn], whereas [zi:] and [sprɛçn] are heard in Kiel. Such differences are not only found at the phonological level – there is no phoneme /z/ in East Franconian – phonetic realizations of the same phoneme also differ. In the North of Germany, for instance, [ʃprɛçn] would probably be pronounced with a uvular [ʁ], whereas in the South the tongue-tip [r] is widely used. Such regional varieties of pronunciation we shall refer to as ACCENTS.[4]

But the speech of Nuremberg and Kiel people differs not only in accent, to a certain extent they also use different words. The Nuremberger would probably say *schau einmal* [ʃɑuʷəmɔːl], the man from Kiel *kucke mal* [kʊkmɑ]. Needless to say, there are also some differences in syntax: some Southern dialects lack the distinction made in North Germany by using the preterite or the perfect tenses, the perfect being used for both (see Chapter 12). Variation caused by differences in vocabulary or grammar we shall refer to as DIALECT (Trudgill, *Sociolinguistics*, 1974: 15–20), although in German the distinction between accent and dialect is often obscured by the use of the terms *Dialekt* or *Mundart* for both.

The concept of dialect is itself still a generalization. The boundary of a dialect area can rarely, if ever, be drawn precisely because every dialect is characterized by a number of features whose distribution rarely coincide. The lack of a voiced fricative /z/ and the lack of a preterite/perfect distinction are both features of East Franconian, but the latter can be observed over a wider area than the former. Precise statements about distribution boundaries can only be made about individual dialect features by mapping ISOGLOSSES. Dialect boundaries can then be said to exist where a number of isoglosses coincide or are very close together. We cannot discuss German dialectology in any detail but the following map from *Abriss der Geschichte der Deutschen Sprache* (Berlin, Akademie Verlag, 1976) may serve to illustrate the distribution of the main German dialects.

German Dialects

0   50   100   150 km

Friesisch
—·—·—·—·—·

Niederfränkisch,
Niederdeutsch
▲▲▲▲▲▲▲▲

Mitteldeutsch
┴┴┴┴┴┴┴

Oberdeutsch

Hochdeutsch

—··—··— Sprachgrenze
zum Romanischen,
Slawischen,
Dänischen

friesisch

Kiel

Rostock

Hamburg   Mecklenburgisch

Saterländ

Nordniedersächsisch   Bremen

Elbe

Märkisch

Amsterdam
Nieder-

Ems

Ost-
Hannover

Weser

Magdeburg

Oder

fränkisch

Münster

West-
fälisch

Saale

Leipzig

Neiße

Brussels
Ripaurisch

Maas

Köln

Kassel

Thüringisch

Dresden

Ober-
sächsisch

Sorbisch
Lausitzisch

Hessisch

Erfurt

Moselfränkisch

Frankfurt

Mainz

Rheinfränkisch

Ostfränkisch

Main

Prag

Neckar

Nürnberg

Südfränkisch

Nord-
bairisch

Rhein

Stuttgart

Schwäbisch

Mosel

München

Mittelbairisch

Donau

Wien

Salzburg

Nieder-

Zürich

alemannisch

Bern

Innsbruck

Graz

Hoch-

Rhône

Südbairisch

9.2.2 *The standard language*

Whenever German television broadcasts a play in Bavarian dialect, this pro-
vokes protests from viewers in the North who complain that the play is unintel-
ligible. Although communication between speakers of different dialects of one
language should always be possible, dialect differences do lead to misunder-
standings. It follows from this that the television authorities in Germany
would be ill-advised to have a national newscast read by a newsreader with
a strong regional accent. This demonstrates the need for a supra-regional
variety to ensure communication over a wide area. This variety of German
is usually called the STANDARD LANGUAGE (HOCHDEUTSCH).[5]

The advantage of the standard lies not so much in its efficiency as a code,

a medium for conveying information, as in its intelligibility over a wide area. While the grammar of East Fraconian would not in itself prevent the Nuremberger from using it to talk about electronics or philosophy, besides football or the family budget, its intelligibility would restrict its use outside Franconia. The standard is preferred, then, not for its intrinsic superiority as a code but for reasons of intelligibility, and so it is best regarded as the supra-regional dialect of the language.

Unquestionably, the standard should be the variety taught to foreigners. It is also the variety that is most commonly described in linguistic analyses. One must, however, remember that it is difficult to define what constitutes the standard. If approached on this matter, most Germans would certainly refer the questioner to the *Duden*. The corpus to which the editors of the *Duden* (*Grammatik*) refer when deciding whether or not a particular usage is acceptable consists largely of literary texts. The spoken language and non-literary texts are seldom used as examples of standard usage, although many linguists have questioned the validity of the written norm. (See also 2.5.2.)[6]

As far as accent is concerned, there is a very strict norm, BÜHNENAUSSPRACHE, which is mainly followed by actors and newsreaders. Most speakers of the standard in Germany still retain a recognizable regional accent. (See also Chapter 10.)[7]

9.2.3 *Social and situational variation*

It would be a mistake to assume that a speaker is either a speaker of standard German or a dialect speaker. Our newsreader will probably not use the 'same language' when talking to his wife or children as he does on the radio. But we need not take such an extreme example: a middle-class Nuremberger, who speaks dialect when talking to Franconian friends, will certainly try to avoid doing so when talking to a Berliner. This brings us back to the influence of the context of situation, which was discussed at length in 5.4.1.[8]

In connection with pragmalinguistic studies we have shown that the situations in which people speak affect the stylistic value of utterances. A lecturer addressing a large audience will use a more formal variety than in a tutorial group, an employee will probably speak more formally when chatting with his boss than when discussing the football results with his workmates. In the context of sociolinguistics we are not only interested in the stylistic factors determined by the context of situation and the social role at the time of speaking but also in the influence these factors have on the dialect and accent of the speaker.[9]

9.2.4 *The standard, dialect and social class*

In order to examine the link between use of the standard and social class, Ammon (*Dialekt*, [2]1973) analyses recordings of 638 speakers (natives of Baden-Württemberg), representative of all social classes and age-groups. The language of the subjects was analysed at the phonemic, morphemic and lexemic levels and the utterances evaluated to assess the dialect level: level 1 being reserved for forms with the minimum geographical distribution ('strong' dialect forms), level 4 for standard forms. Ammon hopes to establish a cline between standard and dialect and to overcome the artificial dichotomy between the two. His results can be summarized as follows:

   (i) High socio-economic status correlates highly with the use of the standard language.
  (ii) Men use the standard more often than women.
 (iii) Young men use the standard more often than older men.

These results, especially (i), suggest a direct link between social class and the language variety used. Dialect and standard, to use Ammon's term, 'symbolize' the lower and upper classes respectively; it is not the variety used that determines social status but social class that determines language use.[10] Ammon (*Dialekt*, [2]1973: 112) suggests that lower-class speakers are often unable to encode the standard just as some upper-class speakers cannot encode dialect. The term SOCIOLECT has been adopted by many sociolinguists to refer to language varieties determined by social class.

    The link between studies of this kind and the discussion of educational reforms mentioned in 9.1 is evident. If at school working-class children are expected to encode the same variety as middle-class children, they must be at a disadvantage because this sociolect is not spoken by their parents, whereas it is typically used by middle-class parents. As Bernstein's 'code theory' has been particularly influential in the recognition of these problems, we shall outline it briefly before coming back to the question of dialect and school in 9.4.

9.3 The code theory

9.3.1 *Bernstein's theory*
The British sociologist Basil Bernstein has postulated two codes which can be used: ELABORATED and RESTRICTED CODES. The largely context-independent elaborated code is used in formal situations and conveys its meanings without drawing heavily on extra-linguistic features (gestures, etc). It is also syntactically elaborate, using many subordinate clauses, passive forms, etc. The other code, the restricted code, which is used in informal situations, draws heavily upon the context and is less explicit. Its syntax is less complex and more predictable than that of the elaborated code.[11] These codes, Bernstein maintains, are used by both middle-class and working-class children; however, some working-class children always use the restricted code. Bernstein himself has not claimed that the use of the restricted code is a sign of low intelligence nor that this code is inferior. His critics have, however, maintained that the term restricted suggests inferiority and in Germany most sociolinguists associate Bernstein with reactionary attitudes.

9.3.2 *The deficit hypothesis*
Oevermann (*Sprache*, 1970: 448) claims that his research confirms the existence
of different class-determined codes. Like Bernstein's own, Oevermann's research is so complex that we can only summarize his conclusions, which are
that the existence of the two codes makes two requirements of the educational
system. Firstly, it must try to compensate for the environment of the working-
class child, which is deficient with regard to learning stimuli. Secondly, it must
recognize that its selection criteria discriminate against the working-class child
with his different behaviour. Since the problems faced by children from different social classes are themselves different, language, which is a response
to these problems, will reflect the social structure. Furthermore, children will
only expand and elaborate a linguistic repertoire in response to new situations.
This fact – according to Oevermann – explains the inadequacy of the American
headstart programme, which aimed to improve linguistic performance without
considering that language is used instrumentally. Oevermann also claims that
children of equal intelligence differ in their verbal strategies because of social
class. The different symbolization of the working-class child is not, in itself,
an inferior use of language.

9.3.3 *Rejection of the code theory*
Many German sociolinguists have condemned the findings of Bernstein and
Oevermann as invalid and/or reactionary.[12] Jäger (*Sprechen*, 1973: 14) says
that Bernstein and Oevermann can only deduce from the surface differences
between the working-class and middle-class codes that there are differences
of social status and that the codes tell us nothing about the speaker's intellectual capacity or social situation. In this pilot study Jäger analyses the spoken
language of a group of schoolchildren by asking them to retell the story of
a silent cartoon film that they have all seen together. He works from the following assumptions:

(i) Traditional grammatical categories must not be used to describe a non-
standard variety.
(ii) The variety must not be compared with the standard.
(iii) Surface differences, of themselves, do not permit the investigator to con-
clude that meaning differences are present.

He suggests that the function of the language analysed can only be appreciated
if the categories of a pragmatic (action-oriented) grammar are applied to it
rather than those of a surface grammar.
   Jäger assumes that thought processes result in two basic structural relationships within utterances: the one between subject and object, the other between
subject and predicate. Since the sentence is an abstraction and cannot be taken
as a unit of analysis in spoken discourse, Jäger speaks of *Ereignisse* (events,
happenings) as the basic relational forms which contain *Ereigniselemente*

(event or happening elements). The following is an example of spoken discourse together with Jäger's (1973: 17) analysis:

> Die Tasche is' ins Wasser geflogen und das Männeken is' hinterher und da kamen alle die Fische zusammen und haben sich das angeguckt.
> (The bag fell into the water and the little man went in after it and then all the fish came and had a look.)

This Jäger transforms into four *Ereignisse*, which themselves comprise ten elements:

(i) (die Tasche) (is' geflogen in) ('s Wasser)
(ii) und (das Männeken) (is' hinterher)
(iii) und da (alle Fische) (kamen zusammen)
(iv) und (die) (haben sich angeguckt) (das)

Jäger draws no firm conclusions from the study apart from those mentioned at the beginning of this section, which deny the validity of the code theory.

It is fair to say that although much sociolinguistic research in Germany has been concerned with the code theory, very little has come of this research. Despite ideologically motivated, though not necessarily invalid, criticisms of Anglo-American research, which have contributed to the popularity of linguistics and to the belief that it might be possible to apply linguistic findings, no progress has been made towards a general theory of German sociolinguistics. We will now turn to the *cause célèbre* of German educational planning in the early seventies, the proposals for the revision of the curriculum (Der Hessische Kultusminister, *Rahmenrichtlinien*, 1972) which for a year or so brought sociolinguistics to the very centre of public interest.

9.4 Language and school

The proposals of the Hessen curriculum development team can be found in the introduction to the *Rahmenrichtlinien Sekundarstufe I Deutsch (RRD)*.[13] Their first demand is that German mother-tongue teaching in the secondary school should increase children's communicative competence, since language and language use are essential both to communication and to social processes in general. Secondly, they claim that, as the primary mode, the spoken language should be stressed. Thirdly, the everyday language of schoolchildren (*Sprachverhalten*) must be the starting-point for all teaching, if emphasis is to be placed on the instrumental function of language (*RRD*, 1972: 6):

> Öffentliche und private Konflikte drücken sich in der Regel auch in Sprache aus. Das Sprachverhalten der Schüler ist darum nur im Zusammenhang mit diesen Konflikten zu sehen.
> (As a rule public and private conflicts also use the medium of language. For this reason the linguistic behaviour of schoolchildren can only be understood in the light of these conflicts.)

Most importantly, it is pointed out that the standard language is not the only dialect that ensures communication. (*RRD*, 1972: 6):

> Dass die Schule besondere Aufgaben zur Sicherung überregionaler Kommunikation zu erfüllen habe, konnte bis zur Verbreitung der Massenkommunikationsmittel als notwendige Aufgabe begriffen werden. Diese Aufgabe stellt sich heute der Schule nicht oder nur in einem sehr abgeschwächten Sinn.
> (Until the mass media had become widespread, it could be argued that the school had special and necessary tasks of ensuring supra-regional communication. This is now not the case or is only marginally important.)

It was this final claim that polarized public opinion. Many teachers and parents saw in this attitude to the standard language a rejection of those principles which *Sprachpflege* (watchfulness with regard to the language) stands for. Whereas the often emotional rejection of loan-words (*Fremdwörter*) and of spelling reform had long been regarded as last ditches in the stand for a 'pure' language, these proposals seemed to many a challenge to the standard language as such. Heinrichs and others ('Die Hessischen Rahmenrichtlinien', 1974) discuss many of the linguistic and educational issues raised by this radical questioning of the aims of mother-tongue teaching. The controversy illustrates particularly well the gulf separating the 'progressive' sociolinguist and the 'no-nonsense' man in the street.[14]

9.5 Concluding remarks

It is tempting, though sometimes misleading, to talk of particular events as turning-points but in retrospect 1972 and the *Rahmenrichtlinien* controversy do seem to have foreshadowed later events. The loss of interest in 'emancipatory' sociolinguistics accompanied a growing disillusionment with educational experiments – in schools and universities. The mood of the mid-seventies was to be one of retrenchment and withdrawal from the enthusiasm of earlier years. A reader in sociolinguistics, published in 1976 under the editorship of W. Viereck (*Sprachliches Handeln*, 1976), illustrates the change in orientation. The contributions include several on research procedures, articles by German- and English-speaking scholars on data collection and urban dialect surveys, as well as articles on discrete problems of language use (the language used in courts, the phonology of Viennese German and an analysis of a conversation). However, not one article is devoted to the Bernstein controversy and indeed Bernstein is only mentioned in passing in a few articles. In future we can probably expect more cooperation between dialectologists and sociolinguists, a greater concentration on empirical research and the growth of a German sociolinguistics which will have emancipated itself from its recent dependence on Anglo-American research.

Part 2

Chapter 10

Phonetics and phonology

10.1 The problem of a standard pronunciation of German

10.1.1 *Bühnenaussprache – an artificial concept*
The first question to be answered when discussing the sound-system of a language is what to take as the basis of the analysis. In Great Britain, the choice is a fairly easy one: most descriptions of British English are based on RECEIVED PRONUNCIATION (RP), known to non-linguists as *Queen's English* or *BBC English*. RP is a non-regional accent of English which is generally spoken by a more or less distinguishable class of people in Britain: university professors, public school students, radio announcers, etc. At least it was before the Second World War, but since then the importance of RP has diminished somewhat and indeed it is regarded by many as old-fashioned or snobbish nowadays. Many educated speakers now speak a variety of standard English with a slight regional accent.[1]

In this respect, Britain has moved closer to the situation in Germany, where indeed most speakers of standard German (we are not discussing dialect speakers in this chapter) retain a noticeable regional accent. This creates great problems when one is discussing the phonology of German. Most pronouncing dictionaries are based on a variety of German called BÜHNENAUS-SPRACHE, which is the outcome of a nineteenth-century movement for a unified pronunciation of German to overcome the considerable differences between German regional accents at the time. Some linguists studied the speech of actors in theatrical performances, which also varied considerably, and tried to establish a binding norm for the pronunciation of German on the stage.[2] One of the most prominent figures within this movement was Siebs, whose *Deutsche Bühnenaussprache* ([11]1915) has since become the standard pronouncing dictionary of German.

Siebs (*Bühnenaussprache*, [11]1915: 4) did not want to see *Bühnenaussprache* restricted to use on the stage, but assumed that educated speakers of German would aim at an approximation of *Bühnenaussprache* in their own pronunciation: the speech of dramatic art was regarded as the purest form of German. It must be pointed out, however, that although Siebs ([11]1915: 20) intended this norm to be introduced in schools, he was well aware of the fact that some regional influences would have to be tolerated.[3] *Bühnenaussprache* can thus be considered a norm for orientation and not an absolute norm; *ie* what Siebs advocated was a kind of modified standard for educated speakers of German.

The main difference between *Bühnenaussprache* and Received Pronunciation lies in the fact that whereas *Bühnenaussprache* is an artificial and codified norm – only valid for one stylistic level – RP is (or was) an accent spoken by a definable group of native speakers.[4] This may explain why accent has not played quite the same role as a social classifier in Germany as in England. It would have seemed inconceivable that the two most prominent statesmen of post-war England should speak varieties of English with regional accents as noticeable as those of Konrad Adenauer and Theodor Heuss – the first chancellor and the first President of the Federal Republic. (Compare 9.2.4.)

In recent years, *Bühnenaussprache* (which was called *Hochlautung* in later editions of the Siebs) has come more and more under attack on these grounds, *ie* that it is an artificial construct and not an actual variety of spoken German. With outspoken irony, Pilch ('Lautsystem', 1966: 248) characterizes the situation in the following way: 'Deutsche Bühnenaussprache ist eine Spielart des Deutschen, von der eines sicher ist: Kein Deutscher spricht sie.' ('German *Bühnenaussprache* is a variety of German of which one thing can be said with certainty: no German uses it.')

10.1.2 *Standardaussprache – Umgangslautung*

On the basis of such considerations, the 1974 edition of the *Duden-Aussprachewörterbuch* (edited by Mangold) makes a distinction between STANDARDAUSSPRACHE and UMGANGSLAUTUNG. The *Duden* (*Aussprachewörterbuch*, [2]1974: 30–61) characterizes *Standardaussprache* as being clear, uniform, supra-regional and based upon the written language. It is a 'Gebrauchsnorm, die der Sprechwirklichkeit nahe kommt' ('a norm of usage, which comes close to the realities of the spoken language'), but it does not reflect the many variations of the spoken language. *Umgangslautung*, on the other hand, is an accent of Standard German (we still exclude dialect speakers) which is used by educated speakers in normal conversation at home, in the street and at work. It is also frequently used by broadcasters when addressing the general public on the radio or on television.

The *Duden Aussprachewörterbuch* ([2]1974: 61–7) establishes a number of rules to relate both varieties, for example:

(i) After a stressed vowel or diphthong [ən] can be replaced by [ŋ] or [n], especially in word-final position: *gehen* (standard: ['geːən], colloquial: ['geːŋ][geːn])

(ii) In stressed monosyllabic words, long vowels can be shortened before a
      consonant: *Bad* (standard: [baːt], colloquial: [bat])
(iii) In a number of positions /p, t, k/ can be realized as /b, d, g/. In most
      cases, a voiceless lenis plosive will be articulated: /b̥, d̥, g̊/. *halte, Halde*
      (colloquial: [hald̥e]).

This *Umgangslautung* is used to cover deviation from standard pronunciation in two respects: certain differences arise from factors caused by fast
speech, etc as is shown by (i) above – the so-called allegro rules. Other variations are caused by regional influences, so (ii) is certainly more common in
the north of Germany, whereas (iii) is typical of Southern German speech
(*cf* Pilch, 1966: 251–2).[5] Variation occurring in *Umgangssprache* – due to
regional, social and individual factors – is so complex that *Umgangssprache*
cannot be described systematically (see *Duden Aussprachewörterbuch*, 1974:
61, and Chapter 9, note 7).

It follows from these considerations that an adequate description of the
pronunciation used by many speakers of German leaves only two possibilities
open: either one describes standard German as it is pronounced by a certain
social group in a particular area or one accepts the principle of generalization
underlying such concepts as *Bühnendeutsch* or *Standardaussprache*. In the following sections, we shall follow the latter alternative, but the reader must remember that this type of *Standardaussprache* is an idealization, which may
be useful for the purposes of linguistic analysis, but which on no account must
be taken as the way educated Germans speak (a factor not to be overlooked
when teaching German to foreigners).

10.2 The phonology of German

10.2.1 *Phonetic description*

Now that we have stated which variant of German pronunciation we shall
attempt to analyse, we are confronted with the problem of how this aim can
best be achieved. The first step towards the description of the sound-system
of a language consists in breaking up the continuum of speech sounds into
a finite set of recurrent items. These sounds, or phones, can be described in
terms of how they are articulated by speakers or decoded by hearers, *ie* according to certain articulatory or auditive properties.[6] The table on *p* 108 – taken
from Kohler (*Einführung*, 1977: 66) – shows how the consonants of German
can be classified by articulatory features, such as manner of articulation (plosive, nasal, etc) and place of articulation (bilabial, labio-dental, etc). A further
feature is the distinction between voiced and voiceless consonants (in the
chart the voiceless variant is always found to the left of the voiced one).[7]

10.2.2 *Phonemes and allophones*

Although a phonetic analysis of German consonants is in itself useful, it seems
legitimate to ask whether these phones can be classified any further. This can

	bilabial	labiodental	alveolar	palatal	velar	uvular	glottal
Plosive	p b		t d		k g		ʔ
Nasale	m	ɱ	n		ŋ		
Frikative	Φ β	f v	enggerillt/weitgerillt s z / ʃ ʒ	ç j	x γ	χ ʁ	h ɦ
laterale Frikative			ɬ				
Laterale			l				
Vibranten			r			R	
Anschläge			ɾ			R	
friktionslose Dauerlaute		ʋ		j	γ	ʁ	

be done, for instance, by regarding the function of a sound in a language;[8] for example, by analysing the effect of the substitution of one sound for another in utterances (or words). All of the following are acceptable standard pronunciations of German words, for example:

[1]a kʊrt   [1]b kʊʁt (*Kurt*)
[2]a kʊrt   [2]b gʊrt (*Gurt*)

The important difference between the two pairs lies in the fact that in the first case every speaker of German would associate the same meaning with [1a] and [b]; ie both forms could be taken as alternative realizations of the same linguistic sign, whereas [2a] and [b] clearly have different meanings. One must recognize on the one hand 'sounds' that can function to distinguish meanings and on the other 'sounds' that cannot fulfil this function (in a particular language). In the terminology, which ultimately originates from the Polish linguist, Jan Baudouin de Courtenay (1845–1929), sounds of the former type are commonly referred to as PHONEMES (cf Jones, *History*, 1957: 3).

The existence of such minimal pairs as [kʊrt]/[gʊrt] enables us to claim phoneme status for /k/ and /g/ in German. Although /r/ must also be considered a phoneme of German ([gʊrt] and [gʊkt] make up a minimal pair, for example), there are not two r-phonemes in German, but merely various alternate pronunciations of the phoneme /r/. Such sounds are called ALLO-PHONES.

A detailed phonetic analysis will reveal that every phoneme can be realized by a number of allophones: /k/, for instance, is most commonly pronounced as an aspirated plosive [kʰ], but – before [s] and [ʃ] – the unaspirated [k] occurs. In this case the choice of the allophone – [k] or [kʰ] – depends on its phonetic environment: these two allophones stand in COMPLEMENTARY DISTRIBUTION. In other cases, allophones of one phoneme can be in FREE VARIATION, as is the case with the variants of /r/, where the choice of allophone depends entirely on the speaker; sometimes the same speaker uses two forms in free variation.[9]

10.2.3 *Allophone or phoneme?*

The consistent analysis of the function of a phone should lead to the establishment of a phoneme inventory for a language. Unfortunately the decision as to whether two phones are allophones of one phoneme or two separate phonemes is not always so straightforward as with /k/ and /g/ or [r] and [ʁ] respectively. For instance, there is considerable disagreement amongst linguists concerning the phoneme status of the voiceless fricatives represented by the grapheme {*ch*} in German. [x] and [ç] are generally distributed as follows:[10]

[x] appears after back vowels ([ax], ['buːx])
[ç] appears after front vowels ([ɪç], ['byːçɐ])

On the basis of these rules, [ç] and [x] could be regarded as being in complementary distribution and thus as allophones of one phoneme. However, some minimal pairs can be established in which these rules are violated: *Kuchen* [x] – *Kuhchen* [ç] or *tauchen* [x] – *Tauchen* [ç].

Does this mean that [x] and [ç] have to be regarded as two separate phonemes? When answering this question, one must bear in mind that the minimal pairs mentioned are exceptional and must be considered marginal cases (in fact it can be doubted whether *Kuhchen* and *Tauchen* are used in present-day German at all),[11] so that these pairs do not present a substantial argument against the allophonic character of [x] and [ç].

The problem remains though that in, for example, *Frauchen* or *Biancachen*, we find the palatal [ç], where our distributional rule (after back vowel) tells us the velar [x] should be used. There is no question of there being a minimal pair here, as with the artificial *tauchen – Tauchen*. How can the palatal be explained here without abandoning an otherwise intuitively and empirically satisfying distributional rule?

It need not follow that [x] and [ç] could not belong to the same phoneme. As the second component of such pairs always consists of the morpheme *-chen*, one could simply expand the rule for the occurrence of [ç] and claim that it was used after front vowels and word- and morpheme-initially, whereas [x] appears in all other environments (*cf* Kohler, 1977: 86). This means, however, that we are using a morphological criterion for the description of phonetic phenomena.

This can be avoided by the introduction of a so-called JUNCTURE PHONEME /+/ so that *Kuchen* and *Kuhchen* could be represented as [kuːxn] and [kuː+çen], if the allophonic rule for [ç] included the juncture phoneme /+/ (*cf* Weinrich 'Phonologie', 1961: 7–8). The phoneme status of juncture, however, must be considered highly controversial, since juncture cannot be regarded as a segment of language in the same way as other phonemes can; it cannot be identified as a segment on a spectrogram, for example (Werner,

Beschreibung, 1973: 88). These and other arguments have led some linguists
to claim phoneme status for both /x/ and /ç/ (cf Pilch, 1966: 254), although
this question remains a matter of dispute among German phoneticians.[12]

10.2.4 One phoneme or two?

A further problem of phonemic analysis is presented by consonant clusters
which can be seen either as a combination of two consonant phonemes or
as one single phoneme. This is the case with the affricates in German [ts], [tʃ],
[dʒ] and [pf], which, phonetically, are made up of a plosive and a following
fricative. Some linguists (*eg* Dieth, *Vademekum*, 1950: 239–40; von Essen,
Phonetik, 1957: 73) hold that these should be regarded as one phoneme,
whereas others argue that affricates are combinations of two phonemes. Not
only are there minimal pairs (*Pfeile–peile–Feile*), there are also cases in which
[t] and [s] belong to different morphemes (*nichts*). Phonetically identical strings
of sounds, however, should not be given two phonemic representations (Hartmann, 'Unterschiede', 1964: 390). From the point of view of generative phonology, the problem of whether affricates should be described as one or two
phonemes is not of primary importance: Vennemann's point of departure
('Affrikaten', 1968: 65–76) is not the traditional minimal pairs approach, but
an examination of diachronically and semantically related groups of words.
He postulates an underlying phoneme (*eg* /p/ in /ʃtaːp/) from which different
realizations can be derived according to phonetic environment and morphological considerations (*eg* /f/, /ff/, /pf/, /p/ in *Stufe, Staffel, stapfen,* and *Stapel*
respectively).

10.2.5 The phonemic system of German

The discussion of some problems presented by the phonological analysis of
German has shown that there can be various opinions as to the final shape
of a German phoneme inventory. The *Duden* (*Ausspracheworterbuch*, 1974:
40) claims the following consonant phonemes for German:[13]

plosives	/p/ /b/	/t/ /d/	/ k/ /g/	
nasals	/m/	/n/	/ŋ/	
fricatives	/f/ /v/	/s/ /z/ /ʃ/ /ʒ/ /ç/ /x/ /j/	/h/	
lateral		/l/		
vibrant		/r/		
affricates	/pf/	/ts/ /tʃ/ /dʒ/		

A similar inventory of German vowel phonemes can be established. The *Duden*
(*Ausspracheworterbuch*, 1974: 31) uses the criterion of the position of the tongue
in the mouth (which can be indicated in the vowel diagram) and the degree
of lip-rounding (○ lips rounded, ● lips spread) to characterize German vowel
phonemes:

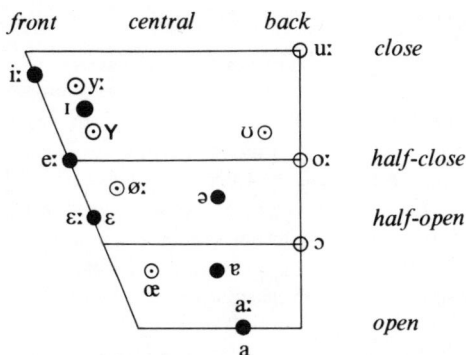

In addition to these monophthongs, there are three diphthongs /ai/, /aʊ/ and /ɔy/. (The nasalized vowels are marginal in the German vowel system, since their occurrence is restricted to a number of non-adapted foreign words.)

An illustration of how this phonemic system is being used in the description of passages of German text is given by the following poem by Peter Härtling ('Erinnerung an eine Landschaft am Mittelmeer', 1977: 9):

Erinnerung an eine Landschaft	ɛɐˈmɐrʊŋ an aɪnə ˈlantʃaft
am Mittelmeer (Sanary-sur-mer)	am ˈmɪt|meːɐ̯ | sanarisyrˈmɛːr||
Ersticken am Schweigen	ɛɐˈʃtɪkn̩ am ˈʃvaɪɡn̩
anderer	ˈandərə
in dieser Landschaft	ɪn ˈdiːzə ˈlantʃaft
mit zuviel Geschichte.	mɪt tsuˈfiːl ɡəˈʃɪçtə||
Sinnvoll wäre es	ˈzɪnfɔl ˈvɛːrə ɛs
alles	ˈaləs
zu vergessen,	tsuː fɛɐ̯ˈɡɛsn̩
Felsen wieder	ˈfɛlzn̩ ˈviːdɐ
zu schichten,	tsuː ˈʃɪçtn̩
Bäume neu	ˈbɔymə ˈnɔy
zu erfinden,	tsuː ɛɐ̯ˈfɪndn̩
Wege	ˈveːɡə
zu löschen	tsuː ˈlœʃn̩
und	ʊnt
jene Stimme	ˈjeːnə ˈʃtɪmə
zu sein,	tsuː ˈzain|
die zum ersten Mal	diː tsʊm ˈeːɐ̯stn̩ ˈmaːl
spricht.	ˈʃprɪçt||

in [P. Härtling (1977) *Anreden. Gedichte aus den Jahren 1972–1977*, 9, Darmstadt, Neuwied: Luchterhand]

10.3 Concluding remarks

It is important to realize that the establishment of these phoneme inventories involves a high degree of abstraction: firstly, the concept of a standard pronunciation of German is an idealization in itself – to a much greater extent than the concept of RP in the analysis of British English. Secondly, the phoneme status of some sounds of German is a matter of dispute amongst linguists. Thirdly, the phoneme is an abstraction in itself, because it represents an ideal concept rather than an actual sound of the language. Fourthly, our analysis has been restricted to the observation of sounds and words in isolation; it is very important, however, to study suprasegmental phones such as rhythm, intonation and stress as well as the influence on sounds of their phonetic environment in fast speech, which leads to the analysis of problems of assimilation, elision and the like.[14] This, however, to a certain extent at least, requires the study of less formal variants of German pronunciation, which leads us back to the first problem. Perhaps the lack of one dialect of German which is the obvious choice, as RP is for English, as the basis for linguistic description is at least partly responsible for the present situation in which many individual fruitful attempts to find solutions to these problems have been made without at the same time their forming a coherent description of the language.

Recommended further reading

Wängler (*Grundriss*, 1960) provides a very detailed phonetic analysis of German. The studies contributed by Ungeheuer (*Materialien*, 1977) and Kohler (*Einführung*, 1977) also deserve attention. A very concise introduction to these problems can be found in the relevant chapters of Werner (*Beschreibung*, 1973).

Chapter 11

The noun: case

11.1 Introduction

One of the most significant features of modern German is that it has retained the originally inflectional character of the Germanic languages.[1] Up to the present day, INFLECTIONAL CASES have remained the most common means used for a task which is fulfilled by the position of a word in an English sentence.[2] In English a change in word order changes the relationship between the lexical items, *eg* [1]. In the German sentence this is not so, *eg* [2].

[1] Manuela saw the old man.
[1]*a* The old man saw Manuela.
[2] Manuela sah den alten Mann.
[2]*a* Den alten Mann sah Manuela.[3]

There is, to be sure, normal word order (subject–verb–object, as in English), but if position and case are – or seem to be – in conflict, as in [3] and [4], a speaker of English would follow the principle of position [3]*a*, a speaker of German the principle of case [4*a*], if they were asked to replace the sentences by the correct or normal form:

[3] *Me saw Manuela. ——→ [3]*a* I saw Manuela.
[4] Mich sah Manuela.——→[4]*a* Manuela sah mich.[4]

Since Antiquity (Greece) the fact that different case forms could easily be distinguished has led linguists to try to assign basic meanings to each case. This is reflected in their traditional names, for example *casus dativus* 'case of giving', etc. But it is not difficult to realize that these concepts are too limited to account for the various uses of the cases termed so.

In the German attempts to describe the case system more appropriately two extreme opinions can be distinguished. One group of linguists, notably the content-oriented grammarians, retain the idea of a general meaning of the cases, trying, however, to find a more suitable common denominator. Of this group, Brinkmann's approach will be presented in 11.2.1. The opposite view is held by the dependency grammarians: they claim that the cases do not normally have a semantic function, but that they are to be regarded as purely structural, syntactic phenomena (11.2.2). However, as we shall see in 11.3, this solution is not totally satisfactory either. In the final section we shall therefore consider some attempts at establishing the relationship between the cases as syntactic and semantic phonemena.

11.2 Semantic vs syntactic view of the cases

11.2.1 *Brinkmann*

Although Brinkmann rejects the traditional case nomenclature, his approach is based on the conviction that a general meaning can be found for each case. According to Brinkmann, this meaning is determined by the interrelationship of the cases, by their position in the case system.[5]

The different meanings can be illustrated best, if two cases occur in the same context, either together (dative and accusative in [5]) or in opposition (dative and accusative in [6] and [7]):

[5] Manuela hat mir einen Brief geschrieben.
[6] Der Arzt schlug ihm auf die Schulter.
[7] Der Arzt schlug ihn auf die Schulter.

Many speakers of German feel a certain difference between [6] and [7] as regards the involvement of the person refered to as *ihm* or *ihn* respectively. In [7] the action is held to be 'more violent'. According to Weisgerber ('Der Mensch im Akkusativ', 1958: 200), in sentences such as [7] the person is seen more as an object (not in the grammatical sense), in [6] more as the partner towards whom an action is directed.[6] Brinkmann deduces that the dative is the case of 'Finalität', the accusative the case of 'Kausalität'. For him sentences such as [5] serve as a confirmation of this view. Here, as well, 'wird (im Akkusativ) das Andere genannt, das vom grammatischen Subjekt in seinem Dasein oder Sosein bestimmt wird, im Dativ die Person, für die der verbale Prozess bestimmt ist.'[7] (Using the accusative we name the other person or thing whose existence or manner of being is determined by the grammatical subject, in the dative case we name the person towards whom the verbal process is directed.) Similar interpretations and definitions were given of the nominative (*Kasus der Identität*) and genitive (*Kasus der Orientierung*).[8]

11.2.2 *Dependency grammar*

Brinkmann's approach has been criticized for various reasons, the most important ones being that his definitions do not coincide with the native speaker's intuition and that his assumptions cannot be wholly justified if the linguistic facts are examined more closely.

As far as the first argument is concerned, Brinkmann's critics[9] find fault
with the vagueness of his terms and claim that the 'common denominators'
are both too embracing and too limited. To be sure, *Finalität* is, as the general
meaning of the dative as a formal case, more abstract and more embracing
than the old term dative understood semantically, but the definition given
above still appears to be too limited. On the one hand, there are many instances
of the dative which cannot be subsumed under the heading of finality, *eg* [8]
and [9] or causality (for the accusative respectively, [10]):

[8] Sei *mir* ja brav!

[9] *Meinem kleinen Bruder* ist es kalt.

[10] Manuela ist *den ganzen Tag* fröhlich.

On the other hand the concept of *Finalität* seems also to apply to some instances of the accusative. Compare, for example,

[11] Er hilft *mir*.   dat

[12] Er unterstützt *mich*. acc

Both sentences are commonly regarded as more or less semantically equivalent. At least the value of *mir/mich* is felt to be the same: a recipient of
help.

As for the second argument concerning Brinkmann's assumptions, the following points have been raised: if the concept of the semantic field is used
at all to determine the meaning of the cases, the investigation should not be
confined to the inflectional cases. It can be shown that there are a considerable
number of instances in which a prepositional group has the same function
as an inflectional case, see [13] and [13a]:

[13]   Erinnerst du dich *des letzten Tages* in Nürnberg? gen

[13]a Erinnerst du dich *an den letzten Tag* in Nürnberg? prep

A further important objection is that semantic distinctions as illustrated
in [6] and [7] are a comparatively isolated phenomenon, and should, therefore,
not be over-generalized. Normally there is no choice. The case is determined
by the governing verb or preposition: *den alten Mann* in [2] is accusative and
not dative for the purely syntactic reason that *sehen* governs the accusative.
'Why' is a question, largely inexplicable and irrelevant for speakers of German.

On the basis of these arguments and some others,[10] many linguists, especially the dependency grammarians, regard the cases – with the few exceptions
mentioned above – as purely syntactic and structural phenomena.

11.3 Case and semantics

As we have seen, there are good arguments for denying that the cases have
meaning. On the other hand there is no doubt that they contribute to the mean-

ing of sentences. These qualities have led Engelen to liken the role of the cases in a sentence to the role of the phoneme in a word: just as the phonemes /g/, /uː/, /t/, which are not meaningful in isolation, 'combine' to form the word [guːt] *gut*, isolated case forms such as *des Mordes* (gen) or *der Staatsanwalt* (nom) or *den Angeklagten* (acc) have – besides their referential meaning 'murder', 'public prosecutor', 'defendant' – no semantic value until they enter into the more complex units of, for example, sentences [14–16]:

[14] Der Staatsanwalt beschuldigte den Angeklagten des Mordes.
[15] Das ist der Staatsanwalt.
[16] Der Staatsanwalt konnte sich des Mordes nicht mehr erinnern.

However, the comparison is not wholly satisfactory. As a rule, we know more about an isolated accusative form such as *den alten Mann* than about an isolated 't', even if the referential meaning is disregarded. If in [2] the word *Manuela* were incomprehensible

[2]*b* (noise) ... sah den alten Mann.

we should be able to recognize the role *den alten Mann* plays in the process of seeing: in any case not that of the agent. This interpretation would be given to *den alten Mann*, even if *sah* became incomprehensible as well. It appears that apart from being structural phenomena the cases are associated with certain roles in the relationships existing between the phenomena of reality which are reflected in a sentence.

Consequently, a comprehensive analysis of the cases must include two levels at least: one level comprising formal syntax, distribution/dependency and another level comprising the reflection of relationships holding between objects of reality. In Germany, Helbig has shown the necessity of taking several levels into account. He distinguishes four levels:

(i) FORMAL LEVEL: distribution, dependency
(ii) LOGICAL LEVEL: According to modern relational logic, cases can be seen as arguments of a function whose relator is the verb. (This approach bears some affinity to the verb-complement model of dependency grammar.)
(iii) SEMANTIC LEVEL: Here Helbig shows that there is no general meaning as, for example, Brinkmann assumes. However, he argues, there can be a 'central meaning'. A case form may adopt in the mind of the language users the semantic qualities it has in the environments in which it occurs most frequently. That is why an isolated *den alten Mann* would be given the interpretation 'not the agent' or 'objective'.
(iv) ONTOLOGICAL LEVEL: the relationships between the phenomena of reality and their reflection in language.

The problem is how these different levels are interrelated.

It is true that in many sentences we do not need the cases as indicators of ontological relationships. The verb *sehen* requires an animate subject (poetry disregarded). Therefore the meaning of [17] would be clear without the formal indicator case:

[17] Manuela sah einen roten Luftballon.

In [2], however, both nouns are animate.

[2] Manuela sah einen alten Mann.

If it were not for the formal indicator case or for some other indicator, the relationship between *Manuela* and *einen alten Mann* would not be determined. The crucial question is which rules or mechanism make us transform what we see as participants in a process such as 'agent', 'non-agent/objective', 'instrument', etc into the formal cases nominative, accusative, etc, or conversely, identify *Manuela* as the person who sees somebody and *einen alten Mann* as the one who is seen as well as *mir* and *mich* ([11] and [12] respectively) as the recipients of help.[11]

The American linguist Fillmore tried to explain this phenomenon by assuming a hierarchy prevailing between the cases on the ontological level (having a TG background, he calls them deep-structure cases). These move up into the formal positions (nominative, accusative, prepositional cases respectively) extant in a sentence in succession. The rule for [18–20]

[18] The worker moved the rock with a bulldozer.
[19] The bulldozer moved the rock.
[20] The rock moved.

would be: 'If there is an A [agent, here: worker], it becomes the subject; otherwise, if there is an I [instrumental, here: bulldozer], it becomes the subject; otherwise the subject is the O [objective, here: rock].'[12]

Which one of these utterances is chosen depends on the number of participants, which is, in turn, not only dependent on the process (verb!) but also on contextual and psychological factors. So is probably the question of which participant becomes subject or object, if more than one solution is possible, see [21–22]:

[21] Manuela rief einen alten Freund an.
[22] Der alte Freund wurde angerufen.

In [22] the mention of *Manuela* may have been felt to be unnecessary or undesirable for some reason or other (previous mention of Manuela's plan, etc). The sentences [21] and [22] also show that changes in the number of participants may entail the choice of a different verb form (sometimes, of a different verb).

Although the investigation of the links between the levels and the conditions which influence them is held to be desirable,[13] German linguistics, probably due to the influence of dependency grammar and its immense practical value, appears to be focused on the formal side of the problem, at best including some remarks on semantic incompatibility, *eg* *Der Stein sah* is impossible, because the semantic features of *Stein* [−animate] and *sehen* [*subj*/+anim] are incompatible.[14] Engelen's view that the case forms in isolation carry many different potential meanings, *ie* are homonymic, and are not dehomonymized until they enter into more complex units is undoubtedly helpful for the interpretation of sentences,[15] but it gives no insight into the production of utterances or the question of why a certain case-verb link is chosen. The investigation of these very complex questions will probably be of considerable importance in the future.

Recommended further reading

Helbig (*Kasus*, 1973) can be read as a comprehensive critical survey of the literature on case functions. For a new view of the formal system of the German cases Bech ('Morphologie', 1963) can be recommended.

Chapter 12

The German verb: tense

12.1 The relation of time and tense

In this chapter on the German verb, we shall first be concerned with the problem of TENSE and the expression of TIME. In German as in English, there is no one-to-one correspondence of TIME and TENSE, since one tense can be used to refer to different time relations as in the following examples, where the Perfect is used to express PAST and FUTURE TIME respectively:

[1] Angelika hat das Buch (gestern) gekauft.
[2] Angelika hat das Buch bis morgen gelesen.

Tense is an obligatory category of the German verb, *ie* the verb has to be marked for tense even if no time relation is to be expressed.[1] Well-known examples of this are sayings or general truths, for instance:

[3] Ein Unglück ist schnell geschehen.
[4] Die Sonne geht im Westen unter.

Here, the Perfect and the Present do not refer to any specific time at which the action takes place. However, these cases are the marginal ones, and we shall mainly be concerned with tense as a means of expressing time.[2]

Apart from tense, however, language provides many other means to express time relations. In sentence [2], for example, the fact that the Perfect refers to Future Time is only made clear by the adverbial *bis morgen*. TIME ADVERBIALS (*bald, morgen*), TEMPORAL PREPOSITIONS (*bis*) or CONJUNCTIONS (*wenn, als*) play a very important part in the linguistic expression of time relations and will also have to be considered in a treatment of tense.

Furthermore, time can also be expressed by nouns such as *Stunde* or *Jahr* and adjectives (*lang*), as well as by the *Aktionsart* of the verb. Compare, for instance:

[5] Angelika arbeitet.
[6] Der Ballon platzt.

The ACTIVITY VERB *arbeiten* in [5] expresses longer duration of the action than the MOMENTARY VERB *platzen* in example [6].[3] In English, *aspect* is another means of expressing the duration of an action (compare Leech, *Verb*, 1971: 18–19).

Tense and most time adverbials belong to the so-called *deictic elements* in language, which, as we have seen in 5.2, have provided the basis for pragmalinguistic theory. We shall, then, attempt to demonstrate some aspects of the pragmalinguistic treatment of the German tense system. This will involve reference to the syntactic model of Burgschmidt and Götz (*Kontrastive Linguistik* 1974) (see 5.4) and our outline is largely based on Wunderlich's *Tempus und Zeitreferenz im Deutschen* (1970a) and some related approaches. This means, of course, that a number of relevant works on tense in German have been neglected; for the most important of these see *pp* 125–6.

12.2 A survey of the tenses in standard German

In pragmalinguistics, a distinction is made between the TIME OF SPEAKING and the TIME OF ACTION (see Wunderlich, *Tempus*, 1970, and Burgschmidt and Götz, 1974: 251)[4]. In the syntactic model developed by Burgschmidt and Götz time relations belong to the MODIFICATION OF THE PROPOSITION, *ie* the speaker can mark the time of the action described in the proposition as either past, present or future in respect to the time of speaking. This relation is referred to as *temporal speaker standpoint* (*temporaler Sprecherstandort*). In

[7] Angelika schrieb Hermann einen bösen Brief.

for instance, the time of action was before the time of speaking. However, other actions can be mentioned in the utterance or the text and be seen not only in relation to the time of speaking, but also in relation to the time of the first action or to the general time frame of the text, which is expressed in the deep structure unit. Therefore this relation is called DSU-*reference* (TSE-*Bezug*). An example of this is

[8] Nachdem Angelika mehrmals versucht hatte, Hermann anzurufen, schrieb sie ihm einen bösen Brief.

where the telephoning took place before the writing of the letter, which is expressed by the use of the Past Perfect in the subordinate clause.

These two relations – time of action to time of speaking (*speaker standpoint*) and time of action to the general time frame of the deep structure unit (DSU-*reference*) – have been used by Burgschmidt and Götz (1974: 253) to set up a table of the following kind to give a broad overview of the German tense system:[5]

Speaker standpoint	DSU-reference	Tense	Example
V	G	Preterite	Angelika *schrieb* einen Brief.
G	G	Present	Hermann *spielt* Fussball.
'Z'		Present (Future I)	Hermann *kommt* morgen. Hermann *wird* nach Fürth *kommen.*
V	V	Past Perfect	Angelika *hatte telefoniert.*
(V	Z)	Present Subj Pret Subj/ werden+Inf Subjunctive	Angelika *telefonierte/ hätte telefoniert/ würde telefoniert haben...*
G	V	Perfect	Angelika *hat* es *gelesen.*
V	V	Future II	Sie *wird* es *gelesen haben.*

Key to symbols:
G Gegenwart (present time)
V Vergangenheit (past time)
Z Zukunft (future time)

'Z' covers the relations Z/G, G/Z and Z/Z, in all of which Present tense is possible, but Simple Future could also be used (see Burgschmidt and Götz, 1974: 253, and Dittmann, *Sprechhandlungstheorie*, 1976).[6]

However the point must be made that this table only describes the use of the tenses in standard German. In the spoken language of the South, only two tenses are used, Present (for G/G and 'Z') and Perfect (for V/G, G/V, V/V); (for this see Lindgren, 'Präteritumsschwund', 1957, and Dal, 'Frage', 1960).

The table set up by Burgschmidt and Götz only serves as a simplified survey, because marginal cases like *historic Present*, etc have not been considered; nor does the table take account of other pragmatic relations which are relevant for the choice of tense. This becomes particularly apparent with the claimed opposition of Preterite and Perfect in standard German.[7]

12.3 The Preterite and the Perfect tense

12.3.1 *Meaning Criteria*

[9] Angelika schrieb Hermann gestern einen Brief.
[10] Angelika hat Hermann gestern einen Brief geschrieben.

In German, there is no such clear opposition of Preterite and Present Perfect as in English, in which the translation equivalents of both [9] and [10] would have to be in the Past tense:[8] *Yesterday, Angelika wrote a letter to Hermann* (see Quirk *et al*, *Grammar*, 1972: 3.37). Both [9] and [10] have the same meaning, denoting that the time of action was before the time of speaking.

However, Preterite and Perfect are not freely interchangeable, since in some contexts there is a meaning distinction between the two, and under certain conditions the one tense would be more frequent than the other. Most attempts to set up oppositions between the Preterite and the Perfect in German have tried to apply only semantic criteria. It would appear, however, that the difference between the two tenses does not lie only in their meaning, but that pragmatic factors ought also to be considered. In the following discussion we shall outline some of the criteria put forward by Wunderlich (*Tempus*, 1970). (For different approaches to the problem of Preterite and Perfect see Kluge, 'Diskussion', 1969, and Trier, 'Unsicherheiten', 1965.)

12.3.2 *Collocation criteria*
Wunderlich claims that there are some cases in which there is a true distinction between the meaning of the two tenses:

[11] Angelika kaufte sich ein neues Fahrrad.
[12] Angelika hat sich ein neues Fahrrad gekauft.

The distinction between these two sentences is that [12] expresses a kind of CURRENT RELEVANCE in that it implies

[13] Angelika besitzt jetzt ein neues Fahrrad

whereas [11] has no such implication. Wunderlich (*Tempus*, 1970: 143) tries to prove this by continuing the text:

[11]*a* Angelika kaufte sich ein neues Fahrrad. Es ist ihr inzwischen aber wieder gestohlen worden.
[12]*a* ?Angelika hat sich ein neues Fahrrad gekauft. Es ist ihr inzwischen aber wieder gestohlen worden.

Whereas [12]*a* sounds rather odd (in standard German), *hat gekauft* suggesting 'is now in possession of', [12]*b* is acceptable.

[12]*b* Angelika hat sich gestern ein neues Fahrrad gekauft. Es ist ihr inzwischen aber wieder gestohlen worden.

The idea of 'current relevance' is the basis of the Burgschmidt and Götz (1974) distinction between V/G and G/V – a distinction between Preterite and Perfect which has been claimed by many grammarians.[9] Wunderlich (*Tempus*, 1970: 144) points out, however, that it only holds for a certain class of verbs, namely the so-called TRANSITIONAL EVENT VERBS (*transformative Verben*)[10] which describe the leading of one state into another (for example: *einschlafen*, *aufstehen*, *herunterfallen*).

Wunderlich (*Tempus*, 1970: 145) posits the following rule for the distinction of the meaning (MEAN) of Preterite and Perfect:

MEAN 1 : Both Preterite and Perfect express the fact that the time of action is before the time of speaking.

MEAN 2 : With transitional event verbs the Perfect indicates that the time of action continues up to the time of speaking or that the result of the action is relevant at the time of speaking.

Connected with this is another distinction between the meanings of Preterite and Perfect (see Wunderlich, *Tempus*, 1970: 149).

[14] Ich habe das bis morgen fertig gemacht.
[15] Ich werde das bis morgen fertig gemacht haben.
[16] *Ich machte das bis morgen fertig.

Again, future reference of the Perfect is only possible with transitional event verbs:

[17] ?Morgen um diese Zeit habe ich gearbeitet.

MEAN 3 : With transitional event verbs the Perfect can also refer to future time (and replace Future Perfect). This is not possible with the Preterite.

12.3.3 *Criteria of preference*

As the opposition in meaning set up by criteria MEAN 2 and MEAN 3 only applies for a certain class of verbs, other criteria to distinguish Preterite and Perfect in German have to be found. According to Wunderlich (*Tempus*, 1970: 146), these depend mostly on regional, social and stylistic factors. There are, however, some collocational restrictions (COLL-rules) on the use of the Preterite and the Perfect.

COLL 1 : The Preterite is not common with *schon, schon oft, schon immer, noch nie* and *seit*.[11]

[18] *Angelika las das Buch schon.
[19] Angelika hat das Buch schon gelesen.

However, with *seit* the Present tense can be used:[12]

[20] Ich warte schon seit drei Stunden auf Brigitte.
[21] Ich habe schon seit drei Stunden auf Brigitte gewartet.
[22] *Ich wartete seit drei Stunden auf Brigitte.

Here a certain parallel with MEAN 2 is apparent, as *schon* or the *seit*-phrase clearly express 'current relevance' at the time of speaking. This explains why the Preterite is possible if a subordinate clause in the Preterite is inserted:

[23] Ich wartete seit drei Stunden auf Brigitte, als sie endlich kam.

COLL 2: In temporal clauses expressing parallel actions, the Preterite is used
rather than the Perfect.

[24] Es hat ununterbrochen geregnet, als Angelika in Schottland war.
[25] *Es hat ununterbrochen geregnet, als Angelika in Schottland gewesen
ist.

COLL 3: When a VERB OF INERT COGNITION (like *wissen, glauben, vermuten*)
is used in the 1st or 2nd person in the Present tense, the perfect is
preferred to the Preterite in the object clause (Wunderlich, *Tempus*,
1970: 147).[13]

[26] Ich weiss, dass gestern das Semester wieder angefangen hat.
[27] ?Ich weiss, dass gestern das Semester wieder anfing.

Criteria COLL 1 and 2 show how the choice of tense is entirely determined
by the collocations of the verb, whereas with COLL 3 only a preference is stated.
This makes COLL 3 a borderline case between collocational criteria and criteria
of a different kind, which state the conditions under which the one or the other
tense would be preferred (PREF-rules). Most of these differences are found
at the level of style, which seems to be very important for the description of
the opposition of the Preterite and the Perfect in German.

The first of these criteria concerns the TYPE OF TEXT in which the utterance
appears: In discussions, essays, etc both Preterite and Perfect are used, but
in narrative texts the Perfect is not common. Weinrich (*Tempus*, 1964: 84)
introduces a *pragmatic* feature [+narrativ], which Baumgärtner *et al*
('Entwurf' 1967) have retermed [− Colloqu]. The following criteria can then
be formulated (see Wunderlich, 1970: 147–8):

PREF 1: In SITUATIONS OF UTTERANCE with the feature [− Colloqu] the Perfect is not used.
PREF 2: In the spoken language, even in narrative, the Perfect will be preferred
to the Preterite.[14]

Apart from the *type of text* and the *situation of utterance*, stylistic considerations may determine the choice of tense.[15]

PREF 3: The Preterite tense is considered more formal than the Perfect (for
this *Ästheten-Präteritum* see *Duden* (*Grammatik*, 1973: 81) and Wunderlich, (*Tempus*, 1970: 148).

Closely connected with considerations of style are morphological questions.
For instance, it is not common to say:

[28] ?Angelika hat gestern arbeiten gemusst.

PREF 4: MODAL VERBS tend to be used in the Preterite only. (See Hauser-Suida
and Hoppe-Beugel, *Vergangenheitstempora*, 1972: 128–50.)[16]

Similarly, problems of articulation have to be considered, because it is likely that in cases where the pronunciation of the Preterite is 'difficult' or 'awkward' (as in *du fochtst*), the Perfect form is preferred.[17]

12.3.4 *Conclusion*

This outline of Wunderlich's treatment of the opposition of Preterite and Perfect has made clear that it is not sufficient to claim a difference in the meaning of these two tenses, as the choice of tense is indeed dependent on quite different factors, which belong to various areas of linguistic description.[18] We have tried to show that it is very difficult to give a systematic account of the use of Preterite and Perfect in that we have had to distinguish criteria which set up an opposition in meaning (MEAN), criteria according to which the choice of tense is entirely dependent on linguistic context (COLL), and criteria which just indicate which tense is probably going to be used (PREF).

These criteria can easily be integrated into Burgschmidt and Götz's model of syntax. The differences in meaning MEAN 2 and MEAN 3 will belong to the MODIFICATION OF THE PROPOSITION as they concern the relation of the time of action and time of speaking, *ie* the speaker can see 'current relevance' in the proposition or not. However, collocational features COLL 1–3 and the criteria of the PREF-type will be found under CONTEXT FEATURES. This treatment of the tenses has shown that an adequate description of the use of Preterite and Perfect in German – unsystematic as it may have to be – will have to take account of pragmatic factors such as the SITUATION OF UTTERANCE, the TYPE OF TEXT and, of course, LINGUISTIC CONTEXT.

Recommended further reading

The great variety in the use of tenses by different speakers of German has been pointed out by J. Trier in his essay 'Unsicherheiten im heutigen Deutsch' (1965), where the author sees it as the task of the linguist to preserve the opposition of Preterite and Perfect (*Sprachpflege*).

Interesting contributions to the question of how the German tense system can best be described can be found in the volume *Der Begriff Tempus – eine Ansichtssache?* In the first article of this collection, H. Gelhaus ('Tempussystem', 1969) suggests treating tenses in terms of semantic components. This approach is supported by Baumgärtner and Wunderlich ('Ansatz', 1969), who develop a similar system of their own. Critical commentaries on Gelhaus's model have been presented by Glinz ('Tempussystem', 1969), and Kluge ('Diskussion', 1969). (For his own ideas on tense, see Kluge, *Perfekt*, 1961.)

A very important work on the German tense system has been provided by H. Weinrich. His *Tempus. Besprochene und erzählte Welt* (1964) has had great influence on other treatments of the question. For a critical discussion of Weinrich, see Gelhaus ('Tempora', 1969).

Gelhaus's (*Futur*, 1975) own approach to the tense problem is outlined in his extensive study of the German Future tense, which is part of the project *Grundstrukturen der deutschen Sprache* carried out by the *Institut für deutsche Sprache (IdS)* in Mannheim. Another comprehensive study of the Future tense has been provided by J. Dittmann (*Sprechhandlungstheorie*, 1976), whose work is an attempt to apply ideas of speech act philosophy to the study of the tense system. Both these works are based on detailed corpus analyses (which distinguishes them from Glinz (*Grammatik I*, 1970) and Wunderlich (*Tempus*, 1970).

Also based on the corpus of the *Institut für deutsche Sprache* is the work of Hauser-Suida and Hoppe-Beugel (*Vergangenheitstempora*, 1972), which is an extremely detailed analysis of how past time is expressed.

For the English-speaking reader, L. Schipporeit (1971) *Tenses and Time Phrases in Modern German* may be particularly useful.

Chapter 13

The subjunctive

13.1 Introduction

The subjunctive is probably the verbal category which has been given the honour of having the most contradictory statements made about it. General insecurity as to the extent of its use and the correct forms to use is also reflected in linguistic literature. One can find there the assumption that the subjunctive is on the way to becoming obsolete (Neuhoff, 'Bemerkungen', 1959). Jäger (*Konjunktiv*, 1971), on the basis of detailed statistical data, has shown this assumption to be incorrect. As far as the correct usage is concerned, it has been claimed that no rules can be given and that the subjunctive should be used according to the speaker's own intuition (Süskind, *Sprachkunstwerk*, 1940: 53). On the other hand many attempts have been made to show 'the simple rules for its use' (Röhrl, 'Konjunktiv', 1962: 289) and recommendations on how to use it can, of course, be found in all grammars. What is it that makes this topic so confusing? Let us consider the following examples:

[1] Wenn das Kapitel fertig wäre, wäre ich froh.
   (If the chapter were finished, I should be happy.)
[2] Du siehst aus, als ob du Gelbsucht hättest.
   (You look as if you have jaundice.)
[3] Wäre er doch schon in Nürnberg!
   (If only he were already in Nürnberg!)
[4] Er sagte mir, dass er im Dezember nach Nürnberg käme.
   (He told me that he would come to Nürnberg in December.)
[5] Er sagte mir, dass er im Dezember nach Nürnberg komme.
   (He told me that he would come to Nürnberg in December.)
[6] Er komme mir nicht mit faulen Ausreden!
   (I don't want to hear his lame excuses!)

This set of examples shows the wide range of the use of the subjunctive. Subjunctive forms can be found in conditional clauses, unreal comparisons and wishes, reported speech and indirect commands. A prominent part in the discussion about the subjunctive has been taken up by the question of what makes these different uses possible, to put it differently, whether there is a 'common denominator' in the semantic features which is present in all instances of subjunctive use.

This is, of course, a rather academic question, which would hardly have inspired such provocative statements as those mentioned above. A second set of examples will show the difficulty the subjunctive creates for the language user, especially the foreign learner. A sentence such as 'Yesterday Hermann said he would be in time today.' could have the following translation equivalents:

[7] Hermann sagte gestern, dass er heute pünktlich kommt/komme/käme.
[8] Hermann sagte gestern, er kommt/komme/käme heute pünktlich.
[9] Hermann sagte gestern, er wird/werde/würde heute pünktlich kommen.

All these sentences would be understood as an equivalent of the English sentence above. The questions here are: Are the nine possible translations [7–9] completely synonymous, or are there (minor) differences in meaning? And, for the foreign learner especially important, which form is the most common one and should consequently be preferred?

In the following we shall first turn to the question of the common denominator (13.2), and then to the question of synonymy (13.3).

13.2 The common denominator

The question as to the basic meaning of grammatical categories is as old as German linguistics (see 1.1). The subjunctive was traditionally believed to be concerned with the degree of reality a speaker attributes to his topic.[1] At least for the forms of KII (= KonjunktivII, ie preterite subjunctive, pluperfect subjunctive, würde + infinitive) a common denominator had been found in the concept of unreality. Thus, sentences [1], [2] and [3] were traditionally classified as an unreal conditional clause [1], unreal comparison [2] and unreal wish [3]. The (realization of the) content was thought to be marked as impossible or at least as improbable by the speaker. However, Flämig (Konjunktiv, 1959: 13) has shown that this is not true of all sentences. Let us compare sentences [1] and [10]:

[1]   Wenn das Kapitel fertig wäre, wäre ich froh.
[1]a Wenn das Kapitel fertig ist, bin ich froh.
      (If/When the chapter is finished, I will be happy.)
[10] Wenn ich ein Vöglein wär', flög ich zu dir.

[10]*a* ?Wenn ich ein Vöglein bin, flieg ich zu dir.
         (If I were a little bird, I would fly to you.)
         (?If/When I am a little bird, I will fly to you.)

The realization of [10] is rather unlikely (except in fairy-tales), whereas I know
for sure that I shall be happy, once my work is done. Of course, I can only
be as sure as one can be when talking about future events which are subject
to a condition. But this is due to the conditional clause, not the subjunctive,
as the sentences [1*a*] and [10*a*] show: compared with [1*a*], [10*a*] is just as 'poetic'
(some would call it odd!) as [10] in comparison with [1]. Unreality or reality
does not depend on the subjunctive, but, first of all, on the content of the
proposition.[2]

The impossibility of having recourse to the old basic meaning has led to
two different reactions. One group of linguists has abandoned the idea of a
common denominator altogether, for example Admoni (*Sprachbau*, [3]1970),
W. Schmidt (*Grundfragen*, 1965) and Duden (*Grammatik*, [3]1973).[3] On the
other hand Jäger (*Konjunktiv*, 1971) and Brinkmann (*Deutsche Sprache*, [2]1971)
have tried to find a new common denominator which can account for the various uses of the subjunctive more suitably than the old concept would. Both
come to the conclusion that KI (= present subjunctive) and KII have distinct
basic meanings, which are prevalent in all contexts.[4]

Brinkmann ([2]1971: 372–80) takes as his point of departure the use of the
subjunctive as demonstrated by sentence [6], and compares it with an instance
of the imperative.

[6] Er komme mir nicht mit faulen Ausreden!
[11] Komm mir nicht mit faulen Ausreden!

The difference between sentences [6] and [11] is that [11] would be addressed
to the person one wants to prevent from making lame excuses, whereas [6]
is addressed to somebody else. In Brinkmann's view the KI transgresses the
horizon given in the speech situation by introducing a third person who is
not a direct participant.[5] The use of KI in indirect speech (see below) confirms
this view of the subjunctive. Here, too, somebody not participating in the
present speech situation is introduced, even if this person is, however, one
of the interlocutors at a different time.

Brinkmann's idea of the transgression of the horizon also provides us with
a link between sentences [1] and [10] above:

[1] Wenn das Kapitel fertig wäre, wäre ich froh.
[10] Wenn ich ein Vöglein wär', flög ich zu dir.

Here the transgression does not consist in the introduction of someone beyond
the limits of the speech situation, but in evoking a situation which the speaker
regards as 'not given' at the moment of speaking:[6] the chapter, alas, has yet
to be completed, and I (HMD) am not a bird. Brinkmann emphasizes that
distinctions such as 'real' or 'unreal' are not appropriate for modern German.[7]

For example sentence [2] *Du siehst aus, als ob du Gelbsucht hättest.* could well
receive an answer such as *Du wirst lachen, ich hab' Gelbsucht.* The speaker
unwittingly guessed the truth. When he made his remark the *Gelbsucht* for
him was a fact 'not given'. Similarly, *er* in [3] *Wäre er doch schon in Nürnberg!*
could well be in Nürnberg, but the speaker may not know about his arrival.
The situation in [4] is rather more difficult (see below), but in this case, too,
there is much to be said for Brinkmann's interpretation.

Jäger (*Konjunktiv*, 1971) comes to similar conclusions.[8] Restating the basic
meaning of KI and KII is, however, only a secondary result of his investigation. Its primary merit consists in being the most detailed empirical study of
the German subjunctive available.[9] Empirical investigation was especially important for the use of the subjunctive in indirect speech, which is very confusing, not only for the foreign learner.

13.3 Subjunctive in indirect speech

13.3.1 *KI vs indicative*
As we saw above, the subjunctive is sometimes regarded as becoming obsolete.
This assumption could not be confirmed by Jäger's statistical data: of 3,720
unambiguous finite verb forms in indirect speech only 15 per cent (544) were
indicative forms, of the rest 57 per cent (2,123) were KI forms, and 27 per
cent (1,053) KII forms (Jäger, *Konjunktiv*, 1971:76, 87, 132). In addition, there
were a large number of ambiguous forms which could have been either indicative or subjunctive. The question is whether these forms are completely equivalent and substitutable for one another or, if not, what the reasons are for
their distribution. We shall first consider the opposition indicative/subjunctive
and then the distinction between KI and KII.

If we try to reconstruct Hermann's original utterance, the indirect representations of which we can see in sentences [7–9], we should probably arrive
at one of the following:

[12]   Ich komme morgen pünktlich.

or

[12]a Ich werde morgen pünktlich kommen.

If we now compare the original sentence with [7–9], we shall notice the following differences:

(i) In [7–9] the utterance is introduced by a reporting clause (RC): *Hermann sagte gestern,*
(ii) The utterance may be connected to the RC by means of a conjunction: *dass*
(iii) There is a shift of pronouns and deictic adverbials: *ich→er, morgen →heute*
(iv) Subjunctive is sometimes used instead of indicative.

As we can see, most of the possible sentences are over-determined in that they contain more than one sign indicating that not the whole sentence should be understood as an original utterance. Therefore, Jäger (*Konjunktiv*, 1971: 75–6) classified the instances of reported speech according to their degree of determination as triple-determined (RC, conjunction, subjunctive), double-determined (RC, subjunctive) and single-determined (subjunctive); for example, as in [13], [14] and [15] respectively:[10]

[13] *Hermann sagte mir gestern, dass* er heute pünktlich kommen *werde.*
[14] *Hermann sagte mir gestern,* er *werde* heute pünktlich kommen.[11]
[15] Hermann hatte nichts einzuwenden. Er *werde* heute pünktlich kommen.

Jäger's counts show that the higher the degree of determination is, the more ambiguous (KI/ind) and indicative forms can be found. These forms are particularly frequent in triple-determined sentences, whereas hardly any ambiguous and no indicative forms can be found in single-determined sentences.[12] This is, perhaps, not very surprising, for the indicative would make a sentence appear to be an original statement, almost certainly in single-determined cases and very often in double-determined ones. It is the frequent use of the KI in triple-determined sentences which is astonishing. Here, the subjunctive is, one might think, redundant. Why is it still used to such an extent? Perhaps the following examples will help to answer this question.

Let us suppose Hermann's utterance [12a] was made on Wednesday morning. His utterance would be reported on Wednesday afternoon as

[13]a Hermann sagte mir heute, dass er morgen pünktlich kommen wèrde.

on Thursday as

[13] Hermann sagte mir gestern, dass er heute pünktlich kommen werde.

on Friday as

[13]b Hermann sagte mir vorgestern, dass er gestern pünktlich kommen werde.[13]

The sentences [13], [13a] and [13b] show that the deictic adverbs change according to the temporal location of the speaker, whereas the tense is unaffected. Let us now replace the subjunctive forms by the indicative ones:

[13]a′ Hermann sagte mir heute, dass er morgen pünktlich kommen wird.
[13]′ Hermann sagte mir gestern, dass er heute pünktlich kommen wird.
[13]b′ *Hermann sagte mir vorgestern, dass er gestern pünktlich kommen wird.

Sentence [13b′] is ungrammatical because the deictic features of *gestern* (= before now) and future tense (= after now) are incompatible. The reason for the difference in acceptability must be sought in the deictic function of the subjunctive: whereas the indicative, like the adverb of time, refers to the temporal location of the speaker (*ich*), KI refers to the temporal location of the original speaker (*Hermann*). As seen from Wednesday morning, Thursday will always remain future. Thus, KI is a means of removing the reported utterance into a temporal distance, of relating to it a different location of the speaker, whereas the use of the indicative suggests that the reported utterance is accepted as also valid for one's own position (Jäger, *Konjunktiv*, 1971: 127–128).[14]

A different point of departure does not mean a reduced tense system. Different temporal relations can be expressed in reported speech just as in direct speech, as the following sentences show:[15]

[16] H. sagte, er sei gekommen.
[17] H. sagte, er komme.
[18] H. sagte, er werde kommen.
[16]*a* H. wird sagen, er sei gekommen.
[17]*a* H. wird sagen, er komme.
[18]*a* H. wird sagen, er werde kommen.

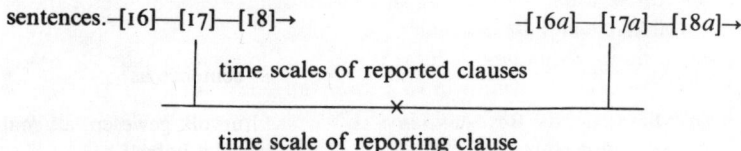

sentences.–[16]–[17]–[18]→   –[16*a*]–[17*a*]–[18*a*]→

              | time scales of reported clauses |
              |_____|
                              ×

                 time scale of reporting clause

× = possible 'now' of speaker of sentences [16–18*a*]

13.3.2 *KI vs KII*

Here, as in Chapter 12, the main difficulty arises with the preterite forms. It is a well-known fact that KI and KII do not mark a temporal difference (see also sentences [7] and [8] above). As in the distinction indicative/KI, the question is what are the reasons for the decision in favour of one form or the other.

Amongst the numerous attempts to explain the difference the following replacement rule takes pride of place[16]: ambiguous KI forms should be replaced by KII forms. However, Jäger's results show that the use of KI or KII cannot be reduced to a simple replacement rule. Apart from the unambiguous forms (see above), he found a considerable number of forms which could not with absolute certainty be assigned to the indicative or KI on the one hand (*Ich sagte, ich rechne damit, dass ...*), or to the preterite indicative or KII on the other (*Ich sagte, ich rechnete damit, dass ...*). It is significant that

 (i) ambiguous forms of KI can occur, even if an unambiguous KII form is available, and
(ii) ambiguous KII forms can occur, even if an unambiguous KI form is available (see Jäger, *Konjunktiv*, 1971: 80, 132–3).

These results suggest that the distribution is not exclusively dependent on morphological ambiguity, other factors have to be taken into account.

There are, of course, cases in which KII must be regarded as having been taken over from the original utterance, for example in sentence [19]

[19] Er sagte mir, wenn er ein Vöglein wär, flög er zu mir.

but cases for which this is only possible – not definite, as above – or not possible at all are the majority.[17] For these cases, Jäger (*Konjunktiv*, 1971; 165), as other grammarians have done before him, claims that KII expresses 'Distanzierung von Sachverhalten' (the speaker's distancing himself from the truth of what is being stated). Whereas KI in indirect speech indicates a temporal distance between the original and the secondary speech act, KII indicates that the speaker has doubts about the truth of the primary statement or the practicability of the proposition (Jäger, 1971: 165). This opinion can be illustrated by the following examples. In Bavaria one might hear this sentence:

[20] Die Bayern sind schon ein Kulturvolk gewesen, als man sich in Preussen noch auf der Bärenhaut gewälzt hat.
(The Bavarians were already civilized, when people in Prussia were still rolling around on bear-skins.)

A neutral newspaper would possibly report this sentence as

[20]*a* Man sagte, die Bayern seien schon ein Kulturvolk gewesen, als man sich in Preussen noch auf der Bärenhaut gewälzt habe.

A 'Prussian', however (in Bavarian usage all Germans north of the river Main are Prussians), would say:

[20]*b* Man sagte, die Bayern wären schon ein Kulturvolk gewesen, als man sich in Preussen noch auf der Bärenhaut gewälzt hätte.

thus showing his disagreement with what he feels to be an example of Bavarian arrogance.

But this is only one of the possible interpretations. A second one is that the 'Prussian' never uses KI, because his dialect system contains only indicative and KII. Many linguists claim that there are regional differences in the use of the subjunctives (see, for example, Glinz, *Grammatik I*, 1970: 118). Kaufmann (*Indirekte Rede*, 1976: 32), following Schwartz (*Modus*, 1973), mentions as further reasons: the influence of sociolects ('elaborated code' has indicative, KI, KII, 'restricted code' only indicative and KII) and the text type (oral: ind/KII; written: ind/KI/KII). One could add various possibilities of interference resulting from this differentiation.[18] Although many informants support Jäger's view, collocational restrictions have, so far, not been found. On the contrary, Kaufmann (1976:56) adduces examples which would contradict a firm rule:

[21] Heute wollte der Zollbeamte mein Portemonnaie sehen. Ich sagte *wahr-heitsgemäss*, es *läge* im Schlüsselfach des Hotels Axmannstein.
(Today the customs officer wanted to see my purse. I told him quite truthfully that it was in the key-rack of the Axmannstein hotel.)
[Erich Kästner, *Der kleine Grenzverkehr*, 50][19]

He concludes that the differentiation is more a possibility than an obligatory rule (Kaufmann, 1976:56).

13.3.3 *Didactic considerations*
So far, the investigations seem to offer little comfort for the student of German who is looking for a general rule or the teacher who wants to avoid teaching forms not commonly used. A fairly simple rule seems to have been replaced by a bundle of linguistic facts which are more apt to create confusion than to help learners to use the subjunctive correctly. This has, of course, also been realized by the linguists concerned,[20] and the whole second part of Kaufmann's book is dedicated to practical considerations intended to help learner and teacher. For his general rule Kaufmann takes into account not only formal ambiguity, but also the new statistical data.

Investigating the distribution of subjunctive forms Jäger had found the following data for the different persons:[21]

	KI (%) of 2,123	KII (%) of 1,053 unambiguous forms
ich	3.2	18.3
du	0.1	1.7
er/sie/es	90.3	47.8
wir	0.2	2.8
ihr	–	0.2
sie	6.3	29.3

The most striking result is the high percentage of subjunctive forms in 3rd sing/pl, especially for KI 3rd sing. This is, however, not so surprising, if we recall what was said about the basic function of KI (see 13.2): KI introduces a third person in the speech situation.[22] The comparatively low percentage of the first and second person may be due to the fact that Jäger's data are based on a written corpus.[23] But on the other hand one can expect that in oral use (informal dialogue) utterances would tend to be reported in direct speech and/or indicative would be used, if necessary with other signs of reported speech (see Kaufmann, *Indirekte Rede*, 1976: 111).[24]

As far as the decision to use KI or KII is concerned, the above table shows clearly that KII is more frequent in all cases except 3rd sing. This suggests morphological reasons: 3rd sing is the only KI form which is morphologically distinct for all verbs. All other forms of German full verbs are not (1st sing/pl, 3rd pl) or not strikingly (2nd sing/pl) different from their indicative counterparts. The modal verbs, *wissen* and *sein* are the important exceptions. The frequency of their morphologically distinct forms must account for the rest of the data found for KI.[25] Consequently, Kaufmann suggests as a rule of thumb (1976: 111):[26]

Exceptions:

3rd pers sing	3rd pers pl	sie seien
1st pers sing pl		ich sei/dürfe/könne/möge müsse/solle/wolle/wisse wir seien
2nd pers sing pl		du seist

KI = ☐   KII = ▨

Summing up one can say that in learning or teaching the following forms should be emphasized:

KI: all forms of *sein*, 1st and 3rd sing of modal verbs, 3rd sing of other verbs

KII: all forms, but especially modal and auxiliary verbs

Other forms can be neglected as far as active knowledge is concerned.

Recommended further reading

Further study of the subjunctive should be based on the works of Jäger and Kaufmann referred to above. In Jäger's *Der Konjunktiv in der deutschen Sprache der Gegenwart* (1971) especially, other treatments of the subjunctive are discussed critically. Kaufmann's *Die indirekte Rede und mit ihr konkurrierende Formen der Redeerwähnung* (1976) is the first volume of the publications prepared for didactic purposes within the project *Grundstrukturen der deutschen Sprache*. Accordingly, it contains, besides a systematic introduction to the topic, chapters on such problems as the deictic pronoun and adverb shift, the tense system in indirect speech and a survey of different ways of reporting utterances. These chapters and a list of reporting clauses will make the book a valuable aid for teachers.

Chapter 14

Modality and negation

14.1 Introductory remarks

In Chapter 13 we saw that a speaker can, under certain circumstances, indicate his doubts as to the truth of what he is saying. If in indirect speech the preterite subjunctive (KONJUNKTIV II) is used rather than the present subjunctive (KONJUNKTIV I) or the present indicative, many speakers of German feel that this suggests that the truth of the repeated utterance is not being vouched for. A speaker can also indicate his degree of certainty as to whether an event has, will or can take place, often using the indicative mood. This can be observed in the following sentences:

[1] Bettina ist Skilaufen gegangen.
[2] Bettina muss Skilaufen gegangen sein.
[3] Bettina ist vielleicht Skilaufen gegangen.
[4] Bettina könnte vielleicht Skilaufen gegangen sein.
[5] Bettina ist nicht Skilaufen gegangen.

In [5], NEGATION can also be said to express 'the attitude of the speaker to what he is saying', ie MODALITY (cf Lyons, Introduction, 1968: 305).

It seems, then, reasonable to claim that between absolute negation and positive absolute assertion there is an area of doubt, possibility, desirability, etc which is frequently discussed under the heading MODALITY. Negation will be discussed in 14.3, but in the next section we shall be concerned with various ways of expressing modality and will outline an attempt to integrate both modality and negation in a modality model (cf Gerstenkorn, 'Modal'-System, 1976).

14.2 Formal means of expressing modality

14.2.1 Modal verbs and modal adverbials

A distinction is sometimes drawn between an objective use and a subjective use of modal verbs. In the first no speaker attitude is implied; here the modal verb is said to express the objective relationship between the subject of the sentence and the non-finite verb. The second function expresses the speaker's attitude – his assessment of possibility, desirability, etc: it is subjective and pragmatic.[1] In [2] the modal verb *müssen* is used subjectively, as is *können* in [4]; *müssen* can in different contexts also be used objectively. The sentence

[6] Bettina will Skilaufen gehen.

illustrates the objective use of a modal verb, here *wollen*.

Modality can also be expressed by other syntactic options. If we consider these sentences

[7] Bettina fährt bestimmt Ski.
[8] Bettina fährt sicher Ski.

we find that whereas [7] is unambiguously modal, [8] is ambiguous – it can be read as meaning Bettina is a confident skier or that she is certainly skiing. Only the latter reading has a modal function. It is then necessary to distinguish between modal adverbials, which Admoni (*Sprachbau*, 1970: 203–4) calls *Modalwörter* and adverbs of manner.[2] Helbig ('Negationswörter', 1970: 398–400) demonstrates the difference between modal adverbials and adverbs of manner by using syntactic tests. He establishes three syntactic criteria:

(i) Only a modal adverbial can be transformed into a matrix clause.

[8]*a* Es ist sicher, dass Bettina Ski fährt.

(ii) Only a modal adverbial can serve as a one-word response to a yes/no question.

[8]*b* Fährt Bettina Ski?–Sicher/hoffentlich/vermutlich!
                    –*Schön/*schlecht/*pünktlich!

(iii) In negated clauses, *nicht* appears before a manner adverb but after a modal adverbial.

[8]*c* Bettina fährt nicht sicher (=unsicher) Ski.
[8]*d* Bettina fährt sicher nicht (=bestimmt nicht) Ski.

A third class of words which can be used to express modality is the class of particles. According to Helbig (1970: 399–400) they have to be considered a separate class since, unlike modal adverbials, they refer to one constituent of a sentence, are not independent constituents and are not permutable with the constituent they modify. Gerstenkorn (1976: 246–7) rejects Helbig's classification and suggest that there is a subclass of particles, modal particles (*Modalpartikeln*), which are sentence and not word particles, for instance *eben* and *ja* in [9] and [10]:

[9] Bettina ist EBEN die beste Skifahrerin in ihrer Familie; niemand kann
sie schlagen.
(She is just the best skier ...)

[10] Bettina fährt JA ausgezeichnet Ski!
(What an excellent skier Bettina is!)

There are, then, various ways of expressing modality, including the use of
modal verbs, modal adverbs (*Modalwörter*) and modal particles.[3]

14.2.2 *The modality model*

Modality, as we have discussed it so far, is one of the ways in which the proposition of an utterance can be modified; for this reason it is given prominence
in the pragmalinguistic model outlined in 5.4.1. A similar approach which
places great emphasis on modality has been taken by Gerstenkorn (1976) who
describes his model – MOD(MAT) – as a modality proposition model.[4] We can
illustrate the basis of Gerstenkorn's model by examining the following six sentences:

[11] Bettina geht Skilaufen.
[12] Bettina geht wahrscheinlich Skilaufen.
[13] Bettina geht vielleicht Skilaufen.
[14] Bettina geht wahrscheinlich nicht Skilaufen.
[15] Bettina geht vielleicht nicht Skilaufen.
[16] Bettina geht nicht Skilaufen.

Between [11], a definitely asserted positive sentence, and [16], a definitely
asserted negative sentence, we have four sentences in which the proposition
Bettina geht Skilaufen is modified.

Following Gerstenkorn we can ascribe to both [11] and [16] the marker
(+ ABSOLUT), a proposition is definitely asserted. [11] will however have
the marker (+ POSITIV) whereas [16] will have the marker (– POSITIV). What
of sentences [12] to [15]? None of them will have the marker (+ ABSOLUT) since
in none of them is a proposition definitely asserted, they are all in some way
modified assertions of a fact. They do, however, differ. Whereas [12] and [14]
suggest that Bettina will [12] or will not [14] go skiing, [13] and [15] leave the
question open. We can say then that [12] tends towards an absolute assertion
which is positive and that [14] tends towards an absolute assertion which is
negative. This tendency we can express using the marker (+ TENDENZ). [13]
and [15] will then have the marker (– TENDENZ). Our sentences [12–15] can
now be ascribed three markers each:

[11] /+ POS/ /+ ABS/
[12] /+ POS/ /– ABS/ /+ TEND/
[13] /+ POS/ /– ABS/ /– TEND/
[14] /– POS/ /– ABS/ /+ TEND/
[15] /– POS/ /– ABS/ /– TEND/
[16] /– POS/ /+ ABS/.

Another surface realization of $/-$ ABS$/$ $/+$ TEND$/$ is *dürfen* (modal verb):

[12]*a* Bettina dürfte Skilaufen gegangen sein.

and of $/-$ ABS$/$ $/-$ TEND$/$ *können* (modal verb):

[13] Bettina könnte Skifahren gegangen sein.

We have, of course, not yet exhausted the modal (modifying) possibilities of the language. Gerstenkorn ('*Modal*'-*System*, 1976: 22–6, 95–116) identifies three optional markers $-/\pm$ POSITIVE$/$ $/\pm$ ABSOLUT$/$ are of course obligatory, every utterance is either positive or negative as well as definitely or not definitely asserted. Consider sentences [17–19]:

[17] Bettina ist wirklich Skilaufen gegangen.
[18] Bettina ist leider Skilaufen gegangen.
[19] Bettina fährt eben Ski.

In [17] the category /EXPRESSIV/ is realized lexically using *wirklich*. This category stands for emphatic stress and is often realized phonologically by contrastive stress as well as by such elements as *wirklich* and *doch*. *Leider* in [18] expresses the value judgement of the speaker, in this case the illocutionary act of regretting: *Ich bedauere, dass Bettina Skifahren gegangen ist* would be a paraphrase of [18]. Gerstenkorn calls this category /PARTIZIPATIV/; it is realized by adverbials such as *zum Glück, glücklicherweise, bedauerlicherweise, freilich*. In [19] the category /EMOTIV/ is expressed by the particle *eben*. Gerstenkorn (1976: 113) recognizes a class of *emotiva* (emotive particles), which never introduce a sentence (unlike *freilich, leider*, etc), never occur as oneword utterances and are never stressed although they express an emotional involvement with what is said.

We have only been able to introduce the basis of Gerstenkorn's model, which deserves the close attention of any linguist anxious to investigate the modal complex. As we have seen, Gerstenkorn regards negation as a modal category and the rest of the chapter will be devoted to this equally complex area of German grammar.

14.3 Negation

14.3.1 *Introductory remarks*
In 14.2.2 we spoke of the modal status of negation, we must now distinguish negation and modality proper. There are good syntactic reasons for doing so. Firstly, $/-$ POS$/$ sentences can also include either $/-$ ABS$/$ or $/+$ ABS$/$, whereas modality proper is only found with $/-$ ABS$/$. In addition $/-$ POS$/$ $/-$ ABS$/$ are also found with the three optional markers and, whereas $/\pm$ TEND$/$ words such as *vielleicht* and *wahrscheinlich* cannot appear together in a clause, they can be used with *nicht*.

Negation is present in these sentences:

[20] Bettina fährt nicht Schlitten.
[21] Bettina hat ihre Skier nicht gekauft.
[22] Bettina hat nicht ihre Skier gekauft.
[23] Niemand sollte rauchen.
[24] Ute mag keine Skilehrer.
[25] Ute flirtet ungern mit Skilehrern.
[26] Skilehrer sind manchmal ungeduldig.

If we consider [20] as it stands, we will find that it is ambiguous. It could be understood as meaning that Bettina is not tobogganing but skiing or that she is simply not tobogganing without any suggestion of what else she might be doing. In the first reading some linguists would claim that the negative word *nicht* affects only *Schlitten*. We might paraphrase the sentence as follows:

[27] Bettina fährt schon Ski, aber nicht Schlitten.

In this case we could talk of word or constituent negation (*Wortnegation*) and in the other reading of sentence or clause negation (*Satznegation*). We shall return to this matter in 14.3.2 and discuss the arguments in favour of distinguishing two kinds of negation.

Negation is then related but not equivalent to modality, it is one extreme on the probability scale. However, the presence of a negative element in a clause does not seem to guarantee that the whole proposition is felt to be negated. Finally, amongst the many negative elements in German, including bound morphemes such as *un-* (*ungern*) and *-los* (*arbeitslos*), *nicht* has a special position. Let us now turn to some aspects of negation in clauses.

14.3.2 *Aspects of negation*

Negative words are a semantic, but not a syntactic class. If we consider sentences [20–26], we find negative elements in various positions; in some cases, as in [20–24], the negative elements could not change their position without either affecting the meaning of the sentences ([20–22]) or creating ungrammatical sentences [23, 24]. Stickel (*Untersuchungen*, 1970: 13–23) examines the syntactic behaviour of a number of common negative words and concludes that they are syntactically) a very heterogeneous class, a class identified only by their semantic properties.[5] However, they do seem to have a deep homogeneity since, as we noted above, there appears to be a systematic relation between each of them and the negative word *nicht*.[6]

Stickel (1970: 55–71) appeals to the insights of TG for a satisfactory explanation of this relationship. He suggests the following deep structure (base) as shown opposite.

I is to be understood as the obligatory sentence type choice – declarative, interrogative or imperative. NUCLEUS is the proposition and NEG the optional negative element. Stickel (1970: 72–96) argues that whereas *nicht* is derived directly from this, all the other negative words are to be understood

```
                          Satz
                           |
        ┌──────────────────┴──────────────────┐
        I                                      S
                                               |
                               ┌───────────────┴───────────────┐
                             NEG                            NUCLEUS
```

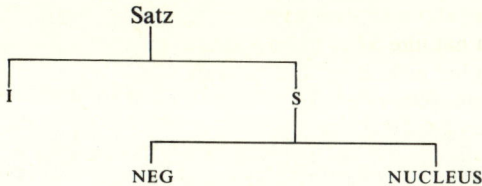

as consisting, in deep structure, of NEG and a non-definite element of NUCLEUS.[7]

We return now to the question of constituent and sentence negation. Admoni ([3]1970: 243) argues that a constituent is negated, and not the whole clause, if a *sondern* (but) or contrastive clause can follow the negated clause, so that if we take *Bettina fährt nicht Schlitten*, (*sondern Ski*), constituent negation is assumed. Similarly with [22] we could take the context *sondern ihre Stiefel* and for [24] *sondern Linguisten*.[8] Stickel argues that if the two surface negations are assumed to result from transformations, the context would be the only factor determining where the negative word was placed. In all cases the validity of the whole sentence is negated, so that in our examples Bettina does not go tobogganing whatever else she may do or not do, and did not buy her skis.

14.3.3 *Final remarks*

We can then identify three main problems in connection with negation. Firstly, how can the focus of negative elements be described and accounted for? Only a pragmatic and textual grammar will allow linguists to answer this question satisfactorily. Secondly, what is the relationship between the negative words we have discussed in 14.3.1 and 14.3.2, which we might call primary negative words, and other negative words and morphemes, such negative elements as *weder … noch*, the affixes *in-*, *un-*, *nicht-*, *-los*, *-frei*, etc and limitation adverbs *kaum*, *nur*, *bloss*, etc? Any treatment of negation will remain inadequate if it limits itself to the primary negative words. Finally, it is necessary to consider both the context of situation and the immediate linguistic context when discussing negation and since no generally accepted pragmatic or textual metatheory is available, investigations of negation which restrict themselves to sentence syntax and semantics must prove inadequate.[9]

Chapter 15

Sentence patterns

15.1 Possible approaches to the classification of sentences

The introduction of so-called SENTENCE PATTERNS is common to many theories of syntactic analysis, they have been called *Grundformen, Satzbaupläne* or *Satztypen*, etc. This phenomenon may be due to the need for classification in the course of linguistic description, but many of the models of sentence patterns have been developed to handle the foreign learner's problems when learning a language. The pedagogic implications of the establishment of descriptively adequate sentence patterns of a language are revealed when one considers the importance of the pattern drill in foreign language learning, a device which is used in almost every textbook or language laboratory programme.[1]

The classification of sentences into a finite number of patterns can, theoretically, be made on the basis of three different levels of linguistic analysis: the levels of linguistic form,[2] content,[3] and function. More complex theories have attempted to link two of these three levels in the course of analysis and have thus developed sentence patterns which are established by formal as well as, for example, semantic criteria. This is true, for instance, of some representatives of *inhaltbezogene Grammatik*; as an example of this approach we shall discuss *die Grundformen deutscher Sätze* as outlined in the 1959 edition of the *Duden* (*Grammatik*, 1959).[4]

In this chapter, we shall compare and contrast the *Duden* sentence patterns with the related, though in some respects quite distinct, approach of the Russian linguist Admoni, who sets up a number of what he calls *logisch-grammatische Satztypen* within a theory emphasizing the role of function in linguistic analysis. What these two approaches have in common is that they do not restrict themselves to a purely formal analysis. This is the main distinction between the patterns elaborated in the *Duden* (*Grammatik*) or by Admoni and the valency-based sentence patterns of dependency grammar (although, as has been shown in Chapter 4, dependency grammarians also consider semantics to be the ultimate aim of linguistic description: the restriction of analysis to linguistic form at this stage is solely for methodological reasons).

15.2 Different sets of sentence patterns

15.2.1 *A valency-based model*
In Chapter 4 we have shown how a theory of sentence patterns can be established on the grounds of the analysis of verb valency. The adverbial *hoffentlich* in a sentence like

[1] Der Linguist gewöhnt Ute hoffentlich das Rauchen ab

has been classified as a circonstant (see 4.2.3), *ie* it is not relevant for the establishment of the sentence pattern. The verb in sentence [1] requires the obligatory actants *der Linguist* (nominative object: 0), *Ute* (dative object: 3) and *das Rauchen* (accusative object: 1), and the sentence as a whole could therefore be classified as belonging to sentence pattern 013.

This is the kind of analysis carried out by Engel,[5] who sets up a model of sentence patterns of German, whose categories have all been established on syntactic grounds only (see 4.2.5 and Engel. 'Satzanalyse', 1970: 111). (As we have seen in Chapter 4, Engel makes a distinction between obligatory and optional actants – take, for example [2] *Ute trinkt einen erlesenen Wein*, where the *einen erlesenen Wein* is an optional actant so that [2] belongs to pattern 0(1) – but this distinction has not been taken account of in table 1.)

Table 1 (*pp* 147–9) shows the sentence patterns listed by Engel (*Syntax*, 1977: 180–1) with his own examples. The +/− symbols indicate whether or not the formal pattern is represented in the models of the *Duden* (*Grammatik*) and Admoni.

15.2.2 *A content-oriented model*
Whereas in Engel's model it is the necessity of including an element in the structure which is considered to be the relevant criterion for inclusion in the sentence pattern *die Grundformen deutscher Sätze* set up in the *Duden* (*Grammatik*, 1959) were developed by the application of the so-called *Abstrichmethode*, a principle devised by Weisgerber (*Weltbild*, 1950: 178), which also takes account of semantic aspects.[8]

As in the 1959 edition of the *Duden* is in the tradition of content-oriented grammar (see Chapter 2), it is only logical that the *Grundformen* do not only state basic grammatical patterns, but are also specified semantically. The reasoning behind this is that form and content are so closely linked with each other that in selecting a certain *Grundform* for the description of an action, etc the speaker already expresses the view he takes of that action *ie* his *Sehweise*; see *Duden* (*Grammatik*, 1959: 465).[9]

The initial classification of sentences is therefore made at the level of content: it is the distinction between sentences expressing *Zustände*, *Vorgänge* or *Tätigkeiten* (states, processes or activities, which we shall abbreviate S) and sentences describing *Handlungen* (actions, henceforth A) (compare *Duden, Grammatik*, 1959: 437–9).[10]

To take an example: within this model, a sentence such as [1] *Der Linguist gewöhnte Ute das Rauchen ab* would be classified as needing a subject, a predicate (verb) as well as a dative and an accusative object. It thus belongs to the category of *Handlungssätze* (A) and its content is characterized as an action which is necessarily directed towards something. ('Handlung, die notwendig einem Etwas zugewandt ist'.) *Duden* (*Grammatik*, 1959: 446–7).

Table 2 (*pp* 150–4) illustrates the sentence patterns of the *Duden* (*Grammatik*, 1959:466–9). The last two columns indicate what we regard as the possible equivalent pattern in Engel's and Admoni's models.

15.2.3 *Sentence patterns and functional roles*
Admoni's sentence patterns shown in Table 3 are based on the criterion of the structural necessity of elements.[11] Although he admits that the same action can be expressed by means of different sentence patterns,[12] he would claim that the sentence pattern also mirrors the facts of the world, *ie* Admoni takes an object-oriented (*sachbezogen*) point of view.[13] He therefore calls his sentence patterns *logisch-grammatische Satztypen* (see Chapter 3, note 18).

Our example [1] *Der Linguist gewöhnt Ute das Rauchen ab* would belong to Admoni's pattern II. [1] contains the obligatory elements subject (nominative) + transitive verb + indirect object (dative) + direct object (accusative). These syntactic elements are described as *Erzeuger der Handlung* (actor) + *Handlung* (action) + *Adressat der Handlung* (beneficiary) + *Gegenstand der Handlung* (goal) (see Admoni, *Sprachbau*, [3]1970: 235). As our translations already suggest, a parallel can easily be drawn here with a functional analysis, for example Halliday's theory or Fillmore's case grammar. Indeed, function is one of the central issues in Admoni's theory of language (see Chapter 3).

15.3 Syntactic or semantic classification?

It is not surprising that a comparison of the three tables reveals some sentence patterns which appear in only one model; Engel's pattern 48 *Es steht nicht gut um unsere Pläne* does not, for instance, have an equivalent in the other two models. Similarly, *Er ist des Diebstahls schuldig* only appears in the *Duden* (*Grammatik*). These differences are a result of the different descriptive procedures and need not really concern us here, although, with the theoretical background of Chapter 4, it must be regarded as a great weakness of Admoni's model that he does not include prepositional objects.

However, the essential difference between the three ways of establishing sentence patterns we have sketched out lies elsewhere. Let us discuss two examples:

[3] Der Linguist bezweifelt die Richtigkeit der Theorie.
[4] Der Linguist zweifelt an der Richtigkeit der Theorie.

In Engel's model, [3] and [4] would be classified as 01 and 04 respectively, and the same formal analysis is provided by the *Duden* (*Grammatik*), which furthermore describes [3] as an action complete in itself ('eine in sich geschlossene Handlung') *Duden* (*Grammatik*, 1959: 467), whereas [4] belongs to the category of sentences expressing states, processes or activities which are either directed towards something or locationally determined ('Zustände, Vorgänge oder Tätigkeiten, die auf ein Etwas gerichtet oder mit einem Etwas lagebestimmt verbunden sind'; (*p* 448). Thus the *Duden* actually ascribes a difference in meaning to [3] and [4], although most speakers of German would probably consider them to be synonymous. A similar problem is presented by the following pair of sentences:

[5] Ute glaubt dem Mediziner (dative).
[6] Ute glaubt die Antwort (accusative).

According to the *Duden* (*Grammatik*, 1959: 439–40), [5] represents the view of states, processes and activities necessarily directed towards something, whereas [6] is an action complete in itself. There are good reasons, however, for doubting the validity of the distinction made in the *Duden*, as in some contexts sentences [5] and [6] can be taken as being functionally equivalent; for example, both could replace *Ute glaubt dem Linguisten die Antwort*.[14]

Whether or not these descriptions seem adequate, we cannot decide here. The problem, however, is quite obvious: has a theory relating syntactic and semantic features in a rather direct way any validity or is it in danger of positing differences where there are none? This is, as we have seen in Chapter 11, a prominent controversy in German linguistics: some linguists, often adherents of dependency grammar, above all Helbig,[15] hold that no easy correspondences between form and content can sensibly be established at all, whereas others point out that denying the possibility of such correspondences would limit the range of syntax further than necessary. This position has, for instance, been adopted by Admoni, who stresses the pedagogic value of a semantic description of formal patterns.[16]

It seems, however, that the question of whether a sentence pattern can be described semantically or not cannot be answered in such a general way. Take, for instance:

[7] Ute wohnt in Nürnberg.
[8] Ute lebt in Franken.
[9] Brigitte reitet im Dartmoor.

This list could be expanded at will and one would still find that all the sentences belonging to pattern 05 are rather similar in meaning. According to Engel ('Satzbaupläne', 1970: 381–3), it is only sentence patterns 05, 06, 07 and 08 which allow a relatively restricted range of semantic representations. A semantic description of these patterns would therefore not present many problems.[17]

With other sentence patterns, however, the situation seems to be much more complicated. This is illustrated by the fact that semantically equivalent sentences can belong to different sentence patterns as, for example,

[10] Der Linguist macht Bettina mit den Blumen eine Freunde.
[11] Der Linguist erfreut Bettina mit den Blumen.

As we have shown in Chapter 4, dependency grammar has provided a solution to this problem by shifting semantic considerations to the description of single verbs (or classes of verbs). It is the great merit of the valency dictionaries to have provided structurally-based descriptions of the use of verbs including their semantic implications without making statements that are either too general to be useful or too specific to be true.[18] It may be interesting to note in this context that the new edition of the *Duden (Grammatik,*[3] 1973) has largely adopted the dependency approach in the discussion of syntactic patterns.

Sentence patterns can perhaps best be regarded as a formal device, which, in some cases, can quite easily be matched with a semantic description. In other cases, however, the semantic value of a pattern is largely determined by the verb or the particular class the verb belongs to. The meaning of an actual sentence (in context) is in any case widely determined by the meaning of its lexical items.

Finally, it must not be forgotten that however great the value of sentence patterns in linguistic analysis and foreign language teaching may be, they are no more than a theoretical construct which can be modified in many ways, both structurally and semantically. Take voice, tense or mood, for instance:

[12] Die Theorie wurde durch den Kakao gezogen.
[13] Der Linguist hat Ute das Rauchen abgewöhnt.
[14] Der Linguist würde die Theorie durch den Kakao ziehen, wenn er nicht viel Geld mit ihr verdienen könnte.
[15] Der Mediziner, nicht der Linguist gewöhnte Ute das Rauchen ab.

This last example also shows that sentence patterns are modified by the formation of more complex sentences; the same process takes place with the inclusion of circonstants. In all these cases, however, the underlying sentence pattern remains the same[19] (compare 4.2.5). Let us consider a final example:

[16] Ute hat der Linguist das Rauchen abgewöhnt.
[17] Das Rauchen hat der Linguist Ute abgewöhnt.

Here, we have changes in meaning which are derived from the theme/rheme structure of a sentence: [14] tends to suggest an implication of the kind *Ute, nicht Brigitte war es, der der Linguist das Rauchen abgewöhnt hat,* whereas [17] might imply that he has been successful in stopping her smoking, but that she still consumes lots of *erlesenen Frankenwein.* As we can see from these examples, word order (and also intonation) make a considerable contribution to the meaning of a sentence; they will be discussed in the next chapter.

Table 1: Engel's *Satzbaupläne*

NOTE: Nominative object is used here rather than the traditional nominative subject, following
Engel's own usage. (Compare Chapter 4, note 26.)

Syntactic classification	No	Example	Duden	Admoni
dummy-subject *es*	–	Es taut.	–	+
accusative object	1	Mich friert/Es friert mich.	–	+
nominative object	0	Johanna fiebert.	+	+
nominative object accusative object	01	Pinkus pfeift den Kaiserwalzer.	+	+
nominative object accusative object accusative object	011	Sie lehrt ihn eine neue Fremdsprache.	+	–
nominative object genitive object	02	Er entledigt sich seiner Kleider.	+	+
nominative object accusative object genitive object	012	Man beschuldigt ihn der Unaufmerksamkeit.	+	–
nominative object dative object	03	Streusalze schaden den Fahrzeugen.	+	+
nominative object accusative object dative object	013	Er sagte ihr, was er dachte.	+	+
nominative object accusative object dative object directional adverbial	0136	Uli bringt dem Vater die Mappe ins Büro.	–	–
nominative object prepositional object	04	Ich denke an dich.	+	–
nominative object accusative object prepositional object	014	Sie überredeten das Opfer zu einer angeblichen Spazierfahrt.	+	–

Syntactic classification	No	Example	Duden	Admoni
nominative object stative adverbial	05	Das Dorf liegt an der Autobahn.	+	−
accusative object stative adverbial	15	Hier gibt es das beste Brot der Welt.	−	−
nominative object accusative object stative adverbial	015	Sie verbrachten drei Tage im Elsass.	−	−
nominative object directional adverbial	06	Wir fahren nach Bamberg.	+	+
nominative object accusative object directional adverbial	016	Sie brachte ihr Gepäck an den Flughafen.	+	−
nominative object identifying complement[6]	07	Dieser Mann ist ein Spion.	+	+
nominative object accusative object identifying complement	017	Man nennt ihn einen Duckmäuser.	+	−
nominative object attributive complement	08	Dieser Mann ist gefährlich.	+	+
nominative object accusative object attributive complement	018	Man nennt ihn zwielichtig.	+	−
nominative object infinitive[7]	09	Ich lasse singen.	−	+
dative object prepositional object	34	Mir graut vor dir.	−	−
nominative object dative object prepositional object	034	Man riet ihm zum Nachgeben.	+	−
nominative object dative object directional adverbial	036	Sie halfen ihm aufs Pferd.	−	−

Syntactic classification	No	Example	Duden	Admoni
nominative object dative object attributive complement	038	Man war ihm unfreundlich begegnet.	–	–
nominative object prepositional object prepositional object	044	Sie sprachen mit den Nachbarn über Utas Haus.	+	–
prepositional object identifying complement	47	Es ist ein Elend mit ihm.	–	–
prepositional object attributive complement	48	Es steht nicht gut um unsere Pläne.	–	–
nominative object prepositional object attributive complement	048	Man ging noch recht sanft mit ihm um.	–	–

Table 2: *Grundformen deutscher Sätze* according to Grebe (*Duden, Grammatik*, 1959: 466–9)

NOTE: The Engel and Admoni columns only list the direct formal correspondences; semantic criteria have not been considered here. Sentence patterns printed in italics appear more than once.

No	Formal description	Content		Example	Engel	Admoni
S1	subject predicate	states, processes or activities	not goal-directed	Die Rosen blühen.	o	I
A1	+ accusative object	an action complete in itself		Der Gärtner bindet die Blumen.	o1	II
S2	subject predicate nominative as complement	states or processes	in which a 'something' is equated with another 'something'	Karl ist mein Freund.	o7	*III*
A2	+ accusative object	actions		Karl nennt mich einen Lügner.	o17	
S3	subject predicate dative object	states, processes or activities	which are necessarily directed towards something	Der Sohn dankt dem Vater.	o3	*III*
A3	+ accusative object	actions		Karl schenkt seinem Freunde ein Buch.	o13	VII

S4	subject predicate genitive object	processes or activities		Ich harre seiner.	02
A4	+ accusative object	actions	to which something contributes	Der Richter beschuldigte den Angeklagten des Diebstahls.	012
S5	subject predicate prepositional object	states, processes or activities	directed towards or positionally linked with	Inge achtet auf ihre Schwester.	04
S5a	+ dative object	processes or activities		Karl spielt mit ihr. Ich rate ihm zum Nachgeben.	014
S5b	+ prepositional object		something (necessarily directed)	Der Forschungsreisende sprach zu den Schulkindern über seine Afrikareise.	044
A5	+ accusative object	actions	(linked with another something)	Er verriet ihn an seine Feinde. Ich bewahre ihn vor seinen Feinden.	014

Table 2 cont'd overleaf

No	Formal description	Content		Example	Engel	Admoni
S6	subject predicate adverbial of place	states, processes or activities	linked to a certain place	München liegt an der Isar.	o5	VI
S6a	+ dative object			Ich klopfe meinem Freund auf die Schulter.	o34	
A6	+ accusative object	actions	(+ necessarily directed towards something)	Ich hänge das Bild an die Wand.	*o14*	
A6a	+ dative object	actions		Karl legte seinem Freunde die Hand auf die Schulter.		
S7	subject predicate adverbial of time	states or processes	which are time-bounded	Die Beratung dauerte zwei Stunden.		
A7	+ accusative object	actions		Er zog das Gespräch in die Länge.	*o14*	

	subject predicate complement	complement		IV
S8		complement	Die Rose ist schön. Wilhelm benimmt sich schlecht.	o8
S8a	+ dative object	(a) necessarily directed towards something	Ich bin diesem Manne fremd. Deine Liebe tut ihm wohl.	*o18*
S8b	+ genitive object	(b) participatory	Er ist des Diebstahls schuldig.	
S8c	+ prepositional object	(c) positionally or directionally determined	Ich bin auf deinen Bericht gespannt.	
S8ca	+ prepositional object + dative object	positionally or directionally determined and directed to something	Er ist mir an Fleiss überlegen.	
S8d	+ adverb of place	place-bound	Er ist in München ansässig.	

states or processes

Table 2 cont'd overleaf

No	Formal description	Content		Example	Engel	Admoni
A8	+accusative object	actions		Die Mutter macht die Suppe warm.	*o18*	
A8a	(equivalent to S8a)		(a)	Ich machte ihm die Beine lang.		
A8b	(equivalent to S8b)		(b)	Der Richter sprach diesen Mann des Diebstahls schuldig.		
A8c	(equivalent to S8c)		(c)	Mein Freund machte mich auf dieses Mädchen aufmerksam.		
S9	subject predicate causal complement	processes or activities	determined by cause	Das Verbrechen geschah aus Eifersucht.	*o4*	
A	subject predicate accusative object accusative object			Herr Meier lehrte uns die französische Sprache.	*o11*	
A	subject predicate accusative object infinitive			Karl hörte seine Schwester singen.		

Table 3: *Logisch-grammatische Satztypen* **according to W. Admoni (***Sprachbau***, 1970: 235–42)**

NOTE: The Engel and Grebe columns only list the direct formal correspondences, no semantic correspondences have been taken account of.

No	Formal description	Semantic description	Examples	Engel	Duden
I	nominative (subject), finite verb as predicate	relating an 'object' and a process (action or state) initiated by this 'object'	Arbeiter arbeiten. Arbeiter haben gearbeitet.	0	S1
II	nominative (subject), transitive verb with either accusative or dative object or both.	initiator of action, action, object of action (or/and recipient of action).	Arbeiter fällen Bäume. Er ist mir begegnet. Er gefällt uns. Er schenkte ihr Bücher.	O1 O3 O13	A1 S3 A3
III	nominative (subject), copula, subject nominal not identical with predicate nominal.	inclusion or integration of the 'individual' or the 'particular' in the 'general', subsuming a restricted concept under a wider concept. naming or identification of people. identity sentence.	Die Rose ist eine Blume. Er ist Student. Dieser Mann ist mein Vater. Die grundlegende Voraussetzung für die Einführung der neuen Methode war die ... völlige Umgestaltung des Produktionsablaufs.	O7	S2
IV	nominative (subject), copula, adjective (not inflected in predicative use).	quality of an 'object'	Die Rose ist schön. Der Schatten dieser Esche ist wohl ein sparsamer. Das Haus ist gross.	O8	S4

Table 3 cont'd overleaf

No	Formal description	Semantic description	Examples	Engel	Duden
V	nominative (subject), copula, genitive predicate.	various meanings: inner state of the subject, state of belonging, quality, predicate genitive of quality.	Er ist guter Laune. Er ist der Meinung. Die Erfindung ist des Dichters. Die Frage ist von grosser Bedeutung. Dieses Substantiv ist männlichen Geschlechts.	02	S6 04
VI	sein (=to be located), temporal and locative adverbials as elements of the extended predicate.	—	Er ist im Garten. Der Tag war da.	05	S6 S7
VII	nominative (subject), modal verb, infinitive. nominal (object). haben, zu-infinitive sein, zu-infinitive	carrier of the state, inner state, which is directed to a usually external process, process, relation between subject and action, modality.	Der Junge muss baden und schwimmen. Wir wollen Frieden. Er will ihr das Buch schenken. Ich beabsichtige zu kommen.	09 01	
VIII	nominative (subject), transitive verb, accusative (object). es gibt, accusative object.	subject–object relation denotes a state, state of the subject. existence of 'thing' denoted by grammatical 'object'.	Ich habe Angst. Es gibt gute Leute. Ich habe Geld. Da hatten wir eine Begegnung.	01	

IX	nominative (subject) following copula with preposed *es* restriction: word-sequence cannot be reversed.	two-element existential sentence: action, process to the fore (verb-meaning), existence of the subject.	Es war einmal ein Mädchen. Es blasen die blauen Husaren.	(o)
X	dummy-subject *es* or no nominative subject when first place occupied by another element.	impersonal sentences	Es schneit. Es hungert mich. Mich hungert. Es wird nicht geraucht. Hier wird nicht geraucht.	$\dfrac{-}{1}$
XI	genitive, copula, word with quantitative meaning.	two-part partitive sentences	Der Gäste waren viele.	
XII	one-part: substantival nominal-word or -group.	one-part existential sentence denoting existence of 'objects' or phenomena.	Laue Wärme, kühle tiefschwarze Nacht und helles Licht.	

Chapter 16

Word order

16.1 Introduction

In the last chapter we saw that sentence patterns, although forming the basis of all sentences, are 'no more than a theoretical construct which can be modified in many ways'. For example, a particular sentence pattern makes no statement about the word order found in a sentence based on it. In this chapter we shall try to shed some light upon one of the bugbears of many learners of German: German WORD ORDER.

Apart from other daunting qualities it may possess, a German sentence based, for example, on Engel's pattern 013 (subject, accusative object, dative object) can have many confusing variants:

[1]*a* Der Boss hat dem Gangster das Geld gestern abend gegeben.
[1]*b* Der Boss hat dem Gangster gestern abend das Geld gegeben.
[1]*c* Der Boss hat das Geld dem Gangster gestern abend gegeben.
[1]*d* Der Boss hat das Geld gestern abend dem Gangster gegeben.
[1]*e* Der Boss hat gestern abend dem Gangster das Geld gegeben.
[1]*f* Der Boss hat gestern abend das Geld dem Gangster gegeben.

Similar sets of six (in cases [2–4]) and of twenty-four variants (in case [5] all four elements right of *hat* can change places) are possible, if *dem Gangster*, *das Geld*, *gestern abend* or *gegeben* change places with *der Boss*:

[2]*a* Dem Gangster hat der Boss das Geld gestern abend gegeben.
[2]*b* Dem Gangster hat der Boss gestern abend das Geld gegeben. etc
[3]*a* Das Geld hat der Boss dem Gangster gestern abend gegeben. etc
[4]*a* Gestern abend hat der Boss dem Gangster das Geld gegeben. etc
[5]*a* Gegeben hat der Boss dem Gangster das Geld gestern abend. etc

All in all, there are 48 possible variants, most of which would be considered 'good German' or, at least, acceptable, some, however, only under very particular conditions.

Stress is one of these conditions. A fairly neutral variant of sentences [1a–5x], for example [1b] would, like most German sentences, contain one element marked by stress as prominent (indicated by *1* above the relevant word or syllable) and elements marked as less important by lesser degrees of emphasis (*2, 3, 4*, etc). Sentence [1b] could be represented as follows:[1]

[1]b Der Boss hat dem Gangster gestern abend das GELD gegeben.

Some variants of [1a–5x] are, at least as isolated sentences outside a given context, only possible if the stress pattern is also different from normal. For example

[5]b GEGEBEN hat der Boss dem Gangster das Geld gestern ABEND.

in which case the sentence would probably or, at least, could be continued by

[6] ..., VERSPROCHEN hatte er es ihm schon LANGE.

The word order as given in [5b], supported by the appropriate stress, is possible if *gegeben/gestern abend* are – explicitly or implicitly – contrasted with other elements.

[5b] would also be possible with emphatic stress on *gegeben* only, with a general reduction of all other stresses, if it is, for example, used as a correction of [7]. In this case it is, however, likely that *Boss*, *Gangster* and *Geld* appear in a pronominalized form [8]. *Gestern abend* may be left out altogether.

[7] Der Boss hat dem Gangster des Geld also gestern abend weggenommen?

[8] Nein, GEGEBEN hat er es ihm!

implying 'not taken away, but given'.[2]

Besides the variants which mostly occur with contrastive or emphatic stress a large number of variants remain, variants without particular stress conditions, but with varying word order. The question is whether these variants are freely exchangeable or, if not, what differences there are between them, and, further, by what conditions the position of an element in a sentence is determined. First of all, however, we shall look for a firm point of departure in our further considerations of word order.

16.2 Firm and unfirm elements in German word order

After an unbiased reading of the first section of this chapter a rather careless reader might assume that anything is possible in German word order. To the distress of every foreign learner of German this is not so. The careful reader will have observed the element that remained consistent in sentences [1–5]. It is the finite part of the verbal group: *hat*.

For the position of *hat* only two changes can be imagined. The first would result in a remarkable change in the communicative function of the sentence: sentence [9] would be interpreted as a question, a change of intonation presupposed (falling intonation in [1–8], rising in [9]).[3]

[9] Hat der Boss dem Gangster gestern abend das Geld gegeben?

The second is only possible under very particular conditions, *ie* if a conjunction is added at the beginning, and the sentence is integrated as a clause into a complex structure:

[10] Es steht fest, DASS der Boss dem Gangster gestern abend das Geld gegeben hat.

In an affirmative proposition, however, the finite part of the verb retains its position as in sentences [1–5].

If there is a non-finite part of the verb, it normally assumes the final position, allowing few elements to follow. Initial position as in [5] depends on contextual conditions, or on particular stress conditions.

Thus, we can draw up a scheme of word order in affirmative sentences showing the frame-constituting function of the verb. The bracketed V_{infin} and final position are not present in all sentences:

Initial position	V_{fin}	*Central position*	(V_{infin})	*(Final position)*[4]
[11]*a* Der Boss	gab	dem Gangster das Geld heute früher	heraus	als gestern.
[11]*b* Der Boss	hat	dem Gangster das Geld heute früher	gegeben	als gestern.
[11]*c* Der Boss	will	dem Gangster das Geld heute früher	geben	als gestern.
[11]*d* Der Boss	gab	dem· Gangster das Geld heute früher		

Having found the firm spot in the position of the verb we can now turn to the other positions: let us begin at the end. The final position can be dealt with in brief, for although it is open to all sorts of elements – especially in the spoken language[5] – the types of elements for which final position is the normal one are very restricted. They usually have corresponding elements in the rest of the sentence (given in brackets), and carry their own intonation centre (*cf* Beneš, 'Ausklammerung', 1968: 294–5):

(i) subordinate clauses (head in main clause)
(ii) infinitive with *zu* depending on verb (verb)
(iii) enumeration (:)
(iv) second component of comparisons with *als* or *wie* (first component, see sentences [11*a–b*])
(v) apposition (head noun)

(vi) parenthesis with *und zwar* (whole sentence)
(vii) second and further components of a multi-componential expression, copulative or adversative (first component)
(viii) elliptic clause corresponding to first part of the sentence

Apart from these cases it is mainly for stylistic reasons that elements are shifted to the final position, *eg* to avoid a weak non-finite component of the verb, which might appear separated from its corresponding finite component by too complex noun phrases. This example is from *Duden* (*Grammatik*, 1973: 625):

[12] Ich drang EIN in die Musik, in die Architektur der Fugen, in die verschlungenen Labyrinthe der Symfonien, in die harten Gefüge des Jazz (Weiss).

Similarly, the initial position can be described briefly for the time being. It contains, at least in neutral written German, a single noun phrase or adverbial phrase, which is sometimes preceded by a conjunction.[6] Thus, it is the central position that contains the bulk of the actants and circonstants. The next sections will be concerned with the principles governing the sequence of the parts of speech in this position, first theoretically (16.3.1), and then practically (16.3.2). Finally, we shall briefly reconsider the initial position (16.3.3).

16.3 Functional Sentence Perspective: the central and the initial positions

16.3.1 *Functional Sentence Perspective*
The concept which has proved most useful in the description of German word order has become known under the name of Functional Sentence Perspective (FSP). It was developed in Czechoslovakia between the wars by the Czech linguist Mathesius and is closely connected with the Czech linguists Firbas, Daneš and Beneš, and the German Boost.[7] Its principal idea is that information is not transmitted in random order, but that the speaker seeks to give his information to his interlocutor in portions, normally starting from what he assumes is common to both (the THEME, topic) and proceeding to what he regards as important new information (the RHEME, comment). In the following we shall mainly follow Firbas's ideas, relegating others to notes and a short discussion in 16.3.3.

First, let us consider the following sentences:

[13] Was gab der Boss dem Gangster?
[14] Der Boss gab dem Gangster das Geld.
[15] Wem gab der Boss das Geld?
[16] Der Boss gab das Geld dem Gangster.

It is significant that the most important items of information – *Geld* in [14], *Gangster* in [16], their importance is evident from the questions – take up the final positions in [14] and [16]. In fact, [16] would not be a suitable answer to [13],[8] and neither would [14] to [15], at least if we ignore stress variation for the time being. As it appears, the difference in word order of [14] and [16] reflects a difference in the 'extent to which a sentence element contributes to the development of the communication' (Firbas, 'Defining the theme', 1964: 270), a difference in what Firbas called the COMMUNICATIVE DYNAMISM (CD) of the respective elements.

This function of word order becomes still clearer if these sentences are matched with equivalent English sentences:

[17] The boss gave the gangster the money.
[18] *? The boss gave the money the gangster.
[19] The boss gave the money to the gangster.

Sentence [18] is odd not because there is, in English, no need to emphasize *the gangster* – this is expressed in [19] – but because this position signals a different syntactic relationship between the elements of the sentence, which in turn is not compatible with our view of the world. The German translation, which is equally odd, will make this clear:

[20]*? Der Boss gab dem Geld den Gangster.[9]

From these and other examples two conclusions can be drawn:

(i) Firstly, indicating different degrees of CD is not the only function of word order. In English, the main function of word order is to signify syntactic relationships. In German, where this function is carried out mainly by inflexional cases, word order can be used to express differences in CD of the sentence elements – at least as far as the central and initial position elements are concerned.

(ii) Secondly, as sentence [19] shows, word order is not the only way of indicating CD. Besides word order syntactic constructions [19], particles (*eg* focusing adjuncts: *eben, sogar; nur; gerade*) and especially phonetic devices (*eg* prominent stress on the element with the highest CD) play an important role, notably in languages which, for syntactic reasons, demonstrate little flexibility with regard to word order.

In German, whose word order is more flexible than English, but still less flexible than Czech or Russian, all possible ways of indicating CD are used. Usually they cooperate: in [14] and [16] stress and position assign the highest CD to *Geld* and *Gangster* respectively.

[14] Der Boss gab dem Gangster das GÉLD.

[16] Der Boss gab das Geld dem GÁNGSTER.

But in the case of the verb stress must suffice, the verbal position being fixed:

[21] Der Boss GÁB dem Gangster das Geld.

Sometimes, the different means (stress, position) conflict, in which case stress overrides word order.

[22] Der Boss gab dem GÁNGSTER das Geld.

As a rule of thumb one can say that the closer the prominent stress moves to the front, and thus away from the position marked as prominent by word order (final, or at least near the end), the more likely it is that the element bears some emotional emphasis and/or is contrasted (see 16.1).

Even though other means of indicating the CD of a sentence element do exist, the close connection between word order and FSP should require some further attention. So far, we have been concentrating on the element with the highest CD, the 'rheme proper' in Firbas's terms. Being marked as the intonation centre of the sentence, this element is particularly easy to distinguish.[10] But if we, with Firbas, assume that each element of a sentence carries its particular load of CD, and that the elements can be ordered as 'theme proper', 'theme', 'transition', 'rheme' and 'rheme proper' on the basis of increasing CD,[11] we are bound to meet difficulties.

How can the CD of a sentence element be determined? How can degrees of CD be measured? Firbas manages to show that the CD is influenced by the interplay of various factors (see Firbas, 'Thoughts', 1959: 42–4):

(i) The BASIC DISTRIBUTION OF CD, which Firbas sees as a continuous rise from the theme proper (lowest CD) at the beginning of a sentence to the rheme proper (highest CD) at the end, if unhampered by other word order principles.

(ii) The CONTEXT (verbal and situational): elements expressing notions 'that are known or may be gathered from the context' are of relatively low CD, new elements of relatively high CD.

(iii) SEMANTIC-CONTEXTUAL FACTORS closely related to the last point: deictic elements (eg personal pronouns), the use of which is only possible in unambiguous contexts (see Chapter 5), tend to have low CD. Similarly, the definite article has – according to Firbas – a dedynamizing effect, the indefinite article a dynamizing one.

As a further semantic-syntactic factor one could add the distinction (obligatory) actants and circonstants, which seems to be the basis of the different influence exerted by different verb classes (Firbas, 1959: 41–2).

Despite many convincing analyses along these lines, Firbas's analysis of sentence elements as theme, transition, etc is still based on (his) linguistic intuition. Attempts to make his analysis susceptible to objective verification, for example by developing question tests, have not, so far, been entirely successful.[12] In longer sentences especially, it is difficult to establish clear boundaries between theme and rheme. Nevertheless, the influence of the distribution of CD must not be ignored in studies of word order. In the last section we shall consider some examples of how the notions theme and rheme (lower/higher

CD) have been applied to the description of German, examining the position of accusative and dative object and the initial position.

16.3.2 *FSP and the position of accusative and dative object*
In the last section we have seen that, due to our inability to measure CD on the basis of testable criteria, it is difficult to assign degrees of CD indisputably, especially in longer sentences. It is probably for this reason that Lenerz (*Abfolge*, 1977) restricts himself to the study of elements in immediate sequence. He manages to show the importance of the CD load for the position of the elements in question, at the same time demonstrating the influence of other factors: definiteness, the sentence frame, and the relative length of the elements.

His first problem in determining the sequence rules of dative (E_3) and accusative (E_1) object is whether the sequences E_3E_1 and E_1E_3 are both equally possible or whether one of them is basic/'unmarked', *ie* possible under all conditions, and the other marked, *ie* possible only under certain conditions. For this purpose, he uses sentences similar to [13–14] to test whether all variants are possible:

[13] Was gab der Boss dem Gangster?
[14] Der Boss gab dem Gangster das GÉLD.
[23] *Der Boss gab das GÉLD dem Gangster.

[15] Wem gab der Boss das Geld?
[16] Der Boss gab das Geld dem GÁNGSTER.
[24] Der Boss gab dem GÁNGSTER das Geld.

The rheme element is indicated by *ı*. Whereas sequence E_3E_1, both for CD distribution lower/higher [14] and higher/lower [24], the sequence E_1E_3 is possible only if the CD distribution is lower/higher [16], or equally high, for example in contrast [25]:

[25] Der Boss gab das GÉLD dem GÁNGSTER und den SCHMÚCK seiner FRÁU.

Consequently, E_3E_1 is the unmarked – normal – sequence (Lenerz, 1977: 43).
So far, Lenerz's results are in agreement with those of the traditional CD analysis, which, however, was founded on the basic distribution of CD, which – according to Beneš ('Thema-Rhema-Gliederung', 1973: 45) – can be found in sentences in which no element is contextually bound (made clear by the indefinite articles and present tense):

[26] Ein Boss gibt einem Gangster Geld.

A further criterion used by Lenerz, however, modifies the traditional view of some FSP linguists that indefinite articles have a dynamizing effect, and should, consequently follow the dedynamizing definite articles (*cf* Boost, *Untersuchungen*, 1955: 52). It can easily be shown that the sequence indefinite–

definite is possible [14a, 24a].[13] Although it is true that the distinction between definite and indefinite article has an influence on word order, the conditions are more complicated, as examples [14–16c] show:

$E_3\acute{E}_1$ [14]   Der Boss gab dem Gangster das GÉLD.
         [14]a Der Boss gab einem Gangster das GÉLD.
         [14]b Der Boss gab dem Gangster GÉLD.
         [14]c Der Boss gab einem Gangster GÉLD.

$\acute{E}_3E_1$ [24]   Der Boss gab dem GÁNGSTER das Geld.
         [24]a Der Boss gab einem GÁNGSTER das Geld.
         [24]b Der Boss gab dem GÁNGSTER Geld.
         [24]c Der Boss gab einem GÁNGSTER Geld.

$E_1\acute{E}_3$ [16]   Der Boss gab das Geld dem GÁNGSTER.
         [16]a *Der Boss gab Geld dem GÁNGSTER.
         [16]b Der Boss gab das Geld einem GÁNGSTER.
         [16]c *Der Boss gab Geld einem GÁNGSTER.

The sequence $\acute{E}_1E_3$ can be left out of consideration as it has already been found to be unacceptable on the grounds of CD distribution. It can be seen that again the marked variant $E_1\acute{E}_3$ is affected by restrictions.

On the basis of these investigations it is possible to formulate the following rules for the sequence of E_3 and E_1 (Lenerz, 1977: 45, 55, 63):

(i) sequence E_1E_3 is impossible if E_1 has a higher CD than E_3.[14]
(ii) sequence E_1E_3 is impossible if E_1 is an indefinite noun phrase.[15]

Two more rules are more of a stylistic nature:

(iii) There is a stylistic tendency to place the more complex element (ie the one containing relatively more words) after the less complex.[16]
(iv) There is a stylistic tendency to avoid – in sentences without a verb frame – 'weightless' endings (cf [27a, 27b]).

For this reason [27] is considered better than [27a].

   [27]   Der Boss gab das Geld dem Gangster, den er seit Jahren kannte und schätzte.
   [27]a Der Boss gab dem Gangster, den er seit Jahren kannte und schätzte, das Geld.

If, however, the final $\acute{E}_1$ in [27a] is supported by the non-finite part of the verb, as in [27b], final position is acceptable:

   [27]b Der Boss hat dem Gangster, den er seit Jahren kannte und schätzte, das Geld gegeben.

In the rest of his book Lenerz applies similar tests to other sequences (accusative object, prepositional object, etc) and concludes that the rules found for E_3E_1 and similar ones also hold for other sequences. His work shows that the rules of German word order can – notwithstanding the rules of CD distribution – possibly not be reduced to a single principle.[17] The set of factors would have become more complicated, if Lenerz had included the position of pronouns in his investigation. As Engel (*Syntax*, 1977: 191) remarks, it is not enough to define word order rules on the basis of sentence elements (objects, adverbial clauses, etc), one has to take their different realizations into account (noun phrases, pronouns, etc).[18]

Apart from this, another important problem remains to be investigated. Lenerz has confined his attention almost exclusively to sequences in which one element is marked by the intonation centre. It will be interesting to know the conditions governing sequences in which neither element is the rheme proper of the sentence.

16.3.3 *FSP: The initial position*

Even if the view that only one element can precede the finite verb must be modified (see note 6), here sequence problems are not as important as in the central position. Neither is it very difficult to decide which elements may occur in initial position: according to Engel most elements occurring in the central position are possible in initial position as well.[19] Therefore discussion has concentrated on the role the initial position plays in FSP, and on the factors that determine how it is filled.

There is general agreement that the element preceding V_{fin} can be part of the rheme (as rheme proper marked by the intonation centre of the sentence), in which case the sentence is marked as expressive and/or emotional, or thematic, the normal, unmarked case.

The thematic status of the initial position has caused considerable confusion, because some linguists (for example Boost, 1955: 26–31) have suggested that the status of theme should be assigned to the element in initial position in all cases.[20] However, if thematic/rhematic are defined as carrying lower/higher CD, the theme (Firbas's 'theme proper') having the lowest, the rheme (Firbas's 'rheme proper') having the highest CD, it can be shown that the first element in a sentence is not necessarily the theme:

[28] Die Zahl der Arbeitslosen ist seit 1970 in allen Ländern Europas gestiegen. In Deutschland lag sie im August 1977 bei 900,000.

In Deutschland, as specification of *Länder Europas*, carries more information than *sie*, which merely takes up *die Zahl der Arbeitslosen*. In FSP, it has therefore been found useful to distinguish between *theme proper* (the element with the lowest CD) and *basis* (the part of the theme in initial position, not necessarily the theme proper).

The choice of basis is mainly determined by the linguistic and/or situational context. The thematic elements can occur freely in initial position without giving special expressive value to the sentence.[21] Which of the thematic elements is finally chosen depends not so much on the CD structure within the theme, but on the prominence an element has in the speaker's mind at the moment at which he starts his sentence. This is, as a rule, an element of the closer context; in German, its syntactic function hardly plays any role. We have then seen that German word order cannot be explained only by CD distribution. When it comes to filling the initial position, contextual factors play a particularly important role. The detailed investigation of the interrelationship of word order and context is another task for the future.[22]

Recommended further reading

For reference: Engel ('Regeln', 1970) on German word order. For an introduction to FSP: Daneš (ed) (*Papers*, 1974), with the contributions to the first international symposium on FSP at Mariánské Lázne (Marienbad) in 1970. To avoid terminological difficulties it is advisable to read the last paper first: Daneš ('Zur Terminologie', 1974).

Notes to chapters

Chapter 1

1 This question is still a matter of discussion today. In modern German grammar we find frequent attempts to match grammatical categories with phenomena of reality (*cf* Admoni's *verallgemeinerter Bedeutungsgehalt*, see 3.2.4) or, similarly, with categories of thought (*cf* Brinkmann's sentence types, see Ch 2)

2 It is true that upper Saxonia played an important role in the development of the standard language, but it was not on the spoken language that *Hochdeutsch* was based, but on the language used in the chancellery of the Elector of Meissen, see Eggers (*Sprachgeschichte*, 1969: 138)

3 Becker's work was only the culmination of a longer development. Glinz (*Geschichte*, 1947) has analysed the emergence and the use of the terms from classical times as well as the philosophical background to Becker's work. The terms syntactic categories and syntactic functions are taken from Lyons (*Introduction*, 1968)

4 It should be noted that the mind is not equivalent to the reason. Contrary to the rationalistic view, in Herder's opinion words were rather created through spontaneous reaction and emotion than through careful planning. In the traditional discussion of the origins of language Herder would be an advocate of 'nature' against 'convention', see Robins (*History*, 1967: 17)

5 Another reason for the flourishing of historical linguistics was undoubtedly the political situation in the German States. At a time when nationalism, which then very often went hand in hand with liberal ideas, was prosecuted in most of the *Partikularstaaten*, the study of the glorified past served as an outlet for suppressed political activity. It is worth noting in this connection that the Grimm brothers took part in the liberal movement and suffered for this: they lost their positions at Göttingen university after criticizing their sovereign for disregarding the constitution. The fact that for J. Grimm linguistics was only one component of the subject of German studies comprising German history, law and literature is emphasized by P. Ganz (*Conception*, 1973)

6 'Die Geisteseigentümlichkeit und Sprachgestaltung eines Volkes stehen in solcher Innigkeit der Verschmelzung ineinander, dass, wenn die eine gegeben wäre, die andere müsste vollständig aus ihr abgeleitet werden.' (Humboldt 'Verschiedenheit' 1830–5: 414.) The suggestion that the mind of a people is reflected in its language had already been uttered by F. Bacon, see Arens (*Sprachwissenschaft*, 1969: 83). The notion that the mother tongue of a person influences his thinking and feeling is a major modification of Kantian ideas, whose influence can be seen elsewhere

in Humboldt's philosophy of language; for links and differences between Humboldt and Kant see Cassirer ('Elemente', 1923) and Robins (*History*, 1967: 176), for the further development of this idea, see 1.3 and Ch 2.

7 'Ihre Verschiedenheit ist nicht eine von Schällen und Zeichen, sondern eine Verschiedenheit von Weltansichten selbst.' (Humboldt, 'Sprachstudium', 1820: 20)

8 The importance of comparative studies is further increased by the fact that no language reflects the world as it is, but each language stamps its own particular view on the world. The comparison of languages is a way to discover the truth, which lies 'zwischen allen Sprachen, und unabhängig von ihnen, in der Mitte'. (Humboldt, 'Sprachstudium', 1820: 20)

9 Sometimes a fourth type is added to these three: the incorporating languages. Robins (*History*, 1967: 25 ff) points out that this type is based on a different classification criterion, namely on sentence structure.

10 Humboldt's topicality can be seen in Chomsky (*Issues*, 1964: 25), who calls his views 'basically Humboldtian', according to Baumann ('Generative Grammatik', 1971) owing to his misunderstanding of Humboldt's terms.

11 Humboldt's pupil Steinthal (*Grammatik*, 1855; *Abriss*, 1871) can be said to belong to the psychological group; similarly, Lazarus (*Leben*, 1856–8), Steinheil (*Lehrgebäude*, 1812) and Becker (*Grammatik*, 1836–9) are representatives of the philosophical direction.

12 The layout of the changes is simplified, see also Lyons (*Introduction*, 1968: 27), Penzl (*Vom Urgermanischen*, 1975: 50–3)

13 Bopp considered Old Slavonic in the second part of his grammar (*Grammatik*, 1833/5/7), Armenian from its second edition (²1857/9/61), Schleicher (*Compendium*, 1861–2) the Celtic languages.

14 The diagram is an adaptation of the ones given in Robins (*Linguistics*, 1964: 321–2). This view of the Indo-European language family did not remain unchallenged. J. Schmidt (*Verwandtschaftsverhältnisse*, 1872) regarded the IE mother-language as a 'scientific fiction' and held the view that the IE languages were dialects from the beginning, attributing the similarities to innovations in one dialect which had spread to its neighbours; see Arens (*Sprachwissenschaft*, 1969: 304). See also the views of Trubetzkoy, who regards the IE languages as a blend of Uralo-Altaic and Caucasian-Mediterranean languages (Arens, 1969: 488–9)

15 Another discovery was Grasmann's Law concerning unchanged *p* and *t* in the combinations *sp* and *st*, see Lehmann (*Linguistics*, 1964: 94)

16 Grimm was also convinced that language was basically regular, although this regularity had become obscured in the course of time. However, he admitted the existence of inexplicable cases, see Glinz (*Geschichte*, 1947: 61, 67)

17 Despite this opinion the *Junggrammatiker* were not quite as anti-semantic as the Bloomfieldians in their heyday; see, for example, the chapters on the change of meaning of words in Paul (*Prinzipien*, ⁵1920)

18 '... aller lautwandel, soweit er mechanisch vor sich geht, vollzieht sich nach ausnahmslosen gesetzen, ... und alle wörter, in denen der der lautbewegung unterworfene laut unter den gleichen verhältnissen erscheint, werden ohne ausnahme von der änderung ergriffen.' (Osthoff and Brugmann, *Untersuchungen*, 1878: XIII)

19 The Germanic sound-shift can be explained by using this theory: when at first IE *bh* (*ph* in Greek) lost its aspiration and became similar to *b*, a number of words which were only distinguished by the contrast *b/bh* were in danger of becoming homonymous. In order to avoid confusion *b* had to change as well (similarly for *b–p/p–f*). A survey of possible causes of sound-change is given in Pinsker (*Grammatik*, ³1969: 97–122)

20 Martinet (*Elements*, 1964) with his theory of maximal distinction could be mentioned for the internal point of view. Labov (*Stratification*, 1966) has shown up social change as one cause of linguistic change: a new standard is arrived at

when the type of language used by a socially rising group of the community loses its class-distinctive character.

21 It is interesting to know that L. Bloomfield excelled as a comparative linguist before he turned to structuralist description. He applied the methods of historical and comparative linguistics to American-Indian languages. F. d. Saussure was an Indo-European scholar and classical philologist, a pupil of Osthoff and Brugmann.

22 Wundt was not the first scholar to attempt the explanation of Humboldt's ideas with the help of psychology. His precursor, Steinthal (*Abriss*, 1871) had, however, used a different model of psychology; for the differences between Steinthal and Wundt, see Ivić (*Trends*, 1965: 54)

23 The fact that linguistic items establish themselves in a language and are used automatically did, in his view, not change the basic quality of language (Vossler, *Schöpfung*, 1905)

24 Vossler found this idea in Croce's writings, see Iordan and Orr (*Romance Linguistics*, 1970: 115–20). Ipsen points out that Vossler's use of the term aesthetics is somewhat unclear: 'Ästhetisch heissen hier ... alle Formen, insofern ihnen ein Sinn innewohnt; zweitens ... das Schaffen des Künstlers; endlich ..., dass das eigentliche Wesen der Sprache Dichtung sei.' (Ipsen, *Sprachphilosophie*, 1930: 18)

25 Due to the criticism it attracted, the second edition appeared with considerable changes under the title *Frankreichs Kultur und Sprache. Geschichte der französischen Schriftsprache von den Anfängen bis zur Gegenwart.* (1929). *Geistesgeschichtliche* studies of Germany and the German language were undertaken by Burdach (for example: *Wissenschaft*, 1934) and H. Naumann ('Geschichte', 1923)

26 More recent investigations have shown that social differentiation of language also has to be taken into account to explain changes in regional distribution; see Robins (*History*, 1967: 188)

Chapter 2

1 For a discussion of colour terms see Gipper ('Inhalt', 1973), Weisgerber (*Vier Stufen*, 1963: 175–84), Lenneberg ('Language', 1971: 548–51), Leech (*Semantics*, 1974: 234–7), Lyons (*Semantics I*, 1977: 25) and Dürbeck 'Untersuchungen', (1975). Another example used by Weisgerber is kinship terms, see Weisgerber (*Grundzüge*, 1962: 63–70), Leech (*Semantics*, 1974: 237–62) and Trudgill (*Sociolinguistics*, 1974: 27–8)

2 The first step in Weisgerber's analysis is the assumption of a *geistige Zwischenwelt*; for this see Weisgerber (*Grundzüge*, 1962: 38–52). The fact that there is no direct correspondence between the linguistic form and objects of the outer world is also illustrated by the semantic triangle of Ogden and Richards (*Meaning*, [4]1936: 11) and by Brekle (*Semantik*, 1972: 34): see also Ch 8.

3 It is very important for an understanding of Weisgerber's theory to bear in mind that he does not look upon language as a pure means of communication; see his discussion of the *Mitteldefinition* in Weisgeber (*Zweimal Sprache*, 1973; 99–104)

4 According to Weisgerber, the study of *content* is the analysis of the *sprachliche Zwischenwelt*. He rejects the term *meaning*; see, for instance Weisgerber (*Grundzüge*, 1962: 120): 'In dem Bemühen der lautbezogenen Grammatik um die *Bedeutungen* und *Funktionen* der Sprachmittel stecken z w e i f o l g e n s c h w e r e I r r - t u m s q u e l l e n. Die eine besteht in der verhängnisvollen Problematik und Ungeklärtheit des Denkens in *Bedeutungen* und *Funktionen*, die andere in der Vorstellung von einem zu einfachen Gleichlauf von Laut und Inhalt, der es rechtfertigte, den Laut als Massstab beim Bemühen um den Inhalt beizubehalten.' Compare also Admoni (*Sprachbau*, [3]1970: 24–6). Weisgerber also rejects *sachbezogene Bedeutungslehre*; for the discussion of other approaches see Weisgerber (*Grundzüge*, 1962: 119–35)

5 For a discussion of Leisi's characterization of language as *Brauch* see Weisgerber (*Gestaltung*, 1962: 47–60)

6 Compare Halliday ('Language Structure', 1970: 141). Such differences in the *sprachliche Zwischenwelt* also exist in different dialects of one language, see Weisgerber (*Muttersprache*, ²1957: 34). For a criticism of Weisgerber's point that the *sprachliche Zwischenwelt* is largely determined by the mother tongue, see Helbig (*Geschichte*, 1974: 141): 'In der Verselbständigung der Sprache als Zwischenwelt verkennt Weisgerber, dass die Sprache als Zeichensystem immer ein *Mittel* im Erkenntnis- und Kommunikationsprozess bleibt . . . Die verschiedenen Weltbilder sind in der Tat nicht Erzeugnisse der Sprache, . . . vielmehr ein Erzeugnis des Denkens, der gesellschaftlich-historischen Erfahrungen der Sprachgemeinschaft.' Compare also W. Schmidt (*Grundfragen*, ⁴1973: 20–1)

7 The *Leistung* of a language is the 'Erschliessung der Welt'. Weisgerber (*Gestaltung*, 1962: 80) takes this idea from Humboldt, who speaks of the 'Umschaffen der Welt,in das Eigentum des Geistes, dem Akt der Verwandlung der Welt in Ideen, die Verwandlung, die die Sprache mit den Gegenständen vornimmt.' Weisgerber introduces the term *sprachlicher Zugriff* for the way in which a language structures reality.

8 Weisgerber (*Inhaltbezogene Grammatik*, 1953: 20) characterizes language acquisition in the following way: 'Was ist das denn, Spracherlernung? Dem Stoff nach: Übernahme der Muttersprache ins Einzelbewusstsein; dem Inhalt nach: Lebendigwerden des muttersprachlichen Weltbilds im Sprachbesitz des Einzelnen.' For a critical discussion of Weisgerber's theory see Helbig (*Geschichte*, 1974: 138–45)

9 For this see Weisgerber (*Gestaltung*, 1962: 80): 'Erschliessen der Welt – das kann gewiss das Aufschliessen vorgegebener Aussenwelt sein, es kann aber auch ein Erschliessen geistiger Welt sein, die erst über diesem Erschliessen ihre geistige Gestalt gewinnt.' Weisgerber (*Zweimal Sprache*, 1973: 167–73) makes a distinction between *sprachliche Zugriffe* and *Ausgriffe*.

10 The study of language as *ergon* is the basis of energetic analysis. A similar distinction is made by transformational grammar in that the object of description has become the competence of the ideal speaker/hearer. For this see Weisgerber (*Zweimal Sprache*, 1973). For a summary and commentary on Weisgerber's analysis, see Bynon ('Four stages', 1966)

11 See Hoberg (*Lehre*, 1970: 59–76) and Geckeler (*Wortfeldtheorie*, 1971: 84) for a discussion of the work of other scholars. Before Trier (*Wortschatz*, 1931), Ipsen ('Der Alte Orient', 1924: 225) had demonstrated that words of similar meaning could be placed in a semantic field, which he compared to a mosaic to suggest the way in which words complement each other.

12 See Weisgerber (*Menschheitsgesetz* ²1964: 70): '*Ein sprachliches Feld* ist ein *Ausschnitt aus der muttersprachlichen Zwischenwelt, der durch die Ganzheit einer in organischer Gliederung zusammenwirkenden Gruppe von Sprachzeichen aufgebaut* wird. Eine solche Gliederung ist durchaus wirksam, auch wenn sie ihren Trägern nicht im einzelnen bewusst und durchschaubar ist.' Even as late as 1963 he affirms the essential function of the word field for content-oriented grammar, see Weisgerber (*Vier Stufen*, 1963: 70): 'Dem Aufzeigen des Bestands und der Struktur der in einer Sprache vorhandenen Wortfelder gilt die Hauptarbeit der inhaltbezogenen Wortlehre.' Trier ('Altes und Neues', 1968: 461) has acknowledged Weisgerber's contribution towards establishing the word field in linguistics.

13 Trier's interest in 1931 was in overcoming the dichotomy between diachronic and synchronic linguistics. He compared conceptual fields at different stages of the language's development hoping to show how the fields' internal structures had changed and how the fields themselves evolved: he examined the 'relative' meanings of the words *wîsheit*, *kunst* and *list* in 1200 and 1300. This procedure, which

he termed *komparative Statik*, he did not, however, follow up in his later work. See also Lehrer (*Semantic Fields*, 1974: 15-19) and Lyons (*Semantics I*, 1977: 250–71) for short discussions in English of Trier's approach.

14 Trier defines the word field as follows (*Wortschatz* 1931: 1): 'Das Wortfeld ist zeichenhaft zugeordnet einem mehr oder weniger geschlossenen Begriffskomplex, dessen innere Aufteilung sich im gegliederten Gefüge des Zeichenfeldes darstellt, in ihm für die Angehörigen einer Sprachgemeinschaft gegeben ist.' For a brief critique of the inadequacies of Trier's definition see Lehrer (*Semantic Fields*, 1974: 17-19). Weisgerber's review of Trier (1931) is reprinted in Schmidt (*Wortfeldforschung*, 1973: 39-40)

15 He distinguishes four kinds of fields, three of them mono-level fields (*einschichtig*). The first of the mono-level fields is sequential or rank ordering (*Reihengliederung*), which can be illustrated by the examination grades *ausgezeichnet, gut, befriedigend, ausreichend, mangelhaft*, or army ranks *general, colonel, major, captain* etc. Spatial ordering (*Flächengliederung*) is illustrated by kinship terms such as *brother, sister, uncle, aunt, cousin* etc, while depth ordering (*Tiefengliederung*) is found with colour words. The many words for dying, the choices of which are governed by considerations of situational and functional appropriacy exemplify a multi-level field. For the four kinds of word field see Weisgerber (*Grundzüge*, ³1962). With respect to the verbs for dying Weisgerber (*Grundzüge*, 1962: 184-185) says that '... die deutsche Sprache einen dreifachen gedanklichen Ring um das Sterben legt. In einem innersten wird das menschliche *sterben* abgehoben von dem *verenden* des Tieres und dem *eingehen* der Pflanze. Das Sterben selbst wird dann von zwei Seiten gefasst ...' These two aspects are the objective – with such words as *erfrieren, ertrinken, verhungern* etc – and the subjective – with such words as *ableben, abkratzen, entschlafen* etc. See also Erben (*Abriss*, 1972: 67) for a discussion of Weisgerber's approach.

16 Weisgerber (*Grundzüge*, 1962: 102) warns that for all its importance the word field should not be over-emphasized. He mentions other forms of determination of content, including derivations, compounds and set phrases. See also Hoberg (*Lehre*, 1970: 90-5)

17 Brinkmann's application of the principles of complementation and interdependence derived from the word field are perhaps best illustrated by his treatment of the modal verbs, see *Sprache* (²1971: 381-402)

18 Erben (*Abriss*, ¹¹1972: 246): 'Im Deutschen herrscht der Typus des Verbalsatzes ... Mit der Wahl des Verbs ... ist die Entscheidung über das grammatische Grundgerüst des Satzes gefallen. Von seiner syntaktischen Wertigkeit ... hängt es wesentlich ab, welche und wie viele Ergänzungsbestimmungen im Vor- und Nachfeld des Verbs auftreten und das Satzschema ausgestalten.' We note that Erben's approach is closer to that of the valency grammarians (see Ch 4) than to Brinkmann's.

19 Glinz (*Geschichte*, 1947: esp 42) examines how the logico-grammatical approach of the nineteenth-century German scholar K. F. Becker imposed alien categories on grammatical description and how Becker's model was used as the basis for pedagogical grammars still in use when Glinz was writing. Glinz (1947: 75) draws the following conclusions: 'Beckers System hat sich in allen wesentlichen Punkten erhalten, obwohl es aus einer Sprachauffassung stammt, welche die Wissenschaft seit 100 Jahren ablehnt. Die Erklärung für diese Langlebigkeit ist bald gefunden: die Sprachwissenschaft hat noch nichts besseres geliefert ... Aber die Lage ist unbefriedigend und fordert heraus zu einem Versuch, von den heutigen sprachwissenschaftlichen Erkenntnissen aus das Problem neu zu behandeln und eine Lehre von den Satzgliedern wie auch von den Wortarten aufzustellen, welche sowohl wissenschaftlich haltbar als praktisch brauchbar ist.' Glinz's *Innere Form* (1952) is the result of his attempt to provide a new grammar of German which describes language in its own right without reference to logic.

20 In later editions Glinz has attached an explanatory appendix to the grammar (see *Innere Form*, ⁵1968: 4, 487–91). Glinz wrote the grammar quite independently of Fries and other structuralists but using structuralist discovery procedures (substitution, transformation and deletion tests). From 1960 onwards Glinz acknowledged a debt to Weisberger, emphasizing that his aim had been to proceed in an *inhaltbezogen* and *leistungbezogen* way (⁵1968: 6–10). Despite this he was in 1952 more concerned with morphology and syntax than with word-content and we have to look to later work (Glinz, *Ansätze*, 1962) for a discussion of the relationship between phonological words (*Wortkörper*) and word-content (*Wortinhalte*)

21 A key term in this monograph is *das Gemeinte* (the intention to give expression to one's experience). As the smallest unit which can itself be regarded as *Gemeintes*, the word is for Glinz of special importance; he does not, however, follow Weisgerber, who ascribes many new word-contents to *Zugriffe* (notes 7 and 9); for him it is the language users' intentions that are paramount – they create new contents for existing phonological words and new phonological words for new contents, see *Ansätze* (1962: 52–5)

22 One of his arguments against this assumption is that it is psychologically unreal. Psychology also plays a part in Glinz's view of the sentence patterns. The 'real' sentence patterns are constituted neither by structural features of the verb nor by the way in which positions in a sentence are filled, but by combinations of structurally exchangeable items with semantic affinities. This can be illustrated by sentences containing verbs of jurisdiction:

Die Zeitung	beschuldigte	ihn	des Mordes
Der Anwalt	verdächtigte	seine Frau	des Diebstahls
Er	...	den Angeklagten	...
...			

23 Glinz (*Ansätze*, 1962: 78–9) illustrates this point with the two verbs *fegen* (to sweep) and *wischen* (to wipe), which have quite contrary meanings in North West Germany and Switzerland. He suggests that the linguist should approach the question of discovering 'contents' by examining texts without preconceived notions. In *Ansätze* (1962: 81–2) he refers to the heuristic value of the *context of situation* (Firth, *Papers*, 1957), seeing in it an independent confirmation of his own proposals.

24 In the 1959 preface Weisgerber and Glinz are mentioned by name, and the uniqueness of every language and the thought-shaping force of the mother tongue are emphasized. In 1973, however, no content-oriented linguist is mentioned in the preface and a description of German syntax based largely on the valency and transformational models is advocated by Grebe. This should not be taken as meaning that *all* the contributions to the third edition differ radically from those of earlier editions; Grebe and Gipper have, however, felt obliged to take note of developments outside the content-oriented approach.

25 Trier and Weisgerber's view of language has much in common with the ideas of the American linguist B. L. Whorf. Like them, Whorf saw a language as imposing a view of the world on a language community, an attitude to language sometimes referred to as linguistic relativity; see Weisgerber (*Sprachliche Erschliessung*, 1954: 254–62); see also Gipper (*Relativitätsprinzip*, 1972) and Whorf (*Language*, 1956). For the principle of linguistic relativity as seen by the German philosopher Herder, see Land (*Signs*, 1974: 69)

26 It must be noted, however, that Chomsky is a universalist, whereas Humboldt is not.

Chapter 3

1 Unless, of course, the utterance was accompanied by certain paralinguistic features. If somebody said *Brigitte!* and made some gestures, she might also know that she is supposed to open the window.

2 Language also reveals something of the social status of the speaker, as Shaw illustrated so graphically in his *Pygmalion*.

3 Translations by Halliday ('Language Structure', 1970: 141). This is, of course, not the only possible division of the functions of language. Halliday himself has suggested a model with a large number of functions, which are subsumed under the heading of *ideational, interpersonal* and *textual functions*, see Halliday (1970) and 'Relevant models of language' (1973). Leech (*Semantics*, 1974: 47–50) uses a model with five functions of language, namely the *informational* (oriented towards subject-matter), the *expressive* (oriented towards speaker/writer), the *directive* (listener/reader), *phatic* (channel of communication) and *aesthetic* (message). For Bühler's tripartite classification of language and Jakobson's modification of it see also Lyons (*Semantics I*, 1977: 51–5)

4 See also Vachek (*Linguistic School*, 1966: 35): 'As a matter of fact, in most instances two or even all of the three functions are found to coexist in the same utterance, but one of them is found to be predominant.'

5 See, however, Vachek (1966: 34) for the functional approach to language adopted by the Prague School of Linguistics in the 1930s.

6 The main points of criticism were: with respect to structural linguistics that it did not take account of meaning, and with respect to the *inhaltbezogene Grammatik* that – in Marxist linguistics – language is a means of communication, not an autonomous force.

7 See, for example, Erben (*Grammatik*, 1968: 30): 'Offensichtlich sind die ... Wörter der deutschen Sprache ... ihrer Grundprägung nach dazu geschaffen und strukturiert, ... Träger bestimmter Funktionen zu werden.' In the early fifties the West German linguist Hamann presented his view of functional grammar. In his model the linguistic form is seen as the function of the content, see Hamann ('Funktionale Grammatik', 1951). This approach is not to be confused with the American type of functional grammar, whose aim is language teaching for practical purposes, based on the view that language has certain functions in everyday life; for this see Lund ('Betrachtung', 1958). See also the use *inhaltbezogene Grammatiker* make of the term function.

8 See F. Schmidt (*Syntax*, 1970: 24), who writes: '... so befindet man sich im Bereich – oder Vorbereich – der Logik und man bekommt Aussageformen mit Variablen: F(x) und F(x, y), wo die in Klammern stehenden Zeichen die Argumente, das unabhängige, der Funktion F die abhängige Variable symbolisiert ... Im Satze wird F durch die Kopula und Prädikatsnomen oder durch Verben, also durch das Prädikat, x durch das Subjekt, x, y, z.B. durch Subjekt und Objekt und durch präpositionale Wendungen ausgedrückt.'

9 'Das Wesen der Kommunikation liegt darin, mittels eines *Mediums* (Code, vehicle usw. – um nur die wichtigsten Termini der modernen Forschung zu benutzen) einen bestimmten Verständigungs*zweck* zu erfüllen, d.h. beim "passiven" Kommunikationspartner einen entsprechenden Kommunikationseffekt auszulösen. Das zu diesem Zweck verwendete Medium ist die *Form*, der von diesem Medium auszulösende Effekt ist die *Funktion* der verwendeten Form.' Meier (*Zéro-Problem*, 1961: 23) uses the term *Medium* in a different way from other linguists!

10 Similar considerations led Austin (*Things*, 1962: 106) to distinguish between locutionary, illocutionary and perlocutionary acts: 'We first distinguished a group of things we do in saying something, which together we summed up by saying we perform a *locutionary act*, which is roughly equivalent to uttering a certain sen-

tence with a certain sense and reference, which again is roughly equivalent to "meaning" in the traditional sense. Second we said that we also perform *illocutionary acts* such as informing, ordering, warning, undertaking, etc, *ie* utterances which have a certain (conventional) force. Thirdly, we may also perform *perlocutionary acts*: what we bring about or achieve *by* saying something, such as convincing, persuading, deterring, and even, say, surprising or misleading.'

11 Meier's *kommunikativer Effekt* seems to subsume Austin's *effect* and *consequence*, referring respectively to illocutionary and perlocutionary acts. By *effect* Austin understands communicating the intended sense of an utterance to an interlocutor; what the interlocutor then does as a result of this Austin (*Things*, 1962: 115–19) terms *consequence*. Compare also Van Dijk's (*Text*, 1977: 175) concept of successfulness.

12 This approach bears a striking resemblance to the behaviouristic model of communication, the only fundamental difference being that Meier uses *Funktion* where Bloomfield (*Language*, 1933: 74) uses meaning. How closely related these models are is shown by the fact that Meier ('Sprachwissenschaft', 1959: 105) uses *Bedeutung* or *Inhalt* to refer to what he later calls *Funktion*: 'Der Form entspricht der Terminus *Kommunikationsmittel*, dem Inhalt entspricht der *kommunikative Effekt* ... Man kommt so zum Schema: Mittel (Form)→Zweck/Effekt (Inhalt).'

13 Meier sets up a dichotomy of form and function, which W. Schmidt adopts in his 1965 grammar (*Grundfragen*, 1965: 30). The linguistic sign is made up of *form* and *function*. W. Schmidt subdivides *Form* into *Lautform* (phonetic structure) and *Formstruktur* (formal structure) and makes a distinction between *logisch-grammatischen* and *kommunikativ-grammatischen* Funktionen, which he adopts from Admoni (*Sprachbau*, ³1970: 5–6)

14 W. Schmidt ('Theorie', 1969: 141) distinguishes three components of the term form: (1) phonemes and phoneme clusters, (2) their dependencies and distribution and (3) suprasegmental, prosodic phonemes.

15 W. Schmidt ('Theorie', 1969: 142): 'Wir verstehen unter Bedeutung die abstrahierende, die invarianten Bestandteile des Erkenntnisprozesses umfassende Widerspiegelung eines Gegenstandes, einer Erscheinung oder einer Beziehung der objektiven Realität im Bewusstsein der Angehörigen einer Sprachgemeinschaft, die traditionell mit der Form zu der strukturellen Einheit des sprachlichen Zeichens verbunden ist.' This is very similar to Wotjak's (*Untersuchungen*, 1971: 47) definition of the *Semem*. Compare Ch 8.

16 There are interesting parallels here with the work of the British linguist J. R. Firth and of the so-called Neo-Firthians, see Robins (*History*, 1967: 220)

17 W. Schmidt ('Theorie', 1969: 143) rejects the introduction of a *cognitive function* as this is already covered by the definition of the linguistic sign as a unit of form and meaning and justifies his view, arguing from a Marxist standpoint: 'Das sprachliche System ist ... die "unmittelbare Wirklichkeit des Gedankens" (K. Marx).'

18 W. Schmidt ('Theorie', 1969: 150) rejects the introduction of a *Bewertungsfunktion* in the sense of Klaus (*Macht*, 1964: 18) as it is only a combination of the *Symptom-* and *Signalfunktion*.

19 Form and meaning here have to be read as form structure (or phonetic structure) and meaning structure, as with utterances etc the communicative function is fulfilled by a chain of linguistic elements.

20 Again, unless it was accompanied by respective paralinguistic features and thus achieved sentence status; see also note 2. In this context it may be interesting to note that the idea of communicative effect is already inherent in Bloomfield's (*Language*, 1933: 139) definition of meaning: 'We have defined the *meaning* of a linguistic form as the situation in which the speaker utters it and the response which it calls forth in the hearer.'

21 W. Schmidt ('Kategorien', 1969: 522): 'Alle anderen lexikalischen und grammatischen Einheiten' – *ie* except for the sentence – 'besitzen zwar Bedeutung, sie
haben jedoch keine relativ eigenständige kommunikative Funktion ..., sondern
lediglich einen spezifischen Anteil am Kommunikationseffekt des Satzes (der
Äusserung).'

22 The fact that the expression of meaning is not the only micro-function is clearly
illustrated by Trubetzkoy's definition of the phoneme, which is a linguistic element
which does not in itself carry meaning, but which has the function of distinguishing
morphemes. For this see Helbig (*Geschichte*, 1974: 54)

23 Compare also Halliday ('Style', 1973: 104): 'The term *function* is used, in two
distinct though related senses, at two very different points in the description of
language. First, it is used in the sense of "grammatical (or 'syntactic') function", ... Secondly, it is used to refer to the "functions" of language as a whole ...'.

24 See also Robins (1967: 204–6 and *passim*) for a discussion of their contributions
to theoretical and descriptive linguistics in the 1930s.

25 See also note 5 above. In earlier work Halliday has developed a systemic description of the English clause and its functions in discourse, and it is perhaps his
emphasis on verbal context (discourse function) that provides the closest link
between his work and that of the Czech linguist Jan Firbas, a former pupil of
Josef Vachek, whose continuing work on Functional Sentence Perspective (corresponding to Halliday's textual function) in English, German and Czech promises
interesting insights. A brief statement of Firbas' work can be found in his
'Thoughts' (1959). For Halliday's work, see Halliday ('Options', 1969) and
('Functional basis', 1973)

26 With the exception of the chapter on the case system the idea that the functions
of language are in some way reflected in its formal system is hardly touched upon.
See Schmidt (*Grundfragen*, 1965: 125–69)

27 Admoni (*Grundlagen*, 1971: 48): 'Ohne sie wäre es sonst schwierig, den Satz
stärker auszuweiten, um etwa einen umfangreichen logisch-grammatischen Inhalt
darzustellen oder die verschiedenartigen Aspekte des Sprechers, z.B. seine kogni-
tive Einstellung ("aktuelle oder kommunikative Gliederung des Satzes") usw. zum
Ausdruck zu bringen.'

28 In Admoni's theory, sentence structure is determined by grammatical rules as well
as by changes due to the situation or personality of the speaker. For instance,
he considers the sentence under seven different aspects, among these, the 'Erkennt-
nisstellung' or the psychological communicative attitude of the speaker, which
would, for example, cover the distinction between theme and rheme, the classification of sentences according to their communicative function and the emotional
content of the sentence. See Admoni (*Sprachbau*, ³1970: 246–55)

29 This cannot be regarded as a criticism of Admoni's grammar, because for him
function is only one of the aspects which ought to be investigated in the analysis
of language, but to restrict himself to one methodological principle would contradict his polydimensional view of language, which implies that language
can only be adequately described, if it is regarded from as many different standpoints as possible. W. Schmidt's more recent work ('Bildung', 1974) goes back to
his original intention: to make function the basic principle of mother-tongue
teaching.

30 This approach shows similarities to Firth's, who 'outlined a programme for
"describing and classifying typical contexts of situation within the context of
culture ... and types of linguistic function in such contexts of situation".' See
Halliday ('Social perspective', 1973: 49)

31 'So even if we start from a consideration of how language varies – how we make
different selections in meaning, and therefore in grammar and vocabulary, according to the context of use – we are led into the more fundamental question of the

relation between the functions of language and the nature of the linguistic system.' Halliday ('Functional basis', 1973: 23)

Chapter 4

1 The Saussurean notion of the linearity of language had already been questioned by Jespersen in his *Analytic Syntax* (1937)
2 These stemmas were introduced by Tesnière. For a brief outline of the basic principles of Tesnière's theory see Brinker (*Modelle*, 1977: 91–8)
3 Predicate logic takes the verb as the relator in the first position: X(A, B) for *A schlägt B*, etc. This principle has been taken over by Fillmore ('Case', 1968: 21–30) and the generative semanticists.
4 For the view of the verb as the structural centre of the sentence see Brinker (*Modelle*, 1977: 102–8). A grammar taking the verb as the highest unit in the hierarchy does not necessarily have to be a dependency grammar, see Engel ('Bemerkungen', 1972). For the question of the arbitrariness of dependency relations see Engel ('Satzbaupläne', 1970: 364–5); for a motivation of the sentence-constitutive character of the verb see Engelen (*Untersuchungen I*, 1975: 58–67)
5 A. W. de Groot used the term valency in his *Structurele Syntaxis* (1949), see Engelen (1975: 38–42)
6 Brinkmann (*Sprache*, [2]1971: 223–9) retains the distinction between subject and object and defines valency as the number of additional elements the verb takes apart from the subject. Basically, he assumes the valencies 0, 1, 2 and 3, but they may be extended, which leads to classifications of the following kind: 'erweitert einstellige Verben mit Dativ (ich danke dir)' or 'erweitert einstellige Verben mit Genitiv (wir gedachten der Toten)'. Critical accounts of Brinkmann can be found in Helbig (*Geschichte*, 1974: 209), Emons (*Valenzen*, 1974: 65) and Stötzel (*Ausdrucksseite*, 1970: 114–16)
7 Erben's (*Grammatik*, 1968: 113–29) *Satzmodelle* are determined structurally by the number of necessary complements of the verb (not more than four) and by semantic considerations. The syntactic structure $\boxed{E_1}$——$\boxed{V}$——$\boxed{E_2}$ (verb V and two complements or *Ergänzungen*) is used in a *Lagesatz*, for instance: *Fritz geht/fährt zum Spital*; Criticism in Helbig (*Geschichte*, 1974: 210) and Admoni ('Satzmodelle', 1974: 40–1)
8 The view that valency is a property of all word classes has already been expressed in the quotation by Bühler and today is mainly held by Soviet Russian linguists: Admoni, Lomtew, Lejkina, Meltschuk; see also Helbig (1974: 213)
9 These definitions go back to Heringer ('Wertigkeiten', 1967: 21), where he takes *sich begnügen* as an example. Helbig uses the term semantic valency to refer to a semantic specification of the *actants*; see Helbig and Schenkel (*Wörterbuch*, 1968: 53)
10 Compare: *Ute wäscht sich/das Geschirr/* etc. For reflexive verbs see Engel and Schumacher (*Kleines Valenzlexikon*, 1976: 42–4)
11 For *es* see Engel and Schumacher (1976: 44–5); compare also Heringer ('Wertigkeiten', 1967) and Helbig and Schenkel (*Wörterbuch*, 1968). Structural valency also changes in some grammatical constructions such as the imperative: *schlafe, lies!*
12 Valency on a logical basis has been favoured by Baldinger, Bondzio and Heger; see, for instance, Heger (*Monem*, 1976). For a criticism see Stötzel (1970: 88–96) and Heringer ('Ergänzungsbestimmungen', 1968: 428). Compare also Schumacher ('Basis', 1976: 278) and Lyons (*Semantics II*, 1977: 486–8, 494–5)
13 A time adverbial is certainly necessary in any answer to: *Wann besucht Ute den Linguisten?*

14 Infinitive constructions and subordinate clauses could be made *actants* within Tesnière's model by the application of a *translation*, which would change their syntactic status. Brinkmann uses Tesnière's distinction, but Erben also allows predicatives and structurally necessary adverbials of place and direction. Grebe, Schulz and Griesbach include adverbials of time, mood and causality when they distinguish between *notwendigen Umstandsergänzungen* and *freien Umstandsangaben* or *Prädikatsergänzungen* and *freien Angaben* respectively.

15 Brinker (1977: 118) concludes that dependency grammar has not yet provided exact criteria for distinguishing between *Ergänzungen* and *Angaben*. For a critical discussion of various criteria suggested see Brinker (1977: 109–14). Brinker's (1977: 114–17) own approach is based on the introduction of a semantic content unit, called *Semantem*. Such sentences as *Der Linguist sieht in Bettina eine Freundin* and *Der Linguist sieht in Nürnberg eine Freundin* can then be distinguished by describing *in Bettina* as 'semantem-konstitutiv' (as it contributes to the meaning of *sehen*), whereas *in Nürnberg* – the deletion of which does not change the semantic structure of the sentence – is 'nicht semantem-konstitutiv'. The problematic character of the distinction between *Ergänzungen* and *Angaben* has also been pointed out by Engel and Schumacher (1976: 18–20). For a discussion of various attempts to distinguish *Ergänzungen* and *Angaben* see Biere ('Ergänzungen', 1976)

16 In order to make these distinctions, Grebe uses the *Abstrichmethode* and Glinz developed the *Weglassprobe* or deletion test; see Helbig and Schenkel (1968: 323) and Heringer (1968: 430–4)

17 See Helbig and Schenkel (1968: 33–40). It may be worth pointing out that the deletion of an optional *actant* can be accompanied by a shift of meaning of the verb: so *Ute raucht eine Zigarette* and *Ute raucht* could be translated into English as *Ute is smoking a cigarette* and *Ute is a smoker*. Whether an *actant* can be deleted or not is widely determined by the context. In order to make the distinction between obligatory and optional *actants* and *circonstants* quite clear, Helbig uses the methods of transformational grammar. The *actants*, both obligatory and optional, appear in the same position in deep structure under the VP node as *enge Verbergänzungen* (EV) (close verb complements). Certain contextual features (previous mention, etc) allow the deletion of optional *actants* in the course of the transformational process. The *circonstants* appear as *freie Verbergänzungen* (FV) (free verb complements) directly under S. So the criterion for distinguishing between *actants* and *circonstants* is found in deep structure, whereas a deletion test in surface structure enables us to separate optional *actants* and *circonstants* from obligatory *actants*.

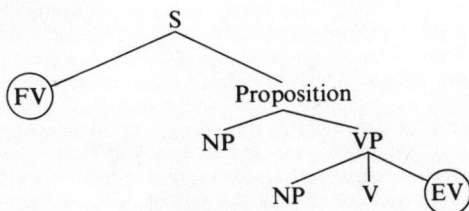

Helbig also claims that *circonstants* are derived from embedded sentences; for a critical discussion of this approach see Emons (1974: 65–7 and 70–1)

18 Engel and Schumacher's valency dictionary is based on purely syntactic criteria of classification. Engel and Schumacher (1976: 274) give the following entry for *trinken:*

| trinken | 0(1 | P1 *Das Baby trinkt (Milch).* |
| trinken | 018 | P1 *Er trinkt sein Glas leer.* |

trinken auf -Akk	o4	P2 *Er trinkt auf meine Gesundheit.*
4: SE mit obligato-	DASS:	*Sie trinken darauf, dass der Plan gelingt.*
rischem Korrelat		
trinken (von–Dat)	o(4	P2 *Das Baby trinkt (von der Milch).*
*Brüderschaft trinken I		Po *Sebastian trank mit allen Brüderschaft.*
mit – Dat		

The second column lists the sentence pattern (see 4.2.5), P1 indicates that E1 (accusative object) can be made the subject of a passive sentence (*Milch wird vom Baby getrunken*), P2 stands for the possibility of an impersonal passive construction (*Es wird auf meine Gesundheit getrunken*) and Po rules out passive constructions (*cf* Engel and Schumacher, 1976: 90–2). One of the most important differences between this valency dictionary and the one provided by Helbig and Schenkel has been characterized by Engel and Schumacher (1976: 11) as follows: 'Verzichtet wurde auch auf eine explizite Einbeziehung der Semantik, da der damalige Forschungsstand eine adäquate semantosyntaktische Beschreibung noch nicht erlaubte. Natürlich wäre es möglich gewesen, im Sinne der Selektionsregeln der Generativen Transformationsgrammatik Besetzungsrestriktionen für die einzelnen Positionen in der Umgebung der Verben zu formulieren. Es hat sich jedoch gezeigt, dass Informationen dieser Art nur wenig zur Lösung der Probleme im Ausländerunterricht beitragen.... Viel wichtiger ist dagegen eine Analyse der Verbinhalte und der Relation zwischen den Inhaltskomponenten und der Umgebung der Verben. An einem solchen Projekt wird z. Zt. am IdS gearbeitet.'

19 According to Helbig ('Zu einigen Spezialproblemen', 1971) stage II resembles Chomsky's subcategorization rules and stage III is equivalent to the selectional restrictions of TG. Semantic components are used in a similar way by Engel (compare our simplified outline in 4.3.3). This use of subcategorization rules has met with considerable criticism from Schumacher ('Basis', 1976: 289), who believes 'dass der Verzicht auf die Explizierung der Verbsemantik und die Ausklammerung der Relationen zwischen den Ergänzungen dazu führen, dass die Erzeugung von ausschliesslich akzeptablen Sätzen nicht gewährleistet ist.' See Schumacher (*Untersuchungen*, 1976) for the basic principles of the establishment of a valency dictionary on a semantic basis.

20 The same reason made Hornby, Gatenby and Wakefield (*ALD*, [2]1963) introduce 25 verb patterns, which are described in structural categories like: Verb Pattern 1: Verb + direct object. *The Advanced Learner's Dictionary* then states the numbers of the verb patterns in which a verb can occur in order to describe its syntactic behaviour. This approach is an attempt to apply the same ideas on which the valency theory in Germany was developed for the description of English.

21 As we have seen, other linguistic schools have put forward models of sentence patterns as well. This outline will be based on the model of sentence patterns suggested by Engel ('Satzbaupläne', 1970) and Engelen (*Untersuchungen I*, 1975), who uses Engel's model with slight modifications.

22 Engel rejects Glinz's definition of *Satzglied* as 'Was sich gesamthaft verschieben lässt' and defines *Satzglieder* as immediate dependents or dependents on the first level. He applies syntactic criteria like substitution tests; see Engel ('Satzbaupläne', 1970: 363–70)

23 This is Engelen's (1975: 90) classification. Engel's model provides a dependent 9 *Verbale* as in: *Ich höre ihn singen*, where Engelen (1975: 69–79) prefers to introduce *Gefügeverb*. Engel labels dependent O nominative object, whereas Engelen calls it subject, which he justifies on structural grounds; see Engelen (1975: 105–8). Identifying complements (*Gleichgrössen*) and attributive complements (*Artergänzungen*) differ in that the deletion of the verb makes no 7 an apposition of the subject (*Ute, eine nette Studentin, ...*), whereas no 8 becomes an adjectival

attribute (*Die müde Ute* ...), see Engelen (1975: 193–5). For the various types of *Ergänzungen* see also Engel and Schumacher (*Valenzwörterbuch*, 1976: 52–79) and Engel (*Syntax*, 1977: 158–79)

24 Compare Engelen (1975: 94–123, 131–60) for further transformational tests.

25 [10a] is possible as a question equivalent of *Ute fährt in/durch Nürnberg/von Nürnberg nach München*/etc. See also [10c]

26 Engel and Schumacher (1976: 27–30) draw a distinction between *Satzmuster* and *Satzbauplan*. Only the *Satzbauplan* illustrates which actants are obligatory and which actants are optional. For a list of *Satzmuster* see also Engel (1977: 180). The problem of impersonal verbs is solved by the introduction of a symbol '–' for sentences without a subject such as *Es regnet*. *Mich friert* or *es friert mich* fall under 1, see Engel ('Satzbaupläne', 1970: 376). Compare also note 11.

27 For a special treatment of *Ausbaupläne* see Engelen ('Möglichkeit', 1968). For *satzförmige Ergänzungen* see Engel and Schumacher (1976: 79–89)

28 Engelen's analysis of the German verb system is an attempt to expand the theory in the direction of semantics: in this work he classifies 5,500 German verbs according to the sentence patterns in which they occur and these groups are then subdivided into lists of verbs (*Verblisten*) by criteria which are partly syntactic distributional, partly semantic. Like Helbig, Engelen includes a semantic description of the *actants* co-occurring with the verbs listed.

29 *Ute besucht* and *besucht den Linguisten* are impossible.

30 Following Hjelmslev, Heringer (*Theorie*, 1970: 107) defines dependency as a co-occurrence relation. Compare Schumacher ('Basis', 1976: 276). Hudson (*Arguments*, 1976: 66) defines dependency in the following way: 'A dependency relation is a relation between two features where one of the features is present only when the other is present – in other words, when one depends for its presence in a structure on the presence of the other.'

31 This is the main argument of those linguists who want to attribute valency to all word classes; see note 8.

32 The first dependency relation Engel ('Bemerkungen', 1972: 142) introduces is an unspecified dependency A–B. A and B stand for syntactic categories of the same level.

33 *Ute ist eine Studentin. Ute ist Studentin.* But *Ute ist eine*. In sentences like *Das hätte ich nicht gedacht*, *das* occurs without a noun, but in this case it is not an article, but a pronoun.

34 The arrangement of the elements does not add any new information to the stemma. The linguist has to introduce a convention concerning the problem of which elements ought to be *regentes* and which elements ought to be *dependentes*. The decision will be taken according to the explanatory value of the different possibilities. See Engel (1972: 146)

35 Semantic features belong to the field of syntax if they influence an element's compatibility with other elements. Stemma I also gives a kind of selectional restrictions, as it would not cover *Ute kauft Obst ein*, because of *Der Händler kauft Vieh ein*.

36 Engel uses small letters for grammatical (bound) morphemes and capital letters for lexical (free, stem-) morphemes.

37 In example [15a] *Eva isst einen Apfel*, however, in addition the stem itself undergoes a change to mark the same grammatical content.

38 Engel uses '=' as a subclassification indicator in a stemma of type II.

39 This formalization of the article and noun dependency is taken directly from Engel (1972: 149)

40 We have already pointed out in 4.1 that a dependency grammar does not necessarily have to be a 'verb' grammar, ie a grammar which makes the verb the highest unit of the hierarchy. The hierarchy in dependency grammar is a hierarchy between elements of the same level of analysis, whereas the hierarchy of a phrase

structure grammar is a hierarchy established by the subclassification of grammatical elements: NP→det + N.

41 The transformational component will also provide for the necessary permutations with verbs like *einkaufen*, where the stem is *einkauf*, but the sentence is *Ute kauft ... ein*. Engel (1972: 151) characterizes projectional rules as follows: 'Die Endkette kann aus dem D-Diagramm unmittelbar abgeleitet werden durch Projektion von Symbolen. Für alle D-Diagramme gilt die folgende P r o j e k t i o n s r e g e l: Alle Symbole, die nicht unmittelbar subklassifiziert werden (d.h. von denen nicht ein nach unten verlaufender Doppelstrich ausgeht), sind auf die Ebene der Endkette zu projizieren.'

42 Gaifman ('Dependency Systems', 1965) and Hays ('Dependency Theory', 1964) have shown the weak equivalence of dependency grammar and phrase structure grammar.

43 Baumgärtner ('Konstituenz', 1970) and Heringer (*Theorie*, 1970) hold that dependency alone is insufficient as a principle of syntactic description. Heringer's reason for this is that in his view a dependency system presupposes a constituency system. See also Brinker (1977: 91), who says: 'Die beiden Prinzipien der Konstituenz und Dependenz ... sind nicht als alternativ, sondern als komplementär zu betrachten.'

44 Heringer's theory includes a dependency system and a constituency system as complementary components. He uses an extremely complicated formalism, see Heringer (*Theorie*, 1970, and *Syntax*, 1970). For Baumgärtner (1970) dependency is a semantic relation to account for 'context activity' (*Kontextaktivität*) – the compatibility of different lexemes. Hudson (1976: 197) describes his own approach of daughter-dependency grammar as 'another attempt to bring the two approaches together'.

45 Robinson ('Dependency Structure', 1970) and Vater ('Model', 1973) use a dependency deep structure, which they transform into a hybrid phrase structure before the transformations are applied. It may be interesting to note that linguists' views as to the role of transformations in dependency grammar vary considerably: Whereas Engel and Schumacher (1976: 12) say that no grammar can do without transformations ('Transformationen sind unverzichtbar, weil eine Grammatik ohne sie alle Dimensionen sprengen würde'), Hudson (*Arguments*, 1976: 177) concludes: 'It is possible to do without transformations provided one also does without phrase-structure rules; and instead of these two types of rule daughter-dependency theory allows for three main types of rule – for classifying, introducing and ordering elements respectively.'

Chapter 5

1 Morris (*Foundations*, 1938) and Schaff (*Introduction*, 1962) can be considered the main representatives of semiotics. Compare also Lyons (*Semantics II*, 1977: 118). For a complex model see also Klaus (*Semiotik*, ²1969: 11–21), who distinguishes between *Sigmatik*, which studies the objects, etc of the real world, and *Semantik*, which analyses the mental conceptions we have of these objects. For a critical discussion of Morris see Wunderlich (*Grundlagen*, 1974: 315–18)

2 For a discussion of pragmalinguistics and pragmatic philosophy see also Klaus (*Macht*, 1964). Klaus is concerned with such terms as *Wahrheit*, *Parteilichkeit*, *Nützlichkeit*, *Evidenz* and *Glaube*. He also gives some examples of language being used for manipulation and propaganda, which also fall under pragmatic analysis, which for Klaus is one component of a comprehensive theory of semiotics.

3 If the degree of familiarity between speaker and hearer allowed the use of *tschüss*,

the *Herr Professor* would be inadequate. If [2] is at all possible, then only in an ironic sense.

4 Although it is self-evident, Wunderlich (*Tempus*, 1970: 80) mentions the fact that the utterance is also determined by the speaker's own abilities and knowledge: if he is not familiar with a certain terminology, he will not be able to use it.

5 Except for a certain cultural context, for this see Firth (*The Tongues of Men*, 1964: 87)

6 Bühler's *Zeigfeld* (*Sprachtheorie*, 1965: 79–148) is an attempt to draw attention to the special place deictic elements should be given in linguistic theory (see also Wunderlich, 'Karl Bühler', 1969). The importance of the context for the meaning of an utterance was also pointed out by Wittgenstein. For this see Savigny (*Philosophie*, 1974: 68–9): 'Was die Äusserung zu einer Äusserung über diese oder jene Person macht, ist die Situation, in der sie getan wird: Wittgensteins Umgebung der Äusserung ... Damit eine Äusserung Bedeutung hat, muss sie also in einer Umgebung getan werden, in der eine solche Äusserung als dieses oder jenes bedeutend aufzufassen ist ... Elemente der Umgebung einer Äusserung können mehr oder weniger dazu beitragen, ihre Bedeutung festzulegen.'

7 In order to support his argument, Wunderlich ('Pragmatik', 1971: 158) discusses IMPLICIT DEIXIS, as in *kommen*. *Brigitte kommt morgen*, for instance, could be paraphrased by *Brigitte wird morgen hier sein*. Or to take another example, the implicit deixis of the verbs *bring* and *take* in English presents considerable difficulty for the German learner, because *bringen* in German can be used with both deictic possibilities – towards and away from the speaker. Wunderlich ('Pragmatik', 1971) also discusses the coherence of texts, presuppositions of *wissen* (which are a part of the meaning of a sentence). For the problem of implicit deixis in contrastive analysis see Burgschmidt and Götz (*Kontrastive Linguistik*, 1974: 118).

8 Firth ('Ethnographic Analysis', 1968: 147–8) establishes a link between Malinowski's work, his own approach and the situation theory developed by the German scholar Wegener (*Untersuchungen*, 1885). For a discussion of Firth and Malinowski see Robins (*Linguistics*, 1964: 25–7) and Palmer (*Papers*, 1968: 1–11, and *Semantics*, 1976; 46–51), for the Neo-Firthians see Robins (*History*, 1967: 221)

9 Many pragmalinguists believe that a linguistic theory of pragmatics has to be based on a general theory of acts (*Handlungstheorie*). Wunderlich (*Sprechakttheorie*, 1976: 31) writes: 'Die Sprechakttheorie ist demnach eine Disziplin, die teils sozialwissenschaftlich, teils philosophisch-wissenschaftsmethodologisch orientiert ist. Der Zusammenhang mit der Sprachwissenschaft besteht darin, dass die pragmatische Fundierung der Sprachtheorie an die Handlungstheorie anzuknüpfen hat, andererseits die linguistische Analyse auch einen Beitrag zur Entwicklung der Handlungstheorie leisten kann.' Wunderlich outlines his point of view in four hypotheses, one of which is that all linguistic utterances have to be regarded as acts in relation to the situation in which they are made. For this see Wunderlich (1976: 30–50). A similar point of view is taken by Heringer, who outlines a formalism of a theory of acts (*Handlungstheorie*) on which he bases a theory of practical semantics (*praktische Semantik*). For this see Heringer (*Praktische Semantik*, 1974: 28–82), see also Ch 8.

10 The utterance can, however, be accompanied by extralinguistic actions, as in the case of the naming of a ship by the breaking of a bottle of champagne, etc.

11 Austin (*Things*, 1962: 5) points out that the true/false distinction only applies for CONSTATIVES, whereas PERFORMATIVES can only be considered happy or unhappy. In Lecture VIII, Austin (1962: 98–101) rejects the notion of constatives and expands the use of the term ILLOCUTIONARY ACT. See also Savigny

(*Philosophie*, 1974: 136–40), Leech (*Semantics*, 1974: 343–5) and Van Dijk (*Text*, 1977: 196–9)

12 Searle (*Speech Acts*, 1969: 24) uses the term SPEECH ACT to cover the ILLOCU-TIONARY ACT and the PROPOSITIONAL ACT, both of which are distinct from pure UTTERANCE ACTS: 'Utterance acts consist simply in uttering strings of words. Illocutionary and propositional acts consist characteristically in uttering words in sentences in certain contexts, under certain conditions and with certain intentions.' For Searle's view of language see Searle (1969: 16). A critical discussion of his theory can be found in Schnelle (*Sprachphilosophie*, 1973: 22–7). See also Dittmann (*Sprechhandlungstheorie*, 1976: 35–50, 70–84)

13 Habermas ('Kompetenz', 1971: 210) elaborates Searle's theory saying that each speech act can be split up into a PERFORMATIVE MATRIX SENTENCE and a dependent PROPOSITIONAL CLAUSE: 'In der elementaren Verknüpfung von Sprechakt und Satz propositionalen Gehalts zeigt sich die *Doppelstruktur umgangssprachlicher Kommunikation*. Eine Verständigung kommt nicht zustande, wenn nicht mindestens zwei Subjekte gleichzeitig *beide* Ebenen betreten: a) die Ebene der Intersubjektivität, auf der die Sprecher/Hörer *miteinander* sprechen, und b) die Ebene der Gegenstände, *über* die sie sich verständigen (wobei ich unter "Gegenständen" Dinge, Ereignisse, Zustände, Personen, Äusserungen und Zustände von Personen verstehen möchte). Der dominierende Satz einer Äusserung dient dazu, den Modus der Kommunikation zu bestimmen und damit den pragmatischen Verwendungssinn für den abhängigen Satz festzulegen.' See also Schnelle (*Sprachphilosophie*, 1973: 42)

14 There has been some discussion on how to integrate illocutionary force into a model of syntax. Ross ('Sentences', 1970) uses a performative matrix sentence (the so-called performative analysis). It is supported by the following observation by Kiparsky and Kiparsky ('Fact', 1971): Whereas it is possible to say: *The book was written by Brigitte and myself*, **The book was written by Brigitte and himself* is not possible unless the governing sentence is replaced by *He said the book was written by Brigitte and himself*. This argument is also used by Wunderlich ('Pragmatik', 1971: 163–4). For a discussion of the performative analysis see Leech (*Semantics*, 1974: 350), who writes: 'Ross himself proposes an alternative to the performative analysis, which he calls the "pragmatic" analysis. The outline of the "pragmatic" analysis is that the subject and performative verb and indirect object are (in Ross's phrase) "in the air" – that is, they belong to the extralinguistic context of the utterance rather than to its actual structure.'

15 For the question of INTENTION and CONVENTION in speech acts see Searle (*Speech Acts*, 1969: 38–49), who says (*p* 48): 'The sentence ... provides a conventional means of achieving the intention to produce a certain illocutionary effect in the hearer.' Compare also Strawson ('Intention', 1964: 38), Savigny (*Philosophie*, 1974: 277–84) and Dittmann (*Sprechhandlungstheorie*, 1976: 74–86)

16 Wunderlich ('Pragmatik', 1971: 180) discusses three possible ways of integrating the *situation of utterance* in deep structure, namely (1) the approach of the generative semanticists: Ross ('Sentences', 1970) and McCawley ('Noun phrases', 1971); compare also Brekle (*Generative Satzsemantik*, 1970); (2) the approach of Sadock ('Hypersentences', 1968), who introduces 'hypersentences'; (3) Wunderlich's own. Wunderlich (*Tempus*, 1970) attributes the components of the situation of utterance to matrix sentences and object clauses following a *verbum dicendi* in the form of syntactic features.

17 This goes back to de Saussure's definition of the sign as consisting of a form-component (*significant*) and a meaning-component (*signifié*). (Compare 8.2.1)

18 Burgschmidt and Götz (1974: 38) write about the possible surface realizations of a DSU: 'Der TSE (DSU) kann auf der Oberflächenstruktur ein Satz entsprechen,

muss es aber nicht. So ist auch ein (deutscher oder englischer) Infinitiv als Satz-bestandteil, z.B. als Ergänzung oder als Subjekt, auf eine TSE zurückzuführen, wenngleich oberflächenstrukturbezogen die Verbergänzungen (Subjekt, Objekt usw.) deletiert sind.'

19 Specific time indicators (*gestern, morgen*, etc) are considered to be optional additions to the proposition. See Burgschmidt and Götz (1974: 39)

20 It is important to note that the P-CORE and its COMPLEMENTS are here postulated on purely semantic grounds; thus the approach differs from Fillmore's and that of syntactically based dependency grammar. For more on the complements see Burgschmidt and Götz (1974: 42): 'Solche "nominale" Valenz-Füller können ihrerseits wieder TSE (DSU) sein; sie werden in der Oberflächenstruktur etwa als Subjekt-, Objektsätze, als Partizipialsätze und deverbale Nomina ausgeführt. Sie behalten dann zwar ihre inneren Valenzen, da sie ja einen Propositionskern haben (etwa *going home wasn't easy*), doch sind keine syntagmatisch notwendigen Beziehungen zur TSE, in die sie eingebettet sind, vorhanden.'

21 It is arguable whether Wunderlich's proposal to integrate situational factors under the nodes of S in a generative transformational model has greater explanatory value than the approach outlined in 5.4.2. Wunderlich develops an extremely complicated formalism to account for the factors of situation of utterance (mainly deictic elements) by means of transformational rules; for this see Wunderlich (*Tempus*, 1970, and 'Pragmatik', 1971: 187–8)

22 Wimmer ('Bedeutung des Regelbegriffs', 1974) shows how the ideas of a theory of *praktische Semantik*, an approach closely related to pragmalinguistics, can be applied to German mother-tongue teaching.

23 For a catalogue of intentions and situations to be used in foreign language teaching, see Denninghaus ('Methoden', 1975). Similar ideas have been developed by Wilkins (*Linguistics*, 1972: 134–59). Hüllen (*Linguistik*, 1976: 28) argues that performance errors do not hinder communication and therefore the importance of the teaching of grammatical correctness should not be over-estimated in foreign language teaching either. 'Die Fähigkeit zur Führung eines situationsbezogenen Dialogs mit der Vielschichtigkeit seiner Kommunikationsakte ist bedeutsamer als die Korrektheit der Syntax.'

24 These curricula combine the study of the structure of an utterance with explanations concerning questions like *when* and *under which conditions* an utterance is made (*Sprechanlässe*), *who* is talking to *whom* (*Rollen*), *where* the utterance is made and *what* is being discussed (*situativer Rahmen*). These aspects show close similarity to the catalogue set up in 5.4.1. For this see Bayerisches Staatsministerium ('Richtlinien', 1974: 723). For another example of the application of pragmalinguistic insights, see Hüllen's (*Linguistik*, 1976: 70 f) discussion of the passive voice in English. How such a lesson could be planned is outlined by Hüllen (1976: 29). For the problem of teacher training, see Burgschmidt ('Überlegungen', 1974)

25 A quite different aspect of pragmatic analysis is revealed in the teaching of pronunciation. Hüllen (1976: 29) indicates the importance of teaching allophonic and intonational differences, as these seem to be particularly important from a pragmatic point of view. Germer ('Bedeutung, 1961) shows that the use of the glottal stop and other features of German English caused by interference make a rather emphatic and decisive impression on the English hearer.

Chapter 6

1 Hartmann ('Texte', 1971: 10) writes: 'Der Text, verstanden als die grundsätzliche Möglichkeit des Vorkommens von Sprache in manifestierter Erscheinungsform, und folglich jeweils ein bestimmter Text als manifestierte Erscheinungsform funk-

tionsfähiger Sprache, bildet das originäre sprachliche Zeichen. Dabei kann die materiale Komponente von jedem sprachmöglichen Zeichenträgermaterial gebildet werden.' Kallmeyer *et al* (*Textlinguistik I*, 1974: 183–4) distinguish between a suprasentential (*transphrastisch*) approach and a text linguistic (*textlinguistisch*) approach to texts. The former, for which the text is a discrete linguistic unit, takes only linguistic facts into consideration and aims solely at extending the boundary of linguistic description beyond the sentence. The text linguistic approach does consider non-linguistic factors.

2 The related questions of whether a finite number of text types can be established and what these text types might be have been widely, if so far inconclusively, discussed in German linguistics. See especially Gülich and Raible (*Textsorten*, 1972, and *Textmodelle*, 1977). We shall restrict our later discussion of text types to the descriptive framework proposed by Werlich (*Typologie*, 1975, and *Text Grammar*, 1976).

3 S. J. Schmidt (*Texttheorie*, 1973: 46) places the linguistic text firmly within a theory of action: 'Ein kommunikatives Handlungsspiel wird konstituiert durch: die globale sozio-kulturelle Einbettung in die Kommunikationsgesellschaft; Kommunikationspartner mit allen sie beeinflussenden Kommunikationsbedingungen und –voraussetzungen; eine einbettende Kommunikationssituation; die geäusserten Texte und faktische oder anschliessbare sprachliche (Kon-) Texte ... Kommunikative Handlungsspiele sind Formen der Realisierung sozialer Kommunitivität (Partnerbezogenheit) sowie komplexer informationeller Prozesse (Informativität).' See also Wunderlich ('Pragmatik', 1971), Habermas ('Kompetenz', 1971: Ch 3 and 5), Maas and Wunderlich (*Pragmatik*, 1972)

4 See especially Kallmeyer *et al* (1974: 115–24) and Weinrich (*Sprache*, 1976: 11–20). For a quite different approach to the question of polysemy see Duden (*Grammatik*, ³1973: 458–65)

5 Compare Halliday's ('Language Structure', 1970) interpersonal, ideational and textual functions. For Firth and Malinowski in this context see note 8 in Ch 5.

6 Kallmeyer *et al* (1974: 54) define coherence as follows: 'Erst in geregelter Kombination sind Textkonstituenten Träger von Referenz- und Konsequenzanweisungen. Entscheidendes Charakteristikum des Texts ist gerade, einen strukturierten Zusammenhang zu bilden. Diese Eigenschaft macht seine Texthaftigkeit aus. Wir bezeichnen diese Form der Verknüpftheit als *Kohärenz*. Äusserungen sind nur "verstehbar", wenn sie als kohärent aufgefasst werden. Konnexionsanweisungen sind also ein wesentliches Mittel der Kohärenzbildung.' See also Van Dijk (*Text*, 1977: 93–129)

7 *Er* could be used to substitute for other masculine nouns, in this text *Sattel, Hut, Alltag*, etc. Harweg ('Pronomina', 1968: 20–35) calls this kind of pronominal substitution two-dimensional. Substitution of the kind *der schwarze Reiter ... der Herr* he calls mono-dimensional. This type is commonly found with proper names and common nouns used generically; for example, *Brigitte hat seit heute früh nichts gegessen. Brigitte hat jetzt Hunger.* Halliday and Hasan (*Cohesion*, 1976: 278–9) use the expression 'reiteration' for this form of substitution. Harweg (1968: 148) attaches such importance to the text-constituting function of substitution forms that he defines the text in terms of pronominalization: '[Der Text ist] ... ein durch eine ununterbrochene Kette zweidimensionaler Substitutionen gebildetes Nacheinander sprachlicher Einheiten.'

8 We could say that pronouns and other words substituting for elements mentioned already are non-referential, they do not refer us to our model of reality, but function solely at the level of connection. *Er* in our texts directs the reader to find an element in the text, or potentially in the situation of utterance, it has *discourse reference*. When more than one nominal can be referred to by a pronoun, semantic congruence must be established. When making a decision of this kind, we take

into account not only the nouns which might be refered to, but also everything predicated of them in the text.

9 See also Halliday and Hasan (1976: 274–92), who come to similar conclusions.

10 Werlich refers to *implicit* and *explicit sequence signals* which correspond to Weinrich's *Regel des Rahmens*. See Werlich (*Typologie*, 1975: 45) and Van Dijk's (*Text*, 1977: 98–108) frame.

11 In addition to Weinrich (1976: 163–98), on whose work our discussion of the articles is based, Dressler (*Einführung*, 1971) and Wunderlich ('Textlinguistik', 1974) have drawn attention to the importance of the articles in creating textual coherence. Weinrich adopts Bühler's distinction between the representational and the conative (internal deixis) function of the linguistic sign, but ascribes more importance to the deictic function than Bühler does. See Weinrich (1976: 187–8)

12 Whereas the possessives are usually anaphoric, the demonstratives can also have a cataphoric function. Unlike the definite articles, the possessives and demonstratives cannot appeal to the hearer/reader's cultural knowledge, but only to the linguistic context or the situation of utterance. To the interrogatives Weinrich ascribes a bridge function between preceding and following information. They are used to elicit necessary complementary information.

13 This section (6.3) is based on Werlich (*Typologie*, 1975) and Werlich (*Text Grammar*, 1976). Werlich (1975: 17) gives this definition of texts: 'Als *textliche Äusserungen* (kurz: *Texte*) fassen wir ... alle jene sprachlichen Äusserungen auf, die durch (sich überlagernde Schichten von) *Kohärenz* und *Kompletion* in der Abfolge ihrer sprachlichen Einheiten gekennzeichnet sind.' Text-structuring is, then, the creation of coherence and completion using initiators and sequence elements. Werlich's descriptive procedures derive largely from scale-and-category grammar, see Halliday ('Language Structure', 1970) and Berry (*Introduction*, 1975–7)

14 Werlich (*Typologie*, 1975: 42) quotes Lenneberg (*Biological Foundations*, 1967: 394) to support his thesis that the processes by which the realized outer structure of a language is created are deeply-rooted, species-specific innate properties of Man's biological nature.

15 Werlich (1976: 44) 'Functional text being situationally autonomous ... The encoder presupposes the addressee to understand the fictional text within its own *internal* fields of reference ... The decoder's understanding of the text depends on how he is able to link the *text-internal model of the world* with his own model of the past ... and now!' Traditionally only poetic (fictional) texts have been regarded as worthy of linguistic analysis. For a brief discussion of the relationship between linguistics and literary criticism see Weinrich (1976: 11–20)

16 Werlich (1976: 107 ff) mentions in addition to comment, scientific argumentation as the other text form of the text type *argumentation*. Narrative text forms are the narrative, the report (the news story being one variant of this text form).

17 In his text grammar of English Werlich has used a systemic approach to textual analysis and to the description of the process of text production. A comparison of his work and Halliday and Hasan (1976) reveals, however, quite different views of the nature of texts. Halliday and Hasan, for example, consider the text to be a semantic whole which is realized but *not* constituted by sentences. There has been much discussion of text types, see especially Gülich and Raible (1972 and 1977), but there is still no consensus on the classification of linguistic texts. This consensus does, of course, exist with regard to many traditonal literary genres.

18 However, Werlich's influence must not be over-estimated, as these proposals are constantly being modified. His applied work has also been heavily criticized for its confusing terminological apparatus.

19 In 5.5.1 we outlined the influence of pragmalinguistic analysis on foreign language teaching. Pragmalinguistics is mainly concerned with the spoken language,

whereas text linguistics often examines written language. In any case, the need for a supra-sentential approach in language teaching has been clearly established. For a similar approach, see also Crystal and Davy (*Conversational English*, 1975: 4): 'The many kinds of linkage which sentences display – using pronouns, articles, adverbials, lexical repetitions, and so on – which are not relevant to the sentence seen in isolation: this is one kind of structural modification which has to be considered. Another involves intonation ...'

Chapter 7

1 Readers who are not acquainted with transformational generative grammar (TG) are advised to consult Lyons (*Chomsky*, 1970) and Allen and Van Buren (*Readings*, 1971) for useful introductions. Huddleston (*Introduction*, 1976) illustrates the application of the theory, while Leech (*Semantics*, 1974) and Lyons (*Semantics II*, 1977) discuss the issues raised by the dispute about the relationship between syntax and semantics.

2 Wunderlich (*Probleme*, 1971: 8) emphasizes the linguistic generation gap. (However not all established *Sprachwissenschaftler* have denied, or do deny the value of the transformational approach): 'Die Theorie der generativ-transformationellen Grammatik – wie auch manche andere Entwicklung – wurde in Deutschland langezeit kaum zur Kenntnis genommen. Dies hat verschiedene, aus der Tradition der deutschen Universitäten her erklärbare Ursachen ...'. Wunderlich then lists these reasons to justify the need for younger scholars to meet regularly so as to promote TG!

3 Coseriu (*Leistung*, 1975: 75): 'Wir werden versuchen, unsere Kritik (*ie* of TG) nicht im transformationalistischen Stil, sondern so nüchtern und objektiv wie möglich zu halten.' We discuss Coseriu's critique in 7.3.

4 Bierwisch (*Grammatik*, 1963) is one of a large number of monographs which have appeared in the *Studia Grammatica* series, many of them written by linguists working under Bierwisch in the *Arbeitsstelle Strukturelle Grammatik der Deutschen Akademie der Wissenschaften* in East Berlin. Bierwisch (1963) like Motsch (*Syntax*, 1964), is based upon the *Syntactic Structures* model of 1957. Using as an example the sentence

   Peter schenkt dem Bruder zu Weihnachten ein Buch.

   Bierwisch shows that elements can be fronted without changing meaning (he excludes stylistic meaning). The grammar will be required to generate sentences so as to show their semantic equivalence; additionally it must make clear the different relations holding between the constituents of such constructions as *Der Verlust der Freunde* (*ist bitter*). One interpretation gives 'X loses friends', the other 'the friends lose X'.

5 Bierwisch (1963: 34–6) comes to the same conclusions as Bach ('Order of elements', 1962) about the position of the finite verb in the terminal string. He gives three syntactic reasons for his decision: firstly, the finite verb forms with separable prefixes or non-finite verbs part of the *Satzklammer* in clause-final position; secondly, the previously finite verb of a non-expanded clause goes as the infinitive to the end of the clause, when a modal or other auxiliary is introduced, see

   Hans kommt um vier Uhr.
   Hans wird um vier Uhr kommen.
   Hans sollte um vier Uhr kommen.

Thirdly, the verb follows other elements not only in subordinate clauses, but in infinitive constructions and cited forms:

die Lust, am Meer in der Sonne zu liegen
Schwimmen bedeutet sich im Wasser fortbewegen.

6 Motsch ('Attributive Adjektive', 1967) is a rebuttal of Winter ('Transforms', 1965) using some syntactic and semantic arguments from Chomsky's *Aspects* model. Winter claims that since some attributive adjectives are not used predicatively, Chomsky's assertion *(Syntactic Structures*, 1957) that the predicative use is primary must be rejected. Winter argues that either kernel strings must be invented in which such attributive adjectives as *bürgerlich* in *bürgerliches Gesetzbuch* are used predicatively, which would be non-intuitive and meaningless, or attributive adjective constructions (at least for some adjectives) must be regarded as primary. Motsch argues that while anomalies exist, the predicative construction must still be regarded as primary.

7 A perhaps over-simplifying view distinguishes interpretive semantics, whose adherents claim that syntax is autonomous, and generative semantics, which derives sentences from a semantic base. This at times esoteric dispute has proved fruitful for theoretical linguistics, but has contributed little of value to descriptive linguistics, since the discussion of semantic universals using features or componential analysis draws on heuristic techniques developed by structural linguists. One version of this analysis is discussed in Ch 8. Lyons (*Semantics II*, 1977: 413–14) does not accept that interpretive semantics and generative semantics are such conflicting theories and claims that they (*ie* the two schools) 'have both accepted that a model of linguistic description should not only generate the set of semantically well-formed sentences, but should also associate with each a semantic interpretation in terms of a universal inventory of sense-components'.

8 Leech (1974: 141) talks of the principle according to which 'meaning seems to overflow sideways from one part of a sentence to another: that certain features of meaning are predictable from environment and that any contradiction of such features will result in an unacceptable utterance'. Selection restrictions or cooccurrence restrictions govern the acceptability of syntagmatic relations.

9 Baumgärtner (1967: 169) '... der Feldbegriff (gilt) ausschliesslich und einheitlich für die jeweiligen Klassen oder Teilklassen von Lexemen unter den vorgegebenen Kategorien – meist untersten "Wortkategorien" ... Die entscheidende Vorbedingung ist, dass man nicht bei der Bestimmung und Betrachtung ganzer Bedeutungen stehenbleibt, sondern zur Analyse von Bedeutungen in ihre kleinsten Bestandteile übergeht ... Der Semantik sind ... nicht Bedeutungen, sondern deren Komponenten zugrunde zu legen.'

10 For a discussion of these disputed semantic procedures, see Lyons (*Semantics II*, 1977: 414–22) and Leech (*Semantics*, 1974: 141–6). Bierwisch ('Semantic universals', 1967: 35) has this to say of componential analysis: 'A semantic analysis of a lexical item is finished only if it leads to a combination of basic elements that are true candidates for the universal set of semantic markers, *ie* that may be interpreted in terms of basic dimensions of the human apperceptive apparatus.'

11 The approach of the *Aspects* model obscures the fact that in both sentences the semantic role of *Ute* is the same, as is that of *der Linguist*. Fillmore ('Case', 1968) redefines the term 'case' to apply to it to deep semantic relations holding between sentence elements, relations which cannot be deduced directly from surface grammatical relations such as grammatical subject, grammatical object, etc.

12 Brekle (*Generative Satzsemantik*, 1970: 15) points out that the phenomena to be described must not be confused with the methods employed to describe them 'Ohne Zuhilfenahme semantischer Kategorien und entsprechender "Überbrük-

kungsregeln" (ist) der Übergang von der Lautkette zur inhaltlichen Struktur unmöglich.'

13 While Bierwisch (1963: 31–3) requires the grammar to derive all the sentences made up of the five constituents *Peter schenkt dem Bruder zu Weihnachten ein Buch* from the same underlying form, he has nothing to say about the grammar's ability to account for these variations.

14 Bierwisch's analysis seems in this case to be inadequate. The acceptability or otherwise of the degree adverbial in connection with *langsam* seems to depend not on the internal semantics of the adjective, but on the context of situation. If, for example, eating slowly were considered a virtue, we might well find *Schau dir Ute an, sie isst doppelt so langsam wie Hans.*

15 Baumgärtner (1969: 3) '. . . die Adjektive sind in diesen Kontexten in ihrer verschobenen, aus den Bereichen der Temperatur, Konsistenz und Form kommenden Bedeutung mit umgangssprachlichen Mitteln nicht zu beschreiben, genauer: nicht durch gleichwertige übliche Lexeme zu ersetzen. Sie erweisen sich unter bestimmter intendierter Meinung trotz ihrer relativ unüblichen Anwendung als notwendig.'

16 Coseriu (1975: 76) points out 'Es wird zwar ganz genau festgestellt [ie in TG], wie Präpositionen in einer Sprache konstruiert werden, es wird aber nicht festgestellt und nicht festzustellen versucht, welches die Funktion der Präpositionen ist, und was uns dazu bringt, gerade diese funktionelle Einheit, die wohl die Grundlage der Beschreibung ist, anzunehmen.'

17 For Coseriu (1975: 26–8) meaning (*Bedeutung*) is given linguistic content, the content given in individual languages (*sprachlich gegeben . . . den einzelsprachlich gegebenen Inhalt*), reference (*Bezeichnung*), the reference to the extralinguistic, that which is denoted (*den Bezug auf das Aussersprachliche . . . auf das Bezeichnete*) and sense or textual meaning (*Sinn*), the level of content which is text-specific (*die texteigene Ebene des Inhalts*).

18 For the discussion of a similar problem, the utterance *the horse miaowed*, see Leech (1974: 142) and Lyons (*Semantics II*, 1977: 414)

19 Wunderlich (*Tempus*, 1970: 164–208) treats tense in the way criticized by Coseriu, ie as an element to be integrated into the sentence.

20 Coseriu (1975: 128–9) argues: 'Sie [ie TG] ist . . . adäquat für das Sprechen und dessen Analyse . . . Es fehlt den Transformationalisten das Bewusstsein, dass sie mit einer Sprache eigentlich eine Linguistik des Sprechens betreiben und nicht eine Linguistik der Einzelsprachen . . . Die transformationelle Grammatik ist deshalb falsch und unannehmbar, weil sie etwas sein will, was sie nicht sein kann, und nicht ausdrücklich das sein will, was sie implizite immer schon gewesen ist.'

21 'Die Schwäche der Sprachkonzeption CHOMSKYS besteht vor allem darin, dass sie das Wesen der menschlichen Sprache allein auf die allgemeinen, biologisch fixierten Grundlagen eines kreativen Zeichensystems zurückführt. . . . Das Wesen einer Sprache kann nur erfasst werden, wenn man ihre konkrete Form als gesellschaftlich-historischen Gebrauch allgemeiner Anlagen versteht.' Motsch (1974: 181)

22 '. . . man befasst sich in erster Linie mit den Grundbegriffen einer semantischen Theorie wie "semantisches Merkmal", "semantische Relation" usw. und kaum mit der weit komplizierteren Frage, wie Bedeutungssysteme einer bestimmten natürlichen Sprache, die in einem bestimmten Zeitraum von einer bestimmten sozialen Gruppe als Instrument der Verständigung verwendet wird, aufgebaut sind. Insbesondere das Problem, welche Beziehungen zwischen semantischen Systemen einer Sprache und Formen des gesellschaftlichen Bewusstseins bestehen, wird ausgeklammert. Hier zeigt sich der grosse Abstand zu Fragen, die für eine marxistisch orientierte Sprachwissenschaft von brennendem Interesse sind.' Motsch (1974: 132)

Chapter 8

1 Many approaches to semantics take account of the fact that semantics is part of the more comprehensive theory of semiotics. Compare, for instance, Brekle, *Semantik*, 1972: 30–7, and Klaus, *Macht*, 1964. For semiotics see also Morris, *Foundations*, 1938, and the Polish scholar Schaff, *Introduction*, 1962, first published in Poland in 1960, and the work of the Italian Eco. For Morris see also Wunderlich, *Grundlagen*, 1974: 315–18.

2 H. J. Heringer's *praktische Semantik* is based on a general theory of acts (*Handlungstheorie*). His basic aim is to set up a pattern of communication in the sense that he intends to set up a systematic description of possible reactions to a speech act. If, for instance, a speaker makes a statement, another speaker can either agree with him and ask for a reason for the statement (*Warum-Frage*) or he can disagree and say so (*Stimmt nicht*). Heringer (*Semantik*, 1974: 175–84) uses this example to set up a pattern of the options a speaker has in the course of such a communication. This is closely related to the pragmalinguistic approach and is quite different from semantics in the traditional sense. Wunderlich (*Grundlagen*, 1974: 311) characterizes this as '... einen Bedeutungsbegriff ..., der auf sprachliche Äusserungen (bzw. Typen von sprachlichen Äusserungen) und nicht auf sprachliche Ausdrücke bezogen ist.' For his discussion of Bloomfield in this context, see Wunderlich (1974: 311–15); for Grice (1974: 326–35)

3 It is not surprising that a lot of work done in Germany is concerned with the criticism and elaboration of various approaches within the model of transformational grammar (see Ch 7). For German approaches applying semantic components as used by Katz and Fodor or Chomsky see, for example, Bierwisch ('Semantic Universals', 1967; 'Semantics', 1970, and 'Semantic Features', 1970) or Hundsnurscher (*Methoden*, 1972). Compare also the approach to componential analysis taken by Baumgärtner ('Struktur', 1967). For an application of the generative semantics approach see Brekle (*Generative Satzsemantik*, 1970, and 'Grammatikmodell', 1970)

4 The semantic component of the natural generative grammar as outlined by Bartsch and Vennemann (*Semantic Structures*, 1972) comprises *sentence semantics* (including word order, morphological markers, intonation and the like), which is part of syntax, and *word semantics* – meaning postulates of words associated with them in the lexicon. Their semantic structure is unordered and, similarly, they do not postulate ordering of the rules in the grammar. Thus Bartsch and Vennemann reject the approach taken by generative semanticists. According to Bartsch and Vennemann (1972: 41) the Strong Naturalness Condition requires 'that all aspects of semantic representations are formulated in a logic which models the linguistically relevant cognitive capacities of human beings'. For the basic principles of natural generative grammar, see Bartsch and Vennemann (1972: 35–44)

5 In our use of the term *Zeichen* (linguistic sign) we follow Brekle (1972: 34), who writes: 'Unter "Zeichen" verstehe ich die einzelsprachlich je verschiedene konventionell feste Korrelation einer Zeichenform *A* mit ihrem Designatum (Bedeutung).' The term sign was also used in this sense by de Saussure, but we should point out that English scholars tend to use sign for what we refer to as *linguistic form* (see, for instance, Palmer, *Semantics*, 1976: 5). For characteristic properties of the linguistic sign see Brekle (1972: 47–50)

6 For a brief discussion of some central terms of semantics like *Bedeutung, Bezeichnung* and *Sinn* see, for example, Coseriu ('Betrachtung', 1976: 7–9). For Frege's use of *Bedeutung* and *Sinn* see Brekle (1972: 62–6) and Wunderlich (*Grundlagen*, 1974: 274–81). For various concepts of meaning see also Ullmann (*Semantics*, 1972: 54–67), Leech (*Semantics*, 1974: 1–9), Lyons (*Introduction*, 1968: 406–12), Palmer (1976: 19–37) or Heger (*Monem*, ²1976: 31–51). See also Leisi (*Wortinhalt*,

1971: 9–24) who defines *Inhalt* as *Gebrauchsbedingungen* of lexical items. For a critical appraisal of the *Gebrauchstheorie* see Brekle (1972: 59–62)

7 Wotjak(*Untersuchungen*,1971:26)usesthefollowingversionofthesemiotictriangle postulated by Ogden and Richards ([4]1936: 11), (see also Lyons, *Semantics I*, 1977: 95)

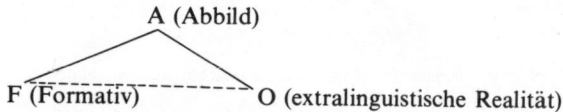

A (Abbild)

F (Formativ) ─ ─ ─ ─ ─ ─ O (extralinguistische Realität)

'Betrachten wir das obenstehende Grundschema der semantischen Zeichenrelation, so ersehen wir daraus, dass das jeweilige Formativ [linguistic form, HHD] nicht unmittelbar für die extralinguistische Realität O, sondern für semBewusstseinsinhalte A steht und damit der Tatsache Rechnung getragen ist, dass das Formativ bzw. das sprachliche Zeichen seiner kommunikativen Funktion nur dank dieses eng mit ihm verknüpften Bewusstseinsinhalts gerechtzuwerden vermag.' Compare Ammer and Meier ('Bedeutung', 1966) and Brekle (1972: 30, 58)

8 If single elements of a set of objects are being referred to in a sentence, the linguistic form must be accompanied by quantifiers. See Brekle (1972: 32)

9 For a distinction between *Intension* and *Extension* see Brekle (1972: 56–7), Heger ([2]1976: 47–51) and Lyons (*Semantics I*, 1977: 158–60)

10 For a discussion of the lexical field in the view of the content-oriented tradition see Gipper ('Die feldhafte Gliederung', 1976). Compare also Coseriu ('Solidaritäten', 1967), Wunderlich (*Grundlagen*, 1974: 281–4) or Seiffert (*Wortfeldtheorie*, 1968: 9–21) and Geckeler (*Wortfeldtheorie*, 1971: 100–66). Compare also our treatment of the word field in Ch 2 and the references given there.

11 For an analysis of *Bedeutungsfelder* as opposed to *Wortfelder* see Baumgärtner ('Struktur', 1967), who also discusses the work of Trier and Porzig and their influence on modern semantics.

12 Although the parallels between phonology and semantics may suggest suitable procedures for the analysis of lexical structure, the case must not be overstated: the analysis of vocabulary requires a much larger number of oppositions than are needed in phonology (compare 8.6), because the lexical structure of a language is much more complex than its phonological structure, as is shown, for example, by the possibility of paraphrases in cases where no primary lexical oppositions exist and also by the fact that one lexeme may belong to more than one word field. Coseriu (1973: 67) points out a further difficulty: 'In der Phonologie gilt, dass gewisse Unterschiede entweder existieren oder nicht existieren, nicht aber, dass sie einmal gemacht werden und einmal nicht ... Im Wortschatz dagegen existieren auch innerhalb einer funktionellen Sprache fakultative Unterschiede.'

13 For equipollent and privative oppositions, see also Lyons (*Semantics I*, 1977: 279)

14 Coseriu (*Probleme*, 1973: 54–5) establishes the following hierarchy: '... am einen Ende stehen die Seme, die auf Grund von minimalen Oppositionen innerhalb eines Wortfeldes festgestellt werden können. Daraus ergibt sich, dass jedes Lexem aus einer Anzahl von Semen besteht. Am anderen Ende steht das Archilexem als Bezeichnung des gesamten Feldes, das seinerseits eine Anzahl von Lexemen enthält. Nur für die Lexeme ist die Existenz eines entsprechenden Wortes erforderlich, während Archilexeme nicht immer durch Wörter bezeichnet werden. Ob es Wörter gibt, die einzelnen Semen entsprechen, erscheint fraglich.' We must add that Coseriu's lexical fields consist of lexemes (*ie* non-compound words); they fall in the category of primary paradigmatic structures. (Some of our examples have violated this principle.) For the distinction between syntagmatic, primary and secondary paradigmatic structures see Coseriu (1973: 52)

15 Note, however, that *der Armleuchter kommt* is only acceptable in a sense that *Armleuchter* (candelabra) is not an *actor* (as *Thea* in *Thea kommt*), but is, say, being delivered by the postman. Similarly, the German verb *essen* always requires a human subject, whereas *fressen*, which is the equivalent verb for animals (*Thea isst. *Der Hund isst. Der Hund frisst*), can be used with a human subject in a very pejorative sense (*eat like an animal*). These facts would not be revealed by an analysis of the kind described in 8.3.2.

16 The distinction between semes and classemes was made by Pottier ('Semantique moderne', 1964), for Pottier see also Wotjak (*Untersuchungen*, 1971: 133–8). Wotjak and Lyons draw a parallel between the seme/classeme distinction on the one hand and the distinction between markers and distinguishers made by Katz and Fodor ('Structure', 1963) on the other. Lyons (*Semantics I*, 1977: 326–7) remarks: 'The distinction between semes and classemes . . . corresponds (in certain respects) at least roughly with the equally controversial, but more familiar, distinction between distinguishers and markers, which, as it was originally drawn by Katz and Fodor (1963), was held to reflect the distinction between what was systematic for a language in the meaning of a lexeme and what was not.' Objections to Katz and Fodor's distinction have been raised by Bierwisch ('Problems', 1969) and by Baumgärtner ('Struktur', 1967: 171). Compare also Bolinger ('Atomization', 1965)

17 Coseriu (1973: 78–85) points out that there are purely semantic classemes (like 'lebende Wesen' or 'menschliche Wesen') and grammatical classemes, for example, masculine gender. Verbs could be marked by such grammatical classemes as 'transitive' and 'intransitive'.

18 Leisi (*Wortinhalt*, 1971: 72) makes a distinction between direct metaphor (*Die Steine reden*) and indirect metaphor (*Die Steine schweigen*). For metaphorical use of lexical items see also Leech (*Guide*, 1969: 150–65). For a comprehensive treatment of co-occurrence conditions of subject and objects of certain verbs see Leisi (1971: 64–70), who compares German and English. (See also our discussion of Leisi in 2.2.2)

19 It is important to note that some linguists, for example Wotjak (1971: 44–5), hold that semes differ in respect to their level of abstraction and in respect to their frequency of recurrence, which enables the linguist to establish hierarchies in which the highly recurrent rather abstract semes occupy a higher rank than more specific and less frequent semes. For this see also Palmer (1976: 88)

20 For a justification of the choice of components see Wotjak (1971: 180–99). In some cases, the table mentions only one component of a binary opposition, so 'vertical' appears, but 'horizontal' does not (see Wotjak, 1971: 190). It must be pointed out that Wotjak's analysis is no more than an attempt to apply componential analysis to the description of a lexical field and that he himself is aware of the inadequacies from which his work may suffer.

21 We do not want to go into the problem of establishing semantic components. For a very detailed discussion of various approaches see Wotjak (1971: 154–75), who outlines different ways of elaborating semantic components using substitution tests, contrastive analysis, gaps and fillers and definition analysis. For an analysis of meaning through collocation, see Neubert ('Analogien', 1966: 108–12). Neubert ('Semantik', 1968) discusses the possibilities of gaining semantic components through contrastive analysis. Both Neubert and Wotjak pay special attention to the *collocation test* developed by Joos.

22 For an outline of the basic principles of componential analysis see Bierwisch ('Semantics', 1970: 168–77) or Leech (*Semantics*, 1974: 95–125), who points out that componential analysis had originally evolved from the analysis of kinship terms in linguistic anthropology. For an example of componential analysis in semantics see Leech (*Description*, 1969). Compare also Lyons (*Introduction*, 1968:

474–80, and *Semantics I*, 1977: 317–21) who draws attention to the fact that in addition to Chomsky and Katz, who have made use of semantic components, Hjelmslev and Jakobson advocate this approach. A rather detailed discussion of the influential paper 'A structure of a semantic theory' by Katz and Fodor (1963) is provided by Bolinger ('Atomization', 1965), but see also Leech (*Description*, 1969: 6–13) or Wotjak (1971: 113–22). See Wotjak (1971: 122–53) for a discussion of the approaches taken by Weinrich and Nida, Bolinger, Pottier, Meier, Greimas and Bierwisch; for Greimas and Pottier see also Geckeler (*Wortfeldtheorie*, 1971: 210–17)

23 G. F. Meier ('Noematische Analyse', 1966: 129) characterizes noemes in the following way: 'Die Noeme müssen ... eindeutig definiert und symbolisch ausgedrückt werden. Sie müssen interlingualen Charakter haben, dh. sie müssen interlingual semantische Informationsquanten speichern. Sie müssen einen hohen Grad an Verallgemeinerung besitzen, nahezu axiomatischen Wert haben. Ihre Anzahl muss so bemessen sein, dass sie alle Sememe einer natürlichen Sprache durch Kombination definieren. Sie müssen allen semantischen Informationen gewachsen sein, also nicht nur den logischen, sondern auch den emotionellen. Die Noeme sind Mengen mit Untermengen.' Wotjak (1971: 141) criticizes Meier's noemes as having a rather low level of abstraction. For an outline of Meier's *Noematik* see also Helbig (*Geschichte*, 1974: 192–6); for the distinction of noemes and semes see Heger (*Monem*, [2]1976: 41–7)

24 Heger ([2]1976: 3) writes: 'Der Terminus "universell" ist dabei in dem relativen Sinn dessen zu verstehen, was nicht von je einzelsprachlichen Bedingungen abhängt, sondern sich auf alle natürlichen Sprachen gleichermassen bezieht bzw. beziehen kann und daher "interlingual" oder "ausereinzelsprachlich" heissen kann.'

25 See Heger ([2]1976: 111–14) for a discussion of Fillmore's case grammar in respect to his own analysis. For a criticism of predication analysis see Heger ([2]1976: 103–5)

26 According to Heger ([2]1976: 105–6 and 48–9) the place of a relator can only be taken by a *diskontinuierlicher Allgemeinbegriff*, by which term he refers to measurable entities (water), one- and multi-place relations (blue, bigger than), states (freedom), events (liberation), etc.

27 In Leech's (1974: 136) model these are referred to as one-place predication (*Jones is ill*) or two-place predication (*The man was in front of the woman*), where the *man, woman* and *Jones* are arguments, whereas *was in front of* and *is ill* are predicates.

28 For a detailed contrastive analysis of *Ball* in English and German see Burgschmidt and Götz (*Kontrastive Linguistik*, 1974: 217–22)

29 Compare G. F. Meier ('Semantische Analyse', 1964: 590): (Es ist sehr nützlich festzustellen) '... wieviel (Noeme) bei der Herstellung einer monosemen Satzbedeutung beteiligt sein müssen ... Sehr allgemeine Noeme sind oft nicht mächtig genug, um Monosemie herzustellen. Bei einem zu geringen Abstraktionsgrad erhöht sich die Zahl der verfügbaren Noeme so sehr, dass sie ihrerseits zergliedert werden müssten.'

30 In some cases syntactic ambiguity can arise: *Spielen* is a verb in *Die Kinder spielen im Garten*, whereas it is a noun in *Die Kinder haben viel Freude an den Spielen, die ihnen der Weihnachtsmann gebracht hat*. For this see G. F. Meier ('Noematische Analyse', 1966: 123–6), who is mainly concerned with machine translation. For an analysis of syntactic ambiguity of the type *Sie nannten den Täter widerwillig* see Agricola ('Problematik', 1968)

31 For other links between semantics and pragmatics see Brekle (*Semantik*, 1972: 99–107)

32 Wotjak ('Invarianz', 1973: 72–3) introduces the term *alloseme* for the actual realization of a sememe in context and writes: '[Es] ... dürfte feststehen, dass in den

Allosemen nie jeweils *alle* Bestandteile des Semems aktualisiert werden, dass die referentiellen Merkmale des begrifflichen Kerns (K e r n s e m e) von Allosem zu Allosem nur geringfügig variieren – etwa insofern als ein Merkmal nicht aktualisert wird, nie jedoch so, dass ein in den Sememen nicht angelegtes bzw. mit den Strukturelementen inkompatibles Merkmal hinzutreten würde.'

33 Neubert ('Semantik', 1968: 206–7) uses this example to illustrate how semes can be elaborated by contrastive analysis and comes to the conclusion that sememes are subcategories of semantic universals. Neubert is also concerned with the pragmatic analysis of political terms, the impact of which may differ in East and West Germany. For the work of the Leipzig school see Neubert and Kade (*Neue Beiträge*, 1973); for a comprehensive discussion of the problems of translation by a representative of the Leipzig school, see Kade (*Zufall*, 1968)

34 Wotjak's view seems to be in accordance with that of Neubert (1968: 202): 'Dabei ist anzumerken, dass die semantischen Merkmale wohl die Komponenten des Bedeutungssystems einer Sprache darstellen, gleichzeitig jedoch die eine Sprache, in der sie jeweils angetroffen werden, transzendieren. Dadurch werden sie gerade übersetzbar. Der Platz dieser "Atome der Bedeutung" ist demnach in einer Metasprache.' For practical purposes, it seems that *seme* and *noeme* are largely interchangeable terms.

35 Another problem of componential analysis can be mentioned only briefly here. Coseriu (*Probleme*, 1973: 62) writes: 'Die grosse Schwierigkeit bei solchen Analysen ist, dass auch für die Wiedergabe der unterscheidenden Züge Wörter oder Zusammensetzungen von Wörtern gebraucht werden müssen. Begriffe wie "Notwendigkeit" oder "Möglichkeit" sind daher in diesem Fall nur als Namen für die entsprechenden semantischen Merkmale zu verstehen. Statt dessen könnten auch andere Wörter oder Symbole, z.B. Pfeile verwendet werden.' The lack of differentiation between metalanguage and object-language is one of the main objections to componential analysis raised by Lyons (*Semantics I*, 1977: 334–5). For an attempt to solve this problem in practical analysis see Leech (*Description*, 1969)

Chapter 9

1 Many of these younger linguists are however very critical both of Bernstein's methods and the conclusions he draws from his research. While Labov's approach is considered more democratic, it too is seen as maintaining the social status quo by Dittmar (*Soziolinguistik*, 1973: especially 307–8); see also Jäger ('Sprachbarrieren', 1972) and Ammon (*Dialekt*, 1973)

2 Radtke ('Stadtsprachen', 1972) emphasizes that German sociolinguistics was still dependent on the theoretical groundwork done by English-speaking linguists. Steger ('Soziolinguistik', 1973: 246) stresses the limited interests of German sociolinguists: 'Der in den 60er Jahren in der BRD aufgenommene Terminus Soziolinguistik wird dort oft beschränkt auf die aus England übernommene Sprachbarrierenproblematik'. German sociolinguists, like the dialectologists, are concerned with a linguistically homogeneous area – problems of bilingualism and languages in contact have only arisen comparatively recently with the influx of many foreign workers. Nor have German linguists benefited from the anthropological tradition in linguistics (Sapir, Malinowski)

3 In a review of the state of German sociolinguistics Steger ('Grundlagen', 1971: 11–13) points to three major deficiencies of dialectology. Firstly, its lack of a sound theoretical base, secondly its superficial and unsystematic interest in the social correlates of language use and thirdly its over-emphasis of geographical variation at the expense of social hierarchical variation. Dialectologists are conscious of

the need to adapt both their research and methodology to developments in linguistics. This is illustrated by the publication of *Germanistische Linguistik*, which has appeared four or so times a year under the aegis of the *Forschungsinstitut für deutsche Sprache, Deutscher Sprachatlas, Marburg*.

4 The definition of what constitutes a language can rarely be based solely on linguistic criteria. See Trudgill (*Sociolinguistics*, 1974: 15–16) for a discussion of the status of German and Dutch as separate languages. In this chapter we follow Trudgill's usage of the terms *accent, dialect* and *variety* (compare Trudgill, 1974: 14–17). The sociolinguist's view of language and its use is necessarily far removed from the unreality of Chomsky's ideal speaker/hearer and Weisgerber's unified language community (*Sprachgemeinschaft*) (see Ch 7 and 2 respectively). For a description of some features of East Franconian dialect see Burgschmidt and Götz ('Konstrastive Phonologie', 1972), who point out that it is the regional dialect and not the standard of L1 which has to be considered in foreign language teaching.

5 In Switzerland and in Austria the standards differ both in lexis and syntax from the German standard. In West Germany there is some concern that the unity of the German standard language may not be preserved as political, cultural and general social developments in the two German republics are widely divergent. This is, of course, most marked in the lexis, for not only have words different referential and connotational meanings, neologisms are beginning to hinder mutual understanding. In Germany which has, like France, a strong tradition of prescriptive usage (embodied in the *Duden* volumes), this state of affairs causes more concern than it does in Britain and America, for example. There is, indeed, more cultural interplay between Britain and the United States than there is between the two German states.

6 In the new, as yet incomplete, *Duden* dictionary (*Das grosse Wörterbuch*, 1976) the criteria used to decide whether words are part of the standard language are discussed at length. This dictionary draws heavily on non-literary sources. Jäger ('Zum Problem', 1971: 163 *passim*) concedes that the *Duden* editors are making more use of non-classical literary texts but claims that the usage of the majority of the population should be established as the norm; Jäger ('Zum Problem', 1971: 165): 'Die kodifizierte Norm richtet sich nach Texten, die sich nach der kodifizierten Norm richten: Im biologischen Bereich nennt man so etwas Inzucht. Dass die Sprache nicht schon längst erstarrt ist, liegt wohl daran, dass den Normern manches entgangen ist und dass sich die Sprache zum Teil der Normierung entzogen hat.' Von Polenz ('Sprachnormung, 1964: 76) had suggested a more conservative basis for the norm: 'Die Art von Sprachgebrauch, die für eine fruchtbare Kritik an den traditionellen Normen herangezogen werden darf, ist die Redeweise klar denkender und im öffentlichen Leben geachteter Menschen im freien, ernsthaften Gespräch, ohne den Zwang schriftlicher Vorlagen oder Vorbilder, allein, unter dem Gesetz der Sprechbarkeit und der Verständlichkeit für den Hörer.' Jäger ('Zum Problem', 1971: 164) rejects this proposal as élitist.

7 Ammon (*Dialekt*, [2]1973: 103–8) gives details of a survey in which people of all ages and from all socio-economic groups were asked to assess their own use of the standard and regional dialects. Over 42 per cent of the highest socio-economic group and 37 per cent of those with a grammar school education replied that they were dialect speakers. A regional accent in Germany, especially in the South, bears little of the stigma that was long attached to most regional accents by English RP-speakers (see also 10.1). See Trudgill (*Accent*, 1975) for an account of the educational implications of accents and dialects in English. A confusing term located somewhere between the two poles *Dialekt* and *Standardsprache* is *Umgangssprache*. Is it to be regarded as the use of a variety, either the standard or a regional standard, for a purpose, *ie* conversation (*Umgang*)? Or is it a variety which is

formally distinct from both the standard and regional dialects? Radtke ('Umgangssprache', 1973: 170) emphasizes the supra-regional function of *Umgangssprache*: 'Wir bezeichnen mit Umgangssprache die gesprochene deutsche Sprache eines jeweiligen synchronen Zeitabschnitts (darin ist also auch die sprach-historische Komponente enthalten), die überregional gesprochen und verstanden wird, nicht fachgebunden (Fachsprache) und verhüllend (Sondersprache) ist, aber durchaus landschaftliche Züge (etwa in den Intonationsverhältnissen) aufweisen kann.' Bichel ('Umgangssprache', 1973: 275) also allows for a definition of *Umgangssprache* as a formally distinct variety: 'Primär bezeichnet "Umgangs-sprache" eine ANWENDUNGSART einer Sprache, nämlich Sprachverwendung im Wechsel mit dem gegenwärtigen anderen: d.h. Umgangssprache bezeichnet die sprachliche Funktion des Gesprächs. In zweiter Linie wird mit "Umgangs-sprache" eine Sprach*form* bezeichnet, die schwerpunktmässig im Umgange, d.h. im Gespräch, in mündlicher Kommunikation möglich ist.'

8 We must not forget that the form of an utterance is also largely determined by the subject-matter. A discussion of problems in electronics or physics, indeed of soccer refereeing, would be impossible without the use of technical terms. The 'languages' of physics, refereeing or hairdressing (to give only a few examples) are then *Fachsprachen*, which in some ways – lexis and syntax – deviate from the common core, the *Gemeinsprache*.

9 Ammon (*Dialekt*, [2]1973: 37–72) like many left-wing sociolinguists rejects the Anglo-American emphasis on roles. He ascribes variations in the use of the standard to class-determined functions of the speaker.

10 Ammon ([2]1973: 103–8) suggests reasons for the disparity in the use of the standard between men and women. He points to the more limited horizon of the housewife and the patriarchal family structure as sources of this disparity. Compare, how-ever, Trudgill's (1974: 92–7) analysis of British English.

11 Trudgill (*Accent*, 1975: 93) uses the following sentences as fictitious examples of the elaborated and the restricted codes respectively:

[1] The blokes what was crossing the road got knocked down by a car.
[2] The gentlemen were crossing the road and a car knocked them down.

While [1] is non-standard English it displays one feature of the elaborated code – a relative clause integrated into the main clause.

12 Dittmar (1973), a critic of the code theory and the Labov school of sociolinguistics, rejects Oevermann's proposals as reactionary. He quotes Marxist sociolinguists who attack all compensatory education as an attempt to exploit the masses by a process of 'embourgeoisement'. We have already mentioned the Marxist rejec-tion of the role hypothesis. For Dittmar, Oevermann and Bernstein are all, how-ever unwittingly, providing pretexts for discriminatory education policies.

13 These proposals were not all accepted by the minister, partly as a result of the bitter controversy that they provoked. It is significant that far-reaching changes proposed in other subjects led to less criticism than in the case of German.

14 The titles of some of the articles written in protest against these proposals reveal the bitterness they provoked: 'Karl Marx im hessischen Schulunterricht', 'Deutschstunde der Ideologen', 'Deutschelend', 'Nieder mit der Hochsprache', 'Bildungskrieg erklärt', 'Richtlinien in Pidgin-Deutsch'. Ermert ('Bibliographie', 1974: 156–60)

Chapter 10

1 Gimson (preface to Jones *EPD*, 1977: x) characterizes the term RECEIVED PRONUNCIATION as used by Daniel Jones as follows: 'The type of speech he had

in mind had for centuries been regarded as a kind of standard, having its base in the educated pronunciation of London and the Home Counties. Its use was not restricted to this region, however, being characteristic by the nineteenth century of upper-class speech throughout the country. Thus, though its base was a regional one, its occurrence was socially determined.' Gimson goes on to illustrate that certain changes in British society – amongst others the use of RP by BBC newsreaders – have led to a situation in which such a concept of RP is 'hardly tenable': 'The result has been a certain dilution of the original concept of RP, a number of local variants formerly excluded by the definition having now to be admitted as of common and acceptable usage. Such an extended scope of usage is difficult to define. A specification in terms of a public boarding-school education is no longer valid, if only because the young are often influenced nowadays by other prestigious accents, eg Cockney or Mid-Atlantic, whatever their educational background. Nor can it be called simply "educated" pronunciation, since not all educated speakers use it nor can all those who use it be safely described as "educated".' A similar view on RP has been taken by Brown (*Listening*, 1977: 1–11). The diminishing importance of RP has also been pointed out by Trudgill (*Accent*, 1975; 56).

2 For the influence of such distinguished scholars as Seume, Sievers and Vietor on the establishment of *Bühnenlautung* see Winkler ('Hochlautung', 1967: 313–14). For Siebs see Winkler (1967: 314–16) and Kohler (*Einführung*, 1977: 30–40), who give an interesting survey of the history of *Bühnen-* and *Hochlautung* in Germany. For attempts made by some GDR linguists (for instance, Krech and Weithase) to take the radio accent as the basis of pronouncing dictionaries and phonetic analysis see Winkler (1967: 316–23) and Kohler (1977: 41–5)

3 Siebs (*Bühnenaussprache*,[11] 1915: 4–5) gives some of the reasons for the introduction of *Bühnenaussprache* as a norm: 'Aber nicht nur für die Bühne, sondern auch für weite Kreise war eine feste Regelung bedeutsam. Wo immer sich die Aussprache über die blosse Mundart erhebt, sei es in der Umgangssprache der Gebildeten, in der Sprache der politischen, lehrenden oder geistlichen Redner oder des deklamatorischen Vortrags, stets geschieht es in der Richtung auf die Sprache der Kunst, der deutschen Bühne. Besonders hat ja die Schule eine über den Mundarten stehende Aussprache zu pflegen und vor allem für den mündlichen Vortrag zu verlangen ... Ein jeder guter Deutsche, dem eine völlige Durchdringung unserer Stämme am Herzen liegt, wird sich über einen solchen weiteren Schritt zur vollkommenen Einigung freuen.'

4 For a comparison of RP and *Bühnendeutsch* see Kohler (1977: 29–33), who points out that RP is acquired mainly by pupils at public schools who are not given actual elocution lessons, whereas actors acquiring *Bühnenaussprache* in Germany are given elocution lessons. Kohler (1977: 32–3) points out a further difference: 'Ausserdem ist RP ein Akzent, der in sämtlichen Sprechsituationen Verwendung findet, der ein sprachlicher Träger für alles ist, was in diesem sozialen Lebensraum kommuniziert wird ... Das Bühnendeutsch hingegen ist auf einen engen Situationsrahmen beschränkt, der die sprachliche Ausprägung bestimmt. Was ausserhalb der Bühne oder einer ihr äquivalenten Sprechsituation gesprochen wird, gilt nicht mehr als Bühnendeutsch.'

5 One weakness of the *Aussprache-Duden* is that – although it lists several examples of regional deviation from *Standardaussprache* – it does not classify these deviations according to the dialect areas of which they are typical. This restricts the usefulness of the pronouncing dictionary for the foreign learner.

6 For a definition of articulatory, acoustic and auditory phonetics see Pilch (*Phonemtheorie I*, 1964: 29–34) and O'Connor (*Phonetics*, 1973).

7 For the distinction between *enggerillt* and *weitgerillt* see Kohler (1977: 63). It is important to note that, as Kohler (1977: 67) points out, some phones of German

are not listed in the table, for example the aspirated plosives [tʰ] or syllabic nasals and liquids such as [ŋ] or [l̩]. For a different account of the sound system of German see Wängler (*Grundriss*, 1960: 63), for a detailed phonetic description of these phones see Wängler (1960: 62–111) and Wängler (*Atlas*, ⁶1976). Compare also Ungeheuer (*Materialien*, 1977: 95–150)

8 For basic terms of phonetics and phonology see v. Essen (*Phonetik*, 1957: 160–7), Wängler (1960: 18–27), Duden (*Aussprachewörterbuch*, 1974: 22–9), Robins (*Linguistics*, 1964: 114–60) and Brown (*Listening*, 1977: 18–37). For the concept of the phoneme see especially Robins (*Linguistics*, 1964: 121–6, and *History*, 1967: 201–24). For the role of Trubetzkoy and other Prague School linguists see Robins (1964: 145–50). For a discussion of various concepts of the phoneme see also Kohler (1977: 91–6), for generative phonology see Kohler (1977: 91–6) and Vennemann ('Affrikaten', 1968)

9 Compare Kohler (1977: 91) for the distribution of the r-allophones. For uvular and tongue-tip trill r see also Trudgill (*Sociolinguistics*, 1974: 160–3)

10 Kohler (1977: 86) makes a further distinction between velar [x] and uvular [χ], [χ] appearing after [a(ː)] and [ɔ], [x] after [uː], [ʊ] and [oː].

11 This objection has been raised by Pilch ('Lautsystem', 1966: 254), who advocates the two-phoneme solution because of the distributional rules. Compare also Pilch (*Phonemtheorie I*, 1964) for conditions of phonematic identity and segmentation.

12 Apart from the [x]–[ç] problem, there is a similar discussion concerning the phonemic status of [h] and [ç], for which only very few and doubtful minimal pairs exist (*hämisch, chemisch*). If a few words such as *Ahorn* and *Uhu* are disregarded, [h] and [ç] could be seen as allophonic variants of one phoneme; [h] appearing in word-initial, [ç] appearing in word-central position. *Cf* Werner (*Beschreibung*, 1973: 82) and Moulton (*Sounds*, 1962)

13 Compare other phonemic descriptions of German; for instance, Ungeheuer (*Materialien*, 1977: 63–78) or Pilch (1964). Kohler (1977: 156), for instance, claims only one phoneme /x/ for [ç], [x] and [χ]. For German vowel phonemes see Kohler (1977: 173–7)

14 For an analysis of phonetic factors beyond the isolated sound see Kohler (1977: 191–230), who discusses problems like intonation, assimilation, elision and weak forms. Compare also Wängler (1960: 111–42). These factors have been taken account of in Brown's analysis of English pronunciation (*Listening*, 1977). A large number of individual studies concerned with these problems have been published in Germany in recent years. Compare, for example, v. Essen (*Grundzüge*, 1964), Heike (*Analyse*, 1969) or the articles published in phonetic journals such as *Phonetica*.

Chapter 11

1 For the possible reason see Dal ('Systemerhaltende Tendenzen', 1962: 74–88)

2 Other means are word order (*Die Mutter schlägt die Tochter* vs *Die Tochter schlägt die Mutter*) and the use of prepositions (*Der Vater sieht aus dem Fenster*). A contrastive survey of the different means of indicating semantic relationships in English and German can be found in Burgschmidt and Götz (*Kontrastive Linguistik*, 1974: 261–5)

3 Possible differences in intonation as well as communicative emphasis have been neglected, see Ch 10.

4 Example after Helbig (*Kasus*, 1973: 53)

5 A different approach was taken by Glinz. After establishing all the possible syntactic environments for a particular case, he tried to find a semantic term comprising all the different uses of a case. However, his terms do not add further information to his syntactic lists, *cf* Glinz (*Innere Form*, 1952)

6 Von Polenz ('Pertinenzdativ', 1969: 170) has shown that the use of the dative in this environment is dependent on several factors, only a limited number of which are considered by Weisgerber and Brinkmann.

7 'With the accusative the other "participant" is named, whose existence or manner of being is determined by the grammatical subject. With the dative the person is named to whom the verbal communication is directed.'

8 For the nominative see Brinkmann (*Deutsche Sprache*, ²1971: 61–4), for the genitive (68–84)

9 See especially Helbig (*Kasus*, 1973: 159–63)

10 For example, the meaning of a sentence does not necessarily change if the case required by a verb changes in the course of time: *cf* 'Wer ruft mir?' (*Faust* I, first scene) and *Wer ruft mich?* or *Wer ruft nach mir?* today. H. Paul was already a supporter of the asemantic view of the cases, see Engelen (*Untersuchungen I*, 1975: 214)

11 For the discussion of participant roles in a sentence see Halliday ('Language structure', 1970: 146–50)

12 Fillmore (*Case*, 1968: 33), also in Quirk *et al* (*Grammar*, 1972: 357). (The bracketed explanations have been added by HHD.)

13 See Helbig (*Kasus*, 1973: 227–30), who also points out the immense difficulty of attempting this. It requires no less than a classification of the phenomena of reality and their interrelationships.

14 See Vater ('Model', 1973) and Baumgärtner ('Konstituenz', 1970). Abraham ('Tiefenstrukturkasus', 1972) seems to be the only German linguist who has attempted to apply Fillmore's ideas to the description of German syntax.

15 See Engelen's discussion of the different functions of the dative (*Untersuchungen I*, 1975: 116–23). Unfortunately, he does not hint at a possible subdivision of the dative object, which thus retains its traditional function as a 'dust bin' for all uses which are not as easily explicable as the *dativus ethicus*. It must be admitted, however, that this problem is not the objective of Engelen's work.

Chapter 12

1 Verbs are marked for tense when referring to the past, even though an adverbial makes the time relation clear; for example, *Angelika schrieb den Brief* GESTERN.

2 The fact that tense alone is not sufficient to express time has been pointed out by Weinrich (*Tempus*, 1964: 16). See also Kluge ('Diskussion', 1969: 61)

3 Burgschmidt and Götz (*Kontrastive Linguistik*, 1974: 250) distinguish between the following *Aktionsarten* (*modes of action*): DURATION: *schlafen, dauern*; ITERATIVITÄT: *hüpfen, hämmern*; PUNKTUALITÄT: *platzen*; TERMINALITÄT: ANFANG: *starten*, ENDE: *erreichen, aufhören*. These time references belong to the CORE OF THE PROPOSITION, whereas nouns, temporal prepositions and conjunctions as well as adverbials are COMPLEMENTS OF THE P-CORE.

4 Wunderlich (*Tempus*, 1970: 25) makes a distinction between PUBLIC TIME (*öffentliche Zeit*) and PERSONAL TIME (*personale Zeit*). Relatively vague time indicators like *neulich* or *bald* belong to PERSONAL TIME, whereas if the speaker says something like *Ich komme am Montag*, he refers to public time. Dittmann (*Sprechhandlungstheorie*, 1976: 142–6) points out that this distinction is insufficient as time relations can be made according to calendar time, so that the time reference is independent of the time of speaking, as in *Am Montag, dem 4. 12. 1973* as opposed to *am Montag voriger Woche*.

5 For this approach see Zimmermann (*Untersuchungen*, 1968), who sets up a tense table for Middle English, in which one tense corresponds to each relation of

speaker standpoint and DSU-reference. Burgschmidt and Götz (*Kontrastive Linguistik*, 1974) do not consider the Future tense to be the expression of illocutionary acts or mood.

6 Dittmann (*Sprechhandlungstheorie*, 1976: 233*f*) points out that Future tends to be used in situations which are more formal than those in which Present tense would be used for the expression of future time. Dittmann's work is a very detailed treatment of the expression of future time in German, based on speech act philosophy, though not explicitly a work within the framework of pragmalinguistics.

7 Burgschmidt and Götz (*Kontrastive Linguistik*, 1974: 254) mention that Southern German dialects express V/Z in indirect speech by a Past Subjunctive: *Er hat g'sagt, du käm(e)st.*

8 Note that in English the Present Perfect tense can only co-occur with adverbials of time related to the present. Thus a sentence such as **I have bought a bike yesterday* is unacceptable. For the use of these tenses in English see Palmer (*Verb*, 1974: 30–80) and Leech (*Verb*, 1971: 30–65)

9 Most linguists discussing the question set up a similar opposition between Preterite and Perfect as in English, see, for instance, Erben (*Grammatik*, 1968: 57–8) or W. Schmidt (*Grundfragen*, ⁴1973: 224–5); compare, however, Admoni (*Sprachbau* ³1970: 185). Trier ('Unsicherheiten', 1965: 13) writes: 'Die Erzählvergangenheit, das Imperfekt, löst von der Gegenwart des Redenden und Hörenden ab. Die Vorgegenwart, das Perfekt, bindet an die Gegenwart.' Glinz (*Grammatik I*, 1970: 151) characterizes actions described in the Preterite as '*vergangen gesehen, jetzt nur im Rückblick*, nur *erinnert*', whereas actions described in the Perfect are seen as '*durchgeführt, ... abgeschlossen*'. See also Glinz ('Tempussystem', 1969: 55). *Duden* (*Grammatik*, ³1973: 84) considers an action in the Preterite to be 'vom Standpunkt des Sprechers entrückt'. Weinrich (*Tempus*, 1964) makes a distinction between *besprochene Welt* (Perfect) and *erzählte Welt* (Preterite). However, Schipporeit (*Tenses*, 1971: 66–7) draws attention to the fact that time adverbials like *jetzt* or *nun* are not restricted to the *besprochene Welt*. Gelhaus ('Tempussystem', 1969: 14) describes actions in the Perfect as 'im Zeitpunkt des Sprechens nicht abgeschlossenes Verfügen über abgeschlossenes Tun'.

10 Wunderlich (*Tempus*, 1970: 145) uses the term *transformatives Verb* to refer to what has traditionally been called *perfektives Verb*. Hauser-Suida and Hoppe-Beugel (*Vergangenheitstempora*, 1972: 55) write: '... [Es] kennzeichnen bestimmte "perfektiv realisierte" Verben (= Verben mit Realisation einer Anfangs- oder Endpunktmarkierung im Kontext) im Perfekt einen "Zustand der Vollendung", der als "Ergebnis für den Zeitpunkt des Sprechens" wirksam ist; in unseren Beispielen handelt es sich u.a. um "perfektiv realisierte Verben", wie finden, werden, geschehen, sterben, erblühen, verändern, vergessen, ausersehen.' They then point out that in these cases the Perfect can usually be substituted by the Present tense (*Zustandspassiv oder präsentische Fügungen*), but not by the Past tense. '"Das ist besonders nett," sagte ich, "dass du's vergessen hast". **...* sagte ich, "dass du's vergassest",' but: '... sagte ich, "dass es vergessen ist."'

11 *schon* can collocate with a Preterite with stative verbs and a temporal clause (according to Wunderlich, *Tempus*, 1970: 148) *Er besass schon eine Glatze, als ich ihn kennenlernte.* With *seit* there is the additional restriction that it cannot co-occur with momentary verbs (see *Tempus*, 1970: 148)

12 Schipporeit (*Tenses*, 1971: 29) writes: 'If used together with a UTN [up-to-now] phrase, the present tense of German durative and iterative verbs always refers to a situation which started in the past and continues into the moment of speaking.' *Wir wohnen in Nürnberg*, etc.

13 See, however, the analysis of Hauser-Suida and Hoppe-Beugel (1972: 57), which is based on the corpus of the *Institut für deutsche Sprache*, who point out that with 'durativ realisierten verba dicendi and sentiendi' both Preterite and Perfect

can be used: 'Wissen Sie, was er da zu mir gesagt hat?' and 'Ich weiss nicht genau, wie Sie ihn ermordeten.' It is striking, however, that all their examples for the Preterite use in this case, contain a negative.

14 The quantitative analysis of Hauser-Suida and Hoppe-Beugel (1972: 79–90) has shown that most uses of Perfect are to be found in dialogue, but that even in dialogue there is equal usage of Preterite and Perfect. It is important to note, however, that the corpus they have used for dialogue analysis consists of a representative selection of contemporary German literature, but no recordings of spoken language. For the corpus, see Hauser-Suida and Hoppe-Beugel (1972: 25–30)

15 Wunderlich (*Tempus*, 1970: 148) points out that in sentences containing a main verb in the Perfect this verb is usually in final position, whereas it occupies the second position in the sentence when it is in the Preterite.

16 Wunderlich (*Tempus*, 1970: 149) claims that these forms are quite common in the spoken language, but that often the particle is replaced by an infinitive: *Angelika hat gestern arbeiten müssen.*

17 Hauser-Suida and Hoppe-Beugel (*Vergangenheitstempora*, 1972: 120–4) point out that the cluster velar + dental + dental is difficult to articulate and therefore will be avoided. Hauser-Suida and Hoppe-Beugel (1972: 63–79) also draw attention to the fact that the meaning of a lexeme may determine the choice of tenses and give a list of examples where either only Preterite or Perfect is possible: *Beim Verhör bewies der Angeklagte, dass er nicht auf den Mund gefallen ist/*dass er nicht auf den Mund fiel* or *Der Wind heulte/*hat geheult. Um Bernies Lippen spielte ein Lächeln/*hat ein Lächeln gespielt.* These restrictions apply only if the lexeme is used with a special, in most cases, an idiomatic meaning and therefore are not so much central issues of a discussion of the tense system, but rather of interest for the study of idiomatics. For problems of articulation see also Glinz (1970: 153)

18 This has also been realized by linguists who do not belong to the pragmalinguistic school. Glinz (*Grammatik I*, 1970: 154) takes the distinction of Preterite and Perfect in German, in which 'besonders viele verschiedenartige Faktoren zusammenwirken' as an example for the fact that the operational approach of structuralism does not provide satisfactory results in all areas of investigation.

Chapter 13

1 *Cf* Admoni's (*Sprachbau*, ³1970: 192) characterization of the function of the subjunctive: 'Der Konjunktiv bezeichnet ... die Einschätzung des Vorgangs als eines nur potentialen oder nur irrealen, dessen Existenz also mehr oder weniger unbestimmt ist.'

2 The content of the proposition is only one of the most prominent reasons why a sentence is unreal, another important one is the temporal location of an event: if something failed to exist or take place in the past, it is unreal in that the event cannot be corrected. [1b] *Wenn das Kapitel fertig gewesen wäre, hätte ich mich gefreut.* There is no possibility of changing the past.

3 In these grammars the traditional terms KONJUNKTIV PRÄSENS and KONJUNKTIV PRÄTERITUM are used as labels for formal categories which can have different functions. Sometimes this treatment is combined with a vague reference to the old concept, see note 1.

4 Flämig (*Konjunktiv*, 1959) adopts a middle position, stating two basic meanings for each KI and KII. The two meanings are distinguished by the presence or absence of a volitional component (in 13.1 present in [3] and [6])

5 'Als Modus der Realisierung überschreitet der Konjunktiv I den gegebenen Hori-

zont. Er wendet sich an einen Dritten, der nicht als Partner anwesend ist.' (Brinkmann, *Deutsche Sprache*, ²1971: 372)

6 'Konjunktiv I überschreitet den gegebenen Horizont wesentlich dadurch, dass ein Dritter eingeführt wird, der in der Situation nicht anwesend ist. Konjunktiv II geht darüber hinaus. Er formuliert, was ausserhalb des gegebenen Horizontes liegt.' (Brinkmann, *Deutsche Sprache*, ²1971: 373.) Similarly, Graf (*Konjunktiv*, 1977: 149): subjunctive designates 'andere Welt'.

7 'Dabei sollte man Unterscheidungen wie "real", "potential", "irreal" für unsere Gegenwartssprache vermeiden; sie sind ihr nicht angemessen.' (Brinkmann, *Deutsche Sprache*, ²1971: 373)

8 Unlike Brinkmann Jäger (*Konjunktiv*, 1971: 205) explains 'unreal' wishes as abbreviated conditional sentences.

9 Jäger's basis was the Mannheim Corpus – fictional and non-fictional books, newspapers and magazines – compiled for the project *Grundstrukturen der deutschen Sprache* by the *Institut für deutsche Sprache*, Mannheim. Other works of this project deal with the passive, the future tense, the past time tenses (see Ch 12, note 13), the sentence patterns (see 4.2.5) and other topics. In accordance with the prominent position of the verb in dependency grammar the investigation of the verbal categories has been given preference over other linguistic phenomena. A second empirical study (Graf, *Konjunktiv*, 1977) based on a corpus of South West German (including Swiss and Austrian dialects) confirms, on the whole, Jäger's results while giving a more detailed account of how factors such as sex, age-group, social class and dialect area are reflected in the use of subjunctive.

   In his theoretical introduction Graf points out that in the past the category mood (*Modus*, ie inflexional property of the verb) has been confused with the sentence type (declarative, interrogative, imperative). He regards the latter as a pragmatic phenomenon, belonging to the level of utterance, the former, however, as belonging to the sentence level of a grammar. For the distinction between sentence type, mood, modality, see Ch 14.

10 Jäger (*Konjunktiv*, 1971: 31–74) regards the shift of deictic pronouns and adverbs as not constitutive of indirect speech, see his detailed discussion of the definition of indirect speech.

11 Jäger has two types of double-determined indirect speech: besides the type illustrated in our sentence [14], sentences such as *Ob er wolle?* can be found (conjunction and KI). This type can be ignored for our purposes, because of its extremely low frequency (31 out of 2,775 instances of indirect speech) (*Konjunktiv*, 1971: 76, 85, 87)

12 For the exact figures, see Jäger (1971: 75–90)

13 Jäger reports that a similar sentence was not accepted as correct by all informants (*Konjunktiv*, 1971: 289, note 80). We found considerable insecurity, but most informants accepted sentence [13*b*]. For the use of deictic adverbials, see Kaufmann (*Indirekte Rede*, 1976: 67*ff*)

14 This interpretation is corroborated by the fact that the use of KI is impossible with 1st person sing pres (unless used as historical present, with future meaning, or modified by modal verbs or negation). *Ich sage, er komme.* is impossible: one cannot assign distance to one's own utterance while making it. (Jäger, *Konjunktiv*, 1971: 101*ff*)

15 Pluperfect (relation: 'before then') can only be expressed lexically. The sentences also show that there is no sequence of tenses in modern German, as some books suggest. There is, however, an affinity between certain lexical representations of the reporting clause and the tense of the reported clause. After verbal expressions such as *ankündigen, drohen, anerbieten, versprechen, voraussagen, vorhersehen* future subjunctive is especially frequent: *Er drohte, er werde* ... (Kaufmann, *Indirekte Rede*, 1976: 14)

204 NOTES TO CHAPTERS THIRTEEN AND FOURTEEN

16 The tense of the reporting clause has also been considered a factor affecting the choice of KI or KII (see also note 13, criticism by Jäger, *Konjunktiv*, 1971: 97), the context (Brinkmann, *Deutsche Sprache*, ²1971: 379), see also Helbig and Buscha (*Grammatik*, 1974): 'Regeln für die Wahl zwischen Konjunktiv Präs. und Prät. einerseits und Konjunktiv Perf. und Plusq. andererseits lassen sich in allgemeingültiger Form nicht geben. (*p* 71)

17 Jäger mentions the possible ambiguity of such sentences as (*a*) *Sie sagten, sie hätten die Feinde gesehen, wenn diese ihr Lagerfeuer angezündet hätten*. This sentence can have two representations in direct speech: (*c*) *Wir haben die Feinde gesehen, wenn diese ihr Lagerfeuer angezündet haben*. and (*b*) *Wir hätten die Feinde gesehen, wenn diese ihr Lagerfeuer angezündet hätten*. If sentence (*a*) is understood as an equivalent of (*b*), the implication 'not given' is taken over from the original sentence; if understood as equivalent of (*c*), the speaker of the reported sentence, according to Jäger (*Konjunktiv*, 1971: 163–5), doubts the truth of the original utterance.

18 After a period of self-observation the author of this chapter (HMD) has noticed that he himself is not totally consistent in his use of KI and KII.

19 Quoted after Kaufmann (*Indirekte Rede*, 1976: 56)

20 *Cf* Kaufmann (*Indirekte Rede*, 1976: 33)

21 Jäger (*Konjunktiv*, 1971: 118–19, 154–5)

22 Of course, this third person introduced could be the hearer or the speaker at a different time: *Ich sagte, ich könne kommen. Du hast doch gesagt, du kämest*.

23 In explaining the low frequency of the first and second person Jäger has recourse to the different speech situation: instances of the second person would presuppose a dialogue (direct speech!)

24 Unfortunately, investigations of reported speech in oral use are not yet available.

25 75.5 per cent of all unambiguous cases of KI are modal verb forms (Jäger, *Konjunktiv*, 1971: 114)

26 There are some additional remarks to be made. In some groups of verbs, some or all KII forms coincide with the respective preterite indicative forms (*ich/er liebte–liebte*, etc); some strong verbs have two possible KII forms(*ich empfähle – ich empföhle*). In these cases in oral speech *würde* + infinitive would be used, in writing indicative forms would be most likely.

Chapter 14

1 See Admoni (*Sprachbau*, ³1970: 165–6) for more on the distinction between objective and subjective use of modal verbs. Fourquet ('Gebrauch', 1970: 154) uses this ambiguous sentence to illustrate the distinction: *Diese Studenten müssen sich längere Zeit in Deutschland aufgehalten haben*. In one reading the modal verb is used objectively and we can translate the sentence as: 'These students must have spent a long time in Germany (if they want to become good teachers of the language).' The other reading will give us: 'These students must have spent a long time in Germany (as their spoken German is excellent).' For the distinction between epistemic modality and factivity see Lyons (*Semantics II*, 1977: 793–809)

2 Admoni's *Modalwörter* (referred to as modal adverbials in the text) do not correspond to the much larger and heterogeneous class *Modaladverbien* proposed in the *Duden* (*Grammatik*, ³1973: 307–10). This latter class comprises not only adverbs of judgement and attitude (*Beurteilung, Einschätzung*) but also adverbs of quality, quantity, intensity, etc. The classification is a syntactic one based on Engel ('Regeln', 1970) and as a result the syntactic classes are semantically heterogeneous. For a more successful attempt to re-classify English adverbials see Quirk *et al* (*Grammar*, 1972: 147–532)

3 The subjunctive mood is only marginally relevant to a discussion of modality
although subjunctive forms of the modal verbs are often used, see for example:
Es könnte morgen regnen. Bettina dürfte die beste Skifahrerin in ihrer Klasse sein.
As we saw in Ch 5 there is no one-to-one fit between function and form. Indicative,
imperative and subjunctive forms can be used to realize the same illocutionary
acts; we find for example *Öffne das Fenster, Das Fenster ist offen* and *Ist das Fenster
offen* used to perform the speech act 'ordering'. We have not given a precise definition of modality since linguists differ in their assessment of modality. Admoni
(*Sprachbau*, [3]1970: 165) uses the term to refer to the verbal mood categories (*Aus-
sageweisen*) as well as for modal verbs and modal words. Weinrich (*Tempus*, 1964:
110) rejects mood as a meaningless term, whereas Kolde ('Funktion', 1970)
attempts to redefine the terms modal, mood and modality.

4 Gerstenkorn (*'Modal'-System*, 1976) tries to avoid the modality definition
dilemma by defining all surface modifications of a basic pre-syntactic proposition – MAT – from deep structure performatives. He describes his model (1976: 71)
as an attempt to account for all the basic speech acts: 'Mein Modell versucht
... Bausteine von illokutiven Akten zu erarbeiten, Illokutionstypen festzustellen'
(1976: 71). See also Gerstenkorn (1976: 306–7)

5 Stickel examines *nicht, nichts, nie, niemals, niemand, nirgends, nirgendwo, kein.*
Only the pairs *nirgends/nirgendwo* and *nie/niemals* are completely interchangeable
according to him (*Untersuchungen*, 1970: 22). Helbig ('Negationswörter', 1970:
393–7) comes to rather different conclusions and criticizes Stickel's failure to
recognize that the valencies and semantic properties of verbs (their secondary
valencies) can affect the positions which a negative word can occupy. So, in the
syntactic environment *Er hat _____ gegessen*, both *nicht* and *nichts* can be inserted. Stickel (1970: 15) chooses his sentences carelessly and concludes that *nicht*
and *nichts* are never syntactically interchangeable. See also Gerstenkorn (*'Modal'-
System*, 1976: 230–42) for a discussion of both Helbig and Stickel's syntactic
classes.

6 Stickel (1970: 36–9) bases this claim on a syntactic argument as well as on the
obvious semantic similarities. In coordinate structures comprising two negative
clauses which are linked by the coordinating conjunction *und ... auch*, the second
coordinated clause can, according to Stickel, always be reduced to a non-finite
clause containing *auch nicht*. If we take these two complex sentences *Ute fährt
nicht gern Schlitten und Bettina fährt auch ungern Schlitten*, and *Der Linguist will
keinen Kuchen essen und seine Freundin will auch keinen*, both can be reduced,
giving us *Ute fährt nicht gern Schlitten und Bettina auch nicht* and *Der Linguist
will keinen Kuchen und seine Freundin auch nicht*. It is interesting to note that if
we had, instead of *nicht gern, ungern* in the first sentence, we should find *Bettina
auch*, not *Bettina auch nicht* in the reduced non-finite clause.

7 Stickel derives this insight from Klima ('Negation', 1964). Bierwisch (*Grammatik*,
1963: 65) has excluded double negatives of the kind *Ich bin nicht nirgends gewesen*
on the basis of context-sensitive rules; Stickel (*Untersuchungen*, 1970: 67–71) finds
Klima's solution better for two reasons. It both explains why double negatives
are not permissible and also overcomes the need to distinguish between constituent
and sentence negation. Stickel (1970: 72–96) discusses the restrictions on the
attachment of NEG to indefinites and also attempts to account for such anomalies
as *ich habe nicht einen Studenten gesehen*. Negation in English has been investigated in some detail by Quirk *et al* (*Grammar*, 1972: 374–84). There are considerable and complex differences between predicate negation in English and German.
Of particular interest to the contrastive linguist are the use of synthetic *He's no
linguist, I've no small change*, and analytical negation *He's not a linguist, I haven't
any small change* and the distribution of the non-assertive/negative words *either,
any*.

8 Admoni (*Sprachbau*, [3]1970: 243): 'Nicht jeder Satz, der eine Negation enthält, ist aber ein negativer (negierender) Satz. Die Negation kann ja auch zu den syntaktischen Beziehungen gehören, die nicht die prädikative Hauptlinie des Satzes bilden ... Es entsteht bei der Negierung eines Satzgliedes überhaupt eine semantische Projektion in der Richtung auf einen positiven analogen Begriff ...' The *Duden* (*Grammatik*, [3]1973: 596) adopts the same position 'Sondernegationen (contituent negation) liegen immer vor, wenn eine Wendung mit *sondern* anschliesst.' The Duden example of a sentence with clause negatives *Ich komme nicht nach Hause* does not present a convincing argument in favour of the two kinds of negation.

9 Stickel (' "Ja" und "Nein" ', 1972, and 'Aspekte', 1975) suggests how the investigation of negation may leave the sentence and draw upon pragmalinguistic insights. The latter article especially provides a considered critique of Stickel's earlier syntactic approach.

Chapter 15

1 It must not be forgotten, however, that the use of basic sentences in a linguistic theory need not necessitate their use in foreign language teaching. In the early phase of transformational grammar, for instance, kernel sentences were introduced, on which the whole generative apparatus was based. Here, quite clearly, basic sentences serve the elaboration of a particular theory of grammar and do not in themselves fulfil a descriptive function. For the role of basic sentences in linguistics, compare also Robins (*Linguistics*, 1964: 222–4)

2 The foremost example of a purely structural analysis is provided by Glinz (*Satz*, [3]1963: 160–8). For Glinz see also Ch 2, note 27.

3 Brinkmann's classification on the level of content has been outlined in Ch 2. It has been taken over – with slight modifications – by W. Schmidt (*Grundfragen*, 1965: 291–302) in his model of functional grammar. For Brinkmann's subclassifications, see Brinkmann (*Deutsche Sprache*, 1971: 519–606)

4 Erben's approach has been referred to in Ch 4. For another model of sentence patterns see Schulz und Griesbach (*Grammatik*, [10]1976: 371–88).

5 Engel ('Satzanalyse', 1970) came to the elaboration of these sentence patterns from the discussion of pedagogic problems in foreign language teaching. See also Engel ('Satzbaupläne', 1970). See Engel ('Satzanalyse', 1970) for the pedagogic possibilities in general. For a more detailed account of Engel's syntactic analysis, see Engel (*Syntax*, 1977), where he uses results of pragma- and text linguistics.

6 Engelen (*Untersuchungen*, 1975: 90) uses the terms *Gleichgrösse* and *Artergänzung*, whereas Engel talks of *Numerabile* and *Comparabile als Ergänzung* ('Satzbaupläne', 1970: 374–5). In Engel (*Syntax*, 1977: 173–4) 7 and 8 are called *Subsumptivergänzung* and *Qualitativergänzung* respectively. For the syntactic classification of *Ergänzungen* see Engel (1977: 158–79).

7 See Ch 4, note 26 for 9.

8 For the *Abstrichmethode* see *Duden* (*Grammatik*, 1959: 434–6). He characterizes this principle in the following way: 'Bei der Frage nach den notwendigen Gliedern in einem Satze darf man nicht nur von den Gliedern ausgehen, die für den grammatischen Bestand unbedingt erforderlich sind, weil man dann beim "Kernsatz" der älteren Grammatik endet. Also nicht:

Der Bauer pflügt den Acker.   Der Vater schreibt an den Sohn.
Der Bauer pflügt.   Der Vater schreibt.

Da jede Benutzung unter einer bestimmten Sehweise erfolgt, gilt es vielmehr, diejenigen Glieder zu ermitteln, die diese Sehweise begründen. Das sind in den obigen

Beispielsätzen zweifellos auch die Glieder "den Acker" und "an den Sohn". Die so verbleibenden Glieder das S a t z g e r ü s t, das mit der betreffenden Grundform identisch ist.' Compare also Weisgerber (*Inhaltbezogene Grammatik*, 1953: 251–8)

9 'Die Grundformen sind Ganzheiten und deshalb nicht weiter reduzierbar. Sie sind dem Sprechenden als geschlossene Einheiten für die Bildung von Sätzen muttersprachlich vorgegeben ... Mit der Wahl einer solchen Ganzheit hat der Sprechende bereits über die Sehweise der Setzung entschieden.' *Duden* (*Grammatik*, 1959: 465)

10 For a definition of the *Handlungssatz* (A) see *Duden* (*Grammatik*, 1959: 875): '*Sätze mit einer Akkusativergänzung*, die ins *Passiv* gewendet werden können ..., ermöglichen es dem Sprechenden, das tätige Verhalten eines Etwas in der Welt, d.h. Handlungen sprachlich zu bewältigen. Man nennt diese Sätze deshalb von ihrer inhaltlichen Leistung her Handlungssätze.' However, some *Handlungssätze* cannot be passivized, see *Duden* (*Grammatik*, 1959: 875). Note that a sentence containing an accusative object need not necessarily be a *Handlungssatz*: Wir besitzen *ein Haus*. See *Duden* (*Grammatik*, 1959: 490)

11 Admoni (*Sprachbau*, [3]1970: 233–4) refers to Glinz in this context.

12 Compare Engelen (*Untersuchungen I*, 1975: 216)

13 Admoni (*Sprachbau*, [3]1970: 230) characterizes the *logisch-grammatischen Satztypen* in the following way: 'Nicht nur die lexikale Semantik und der verallgemeinerte Bedeutungsgehalt der einzelnen Wörter, Wortformen und Wortarten spiegeln also die konkrete Welt, die reale Wirklichkeit wider, sondern auch der grammatische Bau des Satzes als einer geschlossenen Einheit, die Form des Subjekts und die des Prädikats in ihren Wechselbeziehungen. Deswegen nennen wir die entsprechenden Satztypen, die also die im menschlichen Bewusstsein fixierten Sachverhalte der objektiven Welt abbilden, die logisch-grammatischen Typen des Satzes.'

14 One might find that both [5] and [6] could be included under Admoni's pattern II. The great advantage over the *Duden* would then be that both [5] and [6] – although structurally different – belong to the same pattern and show the same (or similar) participant roles.

15 This – and not an a priori neglect of semantics – have led dependency grammarians to establish verb valency on purely formal criteria. See, for instance, Helbig ('Theorie', 1971: 57): 'Was Grebe seinen Grundformen an Inhalt zuschreibt, ist entweder bereits implizit in der Strukturbeschreibung der Grundformen enthalten, oder es ist sachlich nicht zutreffend. So ist durchaus nicht jeder Satz mit Subjekt, Prädikat und Gleichsetzungsnominativ ein "Gleichsetzungssatz" (oftmals handelt es sich ... um eine Klassifikation oder Subsumtion im logischen Sinne; vgl. etwa die Sätze *Paris ist die Hauptstadt Frankreichs* und *Paris ist eine grosse Stadt*); so drückt durchaus nicht jeder Satz mit Subjekt, Prädikat und Akkusativobjekt eine "Handlung" aus (vgl. etwa: *Er bekommt den Brief; er erleidet die Krankheit*). Es gibt keine geradlinige Zuordnung von Grundformen und Inhalten.' Helbig ('Theorie', 1971: 60) also criticizes Admoni: 'Er hält an der "Sachbezogenheit" der sprachlichen Erscheinungen fest und nimmt damit eine unmittelbarere Parallelität der Strukturen an, als sie tatsächlich existiert.'

16 Admoni ('Satzmodelle', 1974: 40): '... in Wirklichkeit ist im Fremdsprachenunterricht die Ausschaltung der semantischen Komponente durchaus unzweckmässig.' Admoni (1974: 39) does not really claim a one-to-one correspondence of form and content/real world: (Es) '... gehört die Asymmetrie zwischen der Form und dem Gehalt gerade zu den wesentlichen Merkmalen der grammatischen Erscheinungen ... Die längst von den Sprachforschern festgestellte Tatsache, dass der Bedeutungsgehalt der LGST (logisch-grammatischen Satztypen) in seiner Konkretheit oft nicht mit Hilfe einer Formel abgetan sein kann, ist kein Einwand

gegen die Notwendigkeit und Möglichkeit, diesen Bedeutungsgehalt zu erforschen...'.

17 Metaphorical use, however, will have to be allowed: *Der Linguist zieht die Theorie durch den Kakao*. (06)

18 For this and for the pedagogical implications of dependency grammar, see also the work of Engelen. In valency dictionaries there should also be a place for the listing of the individual syntactic restrictions on certain verbs, passivization, for example. The new *Duden* (*Grammatik*,[3] 1973: 478–528) establishes structural patterns and has lists of verbs fitting into them.

19 This has been stressed by all linguists, see *Duden* (*Grammatik*, 1959: 465) or Engel ('Satzbaupläne', 1970: 380–1, or 'Satzanalyse', 1970: 105, 118–22). In Admoni's model, sentence patterns are just one of seven aspects of sentence analysis, compare Ch 3, note 42.

Chapter 16

1 The stress patterns given represent our estimate of what could be one possible accentuation of sentences [1]*b*, [5]*b* and [6]. The notation follows that used by Kiparsky ('Akzent', 1966) and Bierwisch ('Intonation', 1966). Attention must be drawn to the fact that the notation is meant to indicate differences in stress (*ie* the 'force exerted in the articulation...', Robins, *Linguistics*, 1964), not in pitch, although these phenomena are closely linked (see Bierwisch, 1966: 100 f). In what follows we shall indicate stress only in so far as this is necessary for our discussion.

2 It is not always easy to decide whether sentences such as [8] follow the emphatic stress pattern or simply have their normal intonation centre (= information centre, rheme, see below) in initial position. For the discussion of the difficulties in distinguishing between normal and emphatic stress, see Fuchs ('Akzent', 1976: 293–312)

3 This word order can also be found in conditional clauses (*Hat er das Geld gebracht, so bin ich zufrieden.*) or in short answers (*Hast du dem Boss das Geld gebracht? – Hab' ich.*; the actants are usually in pronominalized form or are omitted altogether)

4 The German terms are *Vorfeld, Mittelfeld, Nachfeld.* They were introduced by Drach (*Grundgedanken*, [3]1940), the use of the latter two being slightly different, since he counts V_{fin} and accusative object as frame-constituting poles if there is no V_{infin}.

5 Elements a speaker has forgotten when forming the sentence may be added after V_{fin}. For some elements, *eg* obligatory actants (prepositional cases excepted), this seems to be unusual. Even these can, however, occur in the final position, if preceded by a corresponding pronoun within the verb frame (*Ich hab' es ihm schon gegeben, das Geld*). Firbas ('Thoughts', 1959: 58) points out that elements can be more strongly emphasized in final position.

6 Drach suggests that this should not be regarded as an argument against the second position rule. Such elements as *aber, denn*, etc should be regarded as elements linking two sentences and not belonging to either of them. The rule that only one element can precede V_{fin} has been disputed by Betz ('Überprüfung', 1973: 242–67). Judging from the list Beneš gives in 'Besetzung' (1971: 160–1) one can assume that the elements which frequently confine V_{fin} to the third position form a relatively restricted set of items, similar to the one found for the final position.

7 For a historical account of their ideas, see Firbas ('Aspects', 1974), for the Prague School of Linguistics in general see Vachek (*Linguistic School*, 1966)

8 [14] and [16] would be unusual answers to [13] and [15], the most common ones

being probably *das Geld, dem Gangster*. We must hope that our purpose will excuse
our stilted examples.

9 There are sentences in which both sequences are acceptable: *Der Polizist übergab
dem Jungen die Schwester. Der Polizist übergab die Schwester dem Jungen. Der
Polizist übergab der Schwester den Jungen. Der Polizist übergab den Jungen der
Schwester.*

10 According to Daneš ('Intonation', 1960) it can be taken for granted that the centres
of intonation and information coincide, see also Daneš ('Order', 1967)

11 Other definitions distinguish only between theme and rheme. Theme is defined
as 'that which is known or at least obvious in the given situation, and from which
the speaker proceeds' (Mathesius, *Čeština*, 1947: 234 quoted after Firbas, 'Defining the theme', 1964: 268), the first element in a sentence (Boost, *Untersuchungen*,
1955: 26–31), or, in most general terms, 'that about which something is said'
(Beneš, 'Thema-Rhema-Gliederung', 1973: 42). Consequently, rheme is the new
element, the rest of the sentence, 'that which is said about something' (1973: 42).
U. Fries ('Textlinguistik', 1971: 225–31) has collected and discussed the different
definitions of theme and rheme.

12 For the difficulties of finding reliable criteria, see Sgall *et al* (*Topic*, 1973: esp 49–
57). Attempts to determine theme and rheme on the basis of testable criteria have
also been made outside the Prague School tradition, for example in Chomsky
('Deep Structure', 1972: esp 89–103), Posner (*Theorie*, 1972)

13 This did not escape Boost's attention. He later (*Untersuchungen*, 1955: 54) revised
this determination such as to include sentences of the [14*b*] type. The [24*b*] type
remains excluded.

14 There seems to be good sense in this: in $E_3\acute{E}_1$, E_1 is already in the most
prominent position possible from the point of view of both word order and stress,
whereas in $\acute{E}_3E_1$, E_3 can still improve from the point of view of word order,
see Lenerz (*Abfolge*, 1977: 47)

15 This statement is also valid with respect to quantifiers, for example *zwei, viele,
einige*. For word order, a further subclassification of indefinite determiners into
specified, indefinite, generic uses is irrelevant, see Lenerz (1977: 55)

16 This rule has long been known as 'das Gesetz der wachsenden Glieder' (Behaghel,
'Beziehungen', 1909)

17 The idea that German word order is governed by more than one principle can
also be found in Vennemann ('Wortstellungsveränderung', 1974: 265–314), who
distinguishes two types of languages. In the first type the verb is modified by preceding, in the second one by succeeding, elements (structures XV and VX respectively). German is on the way from the XV to the VX type. Thus, the existence
of not only various, but even contradictory principles has to be assumed for German word order.

18 Engel's own suggestion for the sequence E_3E_1 is ... $E1_1$–$E1_3$–$E2_3$–$E2_1$–...–$E3_3$–
... –$E3_1$,
      E1 being unstressed personal pronouns and *man*,
      E2 being stressed personal pronouns and noun phrases with definite article
or demonstrative pronoun, and
      E3 being noun phrases with indefinite article.
As is clear, Engel's model falls short of permitting the possible sequence $E3_2E2_1$
(see above). Nevertheless Engel's work (*Syntax*, 1977, and 'Regeln', 1970) gives
the most detailed account of word order available, and is indispensable for purposes of reference.

19 Exceptions are – according to Engel (1977: 211–12) – $E1_1$, $E1_3$ and circonstants
such as *aber* (in *Der Mann ist aber gross.*), *eben* etc.

20 Halliday ('Language Structure', 1970: 164) substitutes for the principle of CD
two separate, though related distinctions, that between *theme* (= basis) and *rheme*

(the rest of the sentence), and that between *given* and *new* elements. Both pairs belong to the textual function of language.

21 The relative freedom of thematic elements has also been observed by Zemb (*Satz*, 1972), who regards the theme-rheme structure as the reflection of the logical structure of the sentence; theme and rheme are linked by 'modalizators' *ja, nicht, wohl*.

22 Theme-rheme structure has been applied to the study of texts: see Dressler, 'Satz-perspektive' (1974: 87–105), Daneš ('Sentence Persepctive', 1974: 106–28) and Beneš ('Thema-Rhema-Gliederung', 1973), who maintains that theme-rheme structure is not only an inner-sentential, but also a textual, phenomenon, some sentences being able to act as theme for a whole text.

Bibliography

ABRAHAM, W. (1972) 'Tiefenstrukturkasus und ihre Oberflächenrealisation bei zwei-wertigen Sätzen des Deutschen. Eine Skizze'. *Leuvense Bijdragen* 61, 1–12

ADELUNG, J. CH. (1782) *Umständliches Lehrgebäude der deutschen Sprache, zur Erläu-terung der deutschen Sprachlehre für Schulen*. Leipzig

ADELUNG, J. CH. and J. S. VATER (1806–17) *Mithridates oder allgemeine Sprachen-kunde, mit dem Vater unser als Sprachprobe in beinahe fünfhundert Sprachen und Mundarten*, 4 vols. Berlin

ADMONI, W. (³1970) *Der Deutsche Sprachbau*. Munich: C. H. Becksche Verlagsbuch-handlung

(1971) *Grundlagen der Grammatiktheorie*. Heidelberg: Quelle und Meyer

(1974) 'Die Satzmodelle und die logisch-grammatischen Typen des Satzes'. *Deutsch als Fremdsprache* 11, 34–42

AGRICOLA, E. (1968) 'Zur Problematik der syntaktischen Mehrdeutigkeit (Polysyn-taktizität)' in NEUBERT (ed) *Grundfragen*. 1968: 53–61

ALEXANDER DE VILLA DEI (1199) *Doctrinale*, ed D. REICHLING (1893). Berlin

ALLEN, J. P. B. and P. VAN BUREN (eds) (1971) *Chomsky: Selected Readings*. London: Oxford University Press

ALTHAUS, H-P., H. HENNE and H. E. WIEGAND (eds) (1973) *Lexikon der germani-stischen Linguistik*. Tübingen: Niemeyer

AMMER, K. and G. F. MEIER (1966) 'Bedeutung und Struktur', in MEIER (ed) *Zeichen, Band III*. 1966: 5–27

AMMON, U. (²1973) *Dialekt, soziale Ungleichheit und Schule*. Weinheim, Basel: Beltz

ARENS, H. (1969) *Sprachwissenschaft. Der Gang ihrer Entwicklung von der Antike bis zur Gegenwart*. 2 vols. Frankfurt/Main: Athenäum Fischer

ARNOLD, H. E. and V. SINEMUS (eds) (1974) *Grundzüge der Literatur und Sprachwis-senschaft, Band 2: Sprachwissenschaft*. Munich: dtv.

ASCOLI, G. J. (1887) *Sprachwissenschaftliche Briefe*, trans B. GUTERBROCK. Leipzig: Hirzel

AUSTIN, J. L. (1962) *How to Do Things with Words*. Oxford: Clarendon Press

BACH, A. (1934) 'Deutsche Mundartforschung', in *Germanische Philologie. Ergebnisse und Aufgaben. Festschrift für O. Behaghel*. Heidelberg: Carl Winter

BACH, E. (1962) 'The order of elements in a transformational grammar of German'. *Language* 38, 263–9

BACH, E. and R. T. HARMS (eds) (1968) *Universals in Linguistic Theory*. New York: Holt, Rinehart and Winston

BACON, F. (1623) *De dignitate et augmentis scientiarum*, in J. SPEDDING, R. L. ELLIS and D. D. HEATH (1858) *The Works of Francis Bacon*. London. Repr Stuttgart-Bad Cannstatt, 1963: Friedrich Fromman Verlag, Günther Holzboog

BALDINGER, K. (1957) *Die Semasiologie*. Berlin: Akademieverlag

BARTSCH, R. and T. VENNEMANN (1972) *Semantic Structures. A Study in the Relation between Semantics and Syntax*. Frankfurt/Main: Athenäum Fischer

BAUMANN, H. H. (1971) 'Generative Grammatik und Wilhelm von Humboldt'. *Poetica* 4, 1–12

BAUMGÄRTNER, K. (1965) 'Spracherklärung mit den Mitteln der Abhängigkeitsstruktur', *Beiträge zur Sprachkunde und Informationsverarbeitung* 5, 31–53

(1967) 'Die Struktur des Bedeutungsfeldes', in MOSER (ed) *Satz und Wort im heutigen Deutsch*, 1965–97

(1969) 'Synästhesie und das Problem sprachlicher Universalien', *Zeitschrift für deutsche Sprache* 25, 1–20

(1970) 'Konstituenz und Dependenz', in STEGER, H. (ed) *Vorschläge für eine strukturale Grammatik des Deutschen*, 57–77

BAUMGÄRTNER, K., J. KÜHNAST and D. WUNDERLICH (1967) *Entwurf einer Semantik des deutschen Tempussystems*. Mimeographed

BAUMGÄRTNER, K. and D. WUNDERLICH (1969) 'Ansatz zu einer Semantik des deutschen Tempussystems', in GELHAUS (ed) *Der Begriff Tempus – eine Ansichtssache*, 23–49. Düsseldorf: Schwann

BAYERISCHES STAATSMINISTERIUM FÜR UNTERRICHT UND KULTUS (ed) (1974) 'Richtlinien und Curriculare Lehrpläne für die Schulversuche mit der Orientierungsstufe', in *Amtsblatt des Bayerischen Staatsministeriums für Unterricht und Kultus*. Munich

BECH, G. (1963) 'Zur Morphologie der deutschen Substantive'. *Lingua* 12, 177–89

BECHERT, J., D. CLÉMENT, W. THÜMMEL and K. H. WAGNER (²1971) *Einführung in die generative Transformationsgrammatik*. Munich: Hueber

BECKER, K. F. (1836–9) *Ausführliche deutsche Grammatik als Kommentar zur Schulgrammatik*. Prague. Repr 1969, Hildesheim, New York: Olms

BEHAGHEL, O. (1909) 'Beziehungen zwischen Umfang und Reihenfolge von Satzgliedern'. *Indogermanistische Forschungen* 18, 110–42

(1923–8) *Deutsche Syntax*, 4 vols. Heidelberg: Carl Winter

BENEŠ, E. (1968) 'Die Ausklammerung im Deutschen als grammatische Norm und als stilistischer Effekt'. *Muttersprache* 78, 289–98

(1971) 'Die Besetzung der ersten Position im deutschen Aussagesatz', in *Fragen der strukturellen Syntax und der kontrastiven Grammatik*, 160–82. Düsseldorf: Schwann

(1973) 'Thema-Rhema-Gliederung und Textlinguistik', in SITTA and BRINKER (eds) *Studien*, 1973: 42–62

BERNSTEIN, B. (1971) *Class, Codes and Control*, Vol I. London: Routledge and Kegan Paul

BERRY, M. (1975–7) *An Introduction to Systemic Linguistics*, 2 vols. London and Sidney: Batsford

BETZ, W. (1973) 'Zur Überprüfung einiger Wortstellungsregeln' in SITTA and BRINKER (eds) *Studien*, 1973: 243–67

BICHEL, U. (1973) 'Umgangssprache' in ALTHAUS, H-P., H. HENNE and H. E. WIEGAND (eds) *Lexikon der germanistischen Linguistik*, 275–9

BIERE, B. U. (1976) 'Ergänzungen und Angaben', in SCHUMACHER, H. (ed) *Untersuchungen*, 1976: 129–73

BIERWISCH, M. (1963) *Grammatik des deutschen Verbs. Studia Grammatica II*. Berlin: Akademieverlag

(1966) 'Regeln für die Intonation deutscher Sätze', in *Untersuchungen über Akzent und Intonation im Deutschen, Studia Grammatica VII*, 99–201. Berlin: Akademieverlag

(1967) 'Some semantic universals of German adjectives' *Foundations of Language* 3, 1–36

(1969) 'On certain problems of semantic representations'. *Foundations of Language* 5, 153–84

(1970) 'On classifying semantic features', in BIERWISCH, M. and K. E. HEIDOLPH (eds) *Progress*, 1970: 27–50

(1970) 'Semantics', in LYONS, J. (ed) *New Horizons*, 1970: 166–84

BIERWISCH, M. and K. E. HEIDOLPH (eds) (1970) *Progress in Linguistics*. The Hague: Mouton

BLOOMFIELD, L. (1933) *Language*. New York: Holt, Rinehart, Winston. (1935). London: Allen and Unwin

BOLINGER, D. (1965) 'The atomization of meaning'. *Language* 41, 555–73

BONDZIO, W. (1971) 'Valenz, Bedeutung und Satzmodelle', in HELBIG, G. (ed) *Beiträge*, 1971: 85–103

BOOST, K. (1955) *Neue Untersuchungen zum Wesen und zur Struktur des deutschen Satzes*. Berlin: Akademieverlag

BOPP, F. (1816) *Über das Conjugationssystem der Sanskritsprache in Vergleichung mit der griechischen, lateinischen, persischen und germanischen Sprache*. Frankfurt/Main

(1833/5/7, ²1857/9/61) *Vergleichende Grammatik des Sanskrit, Zend, Griechischen, Lateinischen, Latauischen, Altslavischen, Gotischen und Deutschen*. Berlin

BREKLE, H. E. (1970) *Generative Satzsemantik und transformationelle Syntax im System der englischen Nominalkomposition*. Munich: Fink

(1970) 'Generative Satzsemantik versus generative Syntax als Komponenten eines Grammatikmodells'. *Linguistik und Didaktik* 1, 129–36

(1972) *Semantik*. Munich: Fink

BRINKER, K. (1977) *Modelle und Methoden der strukturalistischen Syntax*. Stuttgart: Kohlhammer

BRINKMANN, H. (²1971) *Die deutsche Sprache. Gestalt und Leistung*. Düsseldorf: Schwann

BROWN, G. (1977) *Listening to Spoken English*. London: Longman

BRÜCKE, E. (1856) *Grundzüge der Physiologie und Systematik der Sprachlaute für Linguisten und Taubstummlehrer*. Vienna: Carl Gerold's Sohn

BÜHLER, K. (1965) *Sprachtheorie*. Stuttgart: G. Fischer. (1934), Jena: G. Fischer

BURDACH, K. (1934) *Die Wissenschaft von deutscher Sprache*. Berlin: de Gruyter

BURGSCHMIDT, E. (1974) 'Überlegungen zur Lehrerfortbildung im Bereich "Neusprachlicher Unterricht"'. *Praxis des Neusprachlichen Unterrichts* 21, 115–21

BURGSCHMIDT, E. and D. GÖTZ (1972) 'Kontrastive Phonologie Deutsch/Englisch und Mundartinterferenz'. *Linguistik und Didaktik* 11, 209–25

(1974) *Kontrastive Linguistik Deutsch/Englisch*. Munich: Hueber

BURGSCHMIDT, E., D. GÖTZ, H. G. HOFFMANN, H. O. HOHMANN and H. SCHRAND (1975) *Zielsprache Englisch. Handbuch des Englischunterrichts, unter besonderer Perücksichtigung der Weiterbildung*. Munich: Hueber

BYNON, T. (1966) 'Leo Weisgerber's four stages in linguistic analysis', *Man. The Journal of the Royal Anthropological Institute, London. New Series* 1, 468–83

CARNAP, R. (1942) *Introduction to Semantics*. Cambridge, Mass and London: Milford

(1947) *Meaning and Necessity*. Chicago: University of Chicago Press, Cambridge: Cambridge University Press

CASSIRER, E. (1923) 'Die Kantischen Elemente in Wilhelm von Humboldts Sprachphilosophie', in *Festschrift für Paul Hensel*, 105–27. Greiz

(1923–31) *Philosophie der symbolischen Formen*. Berlin: B. Cassirer

CHOMSKY, N. (1957) *Syntactic Structures*. The Hague: Mouton

(1964) *Current Issues in Linguistic Theory*. The Hague: Mouton

(1965) *Aspects of the Theory of Syntax*. Cambridge, Mass: MIT Press

(1970) 'Remarks on nominalization', in JACOBS, R. A. and P. S. ROSENBAUM (eds) *Readings*, 1970: 184–221

(1972) 'Deep structure, surface structure and semantic interpretation', in CHOMSKY, N. (1972) *Studies on Semantics in Generative Grammar*, 62–119. The Hague: Mouton

COSERIU, E. (1967) 'Lexikalische Solidaritäten'. *Poetica* 1, 293–303

(1973) *Probleme der strukturellen Semantik*. Tübingen: TBL Günter Narr

(1975) *Leistung und Grenzen der Transformationsgrammatik*. Tübingen: TBL Günter Narr

(1976) 'Die funktionale Betrachtung des Wortschatzes', in MOSER (ed) *Probleme*, 1976: 7–25

COSERIU, E. and H. GECKELER (1974) 'Linguistics and Semantics', in SEBEOK, *Trends*, 1974: 103–71

CROCE, B. (1905) *Ästhetik als Wissenschaft des Ausdrucks und allgemeine Linguistik*, trans H. FEIST and R. PETERS. Tübingen: Mohr

CRYSTAL, D. and D. DAVY (1975) *Advanced Conversational English*. London: Longman

DAL, I. (1960) 'Zur Frage des süddeutschen Präteritumsschwundes', in *Indogermanica. Festschrift W. Krause*, 1–7. Heidelberg: Carl Winter

(1962) 'Systemerhaltende Tendenzen in der Kasusmorphologie', in MOSER, H. (ed) *Ringen*, 1962: 74–88

DANEŠ, F. (1960) 'Sentence Intonation from a Functional Point of View'. *Word* 16, 34–54

(1967) 'Order of Elements and Sentence Intonation', in *To Honour Roman Jakobson*, Vol 1, 499–512. The Hague: Mouton

(1974) 'Functional sentence perspective and the organization of the text', in DANEŠ (ed) *Papers*, 1974: 106–28

(1974) 'Zur Terminologie der FSP', in DANEŠ (ed) *Papers*, 1974: 217–22

(ed) (1974) *Papers on Functional Sentence Perspective*. Prague: Academia, The Hague: Mouton

DANTE ALIGHIERI (1305) *De vulgari eloquentia libri II*, ed L. BERTALOT (1917). Friedrichsdorf: Editor

DARWIN, C. (1859, 1968) *The Origin of Species by Means of Natural Selection*. Harmondsworth: Penguin

DELBRÜCK, B. (1884) *Einleitung in das Sprachstudium*. Leipzig: Breitkopf and Härtel (⁴1904) *Einleitung in das Studium der indogermanischen Sprachen*. Leipzig: Breitkopf and Härtel

DENNINGHAUS, F. (1975) 'Methoden der expliziten Lernzielbestimmung'. *Praxis des neusprachlichen Unterrichts* 22, 127–41

DEUTSCHER SPRACHATLAS (1927–56) begun by G. WENKER, ed F. WREDE, W. MITZKA, B. MARTIN. Marburg

DIETH, E. (1950), *Vademekum der Phonetik*. Bern: Francke

DIJK, T. A. VAN (1977) *Text and Context. Explorations in the Semantics and Pragmatics of Discourse*. London: Longman

DINSER, G. (ed)(1974) *Zur Theorie der Sprachveränderung*. Kronberg: Scriptor Verlag.

DITTMANN, J. (1976) *Sprechhandlungstheorie und Tempusgrammatik. Futurformen und Zukunftsbezug in der gesprochenen deutschen Sprache*. Munich: Hueber

DITTMAR, N. (1973) *Soziolinguistik*. Frankfurt: Athenäum Fischer

DONATUS (c 350) *Ars Grammatica*, ed H. KEIL (1864). Leipzig

DRACH, E. (³1940) *Grundgedanken der deutschen Satzlehre*. Frankfurt/Main: Diesterweg

DRESSLER, W. (1973) *Einführung in die Textlinguistik*. Tübingen: Niemeyer

(1974) 'Funktionale Satzperspektive und Texttheorie', in Daneš (ed) *Papers*, 1974: 87–105

DRESSLER, W. and S. J. SCHMIDT (1973) *Textlinguistik. Kommentierte Bibliographie*. Munich: Fink

DUDEN (1959, ²1966, ³1973) *Der Grosse Duden Band IV. Grammatik der deutschen Gegenwartssprache*, ed P. GREBE. Mannheim: Bibliographisches Institut

(1962, ²1974) *Der Grosse Duden Band VI. Aussprachewörterbuch*, ed M. MANGOLD. Mannheim: Bibliographisches Institut

(1976-   ) *Das grosse Wörterbuch der deutschen Sprache in sechs Bänden*, ed G. DODREWSKI. Mannheim: Bibliographisches Institut

DÜRBECK, H. (1975) 'Neuere Untersuchungen zur Sapir-Whorf-Hypothese'. *Linguistics* 145, 5–45

EGGERS, H. (1969) *Deutsche Sprachgeschichte III*. Hamburg: Rowohlt

EMONS, R. (1974) *Valenzen englischer Prädikatsverben*. Tübingen: Niemeyer

ENGEL, U. (1970) 'Die deutschen Satzbaupläne'. *Wirkendes Wort* 20, 361–92

(1970) 'Regeln zur Wortstellung'. *Forschungsberichte des Instituts für deutsche Sprache* 5, 7–148

(1970) 'Satzbaupläne und Satzanalyse'. *Zielsprache Deutsch* 3, 104–22

(1972) 'Bemerkungen zur Dependenzgrammatik'. *Sprache der Gegenwart. Jahrbuch des Instituts für deutsche Sprache*, 111–51

(1977) *Syntax der deutschen Gegenwartssprache*. Berlin: Schmidt

ENGEL, U. and H. SCHUMACHER (1976) *Kleines Valenzlexikon deutscher Verben*. Tübingen: TBL Günter Narr

ENGELEN, B. (1968) 'Zur Semantik des deutschen Verbs', in *Forschungsberichte des Instituts für deutsche Sprache* 1, 55–83

(1968) 'Eine Möglichkeit zur Beschreibung komplexer Sätze', in *Sprache – Gegenwart und Geschichte. Jahrbuch des Instituts für deutsche Sprache, Sprache der Gegenwart* 5, 159–70. Düsseldorf: Schwann

(1975) *Untersuchungen zu Satzbauplan und Wortfeld in der geschriebenen deutschen Sprache der Gegenwart*, 2 vols. Munich: Hueber

ERBEN, J. (1968) *Deutsche Grammatik. Ein Leitfaden*. Frankfurt/Main: Fischer

(¹¹1972) *Deutsche Grammatik. Ein Abriss*. Munich: Hueber

ERMERT, K. (1974) 'Bibliographie zur Didaktik der deutschen Sprache im primärsprachlichen Unterricht'. *Germanistische Linguistik* 1–2, 97–179

VON ESSEN, O. (1957) *Allgemeine und angewandte Phonetik*. Berlin: Akademieverlag

(1964), *Grundzüge der hochdeutschen Satzintonation*. Ratingen: Henn

FILLMORE, C. J. (1968) 'The Case for Case', in BACH and HARMS (eds) *Universals*, 1968: 1–88

FIRBAS, J. (1959) 'Thoughts on the Communicative Function of the Verb in English, German and Czech'. *Brno Studies in English* 1, 39–68

(1964) 'On defining the theme in Functional Sentence Analysis', in *Travaux Linguistique de Prague* 1, 267–80

(1974) 'Some aspects of the Czechoslovak approach to problems of functional sentence perspective', in DANĚS (ed) *Papers*, 1974: 11–37

FIRTH, J. R. (1957) *Papers in Linguistics 1934–1951*. London: Oxford University Press

(1964) *The Tongues of Men and Speech*. London: Oxford University Press

(1968) 'Ethnographic analysis and language with reference to Malinowski's views', in PALMER (ed) *Papers*, 1968: 137–67

FLÄMIG, W. (1959) *Zum Konjunktiv in der deutschen Sprache der Gegenwart: Inhalte und Gebrauchsweisen*. Berlin: Akademieverlag

FODOR, J. A. and J. J. KATZ (eds) (1964) *The Structure of Language. Readings in the Philosophy of Language*. Englewood Cliffs. N.J.: Prentice Hall

FOURQUET, J. (1970) 'Zum "subjektiven Gebrauch" der deutschen Modalverba', in *Studien zur Syntax des heutigen Deutsch. Paul Grebe zum 60. Geburtstag*, 154–61. Düsseldorf: Schwann

FRIED, V. (ed) (1972) *The Prague School of Linguistics and Language Teaching*. London: Oxford University Press

FRIES, C. C. (1957) *The Structure of English*. London: Longman

FRIES, U. (1971) 'Textlinguistik'. *Linguistik und Didaktik* 7, 219–34

FUCHS, A. (1976) 'Normaler und "kontrastiver" Akzent'. *Lingua*, 38, 293–312

GAIFMAN, H. (1965) 'Dependency systems and PS-Systems. *Information and Control* 8, 304–37

GANZ, P. F. (1973) *Jacob Grimm's Conception of German Studies*. An inaugural lecture delivered before the University of Oxford 18 May, 1973. Oxford: Clarendon Press

GARDINER, A. H. (1932) *The Theory of Speech and Language*. Oxford: Clarendon Press

GECKELER, H. (1971) *Strukturelle Semantik und Wortfeldtheorie*. Munich: Fink

GELHAUS, H. (1969) 'Sind Tempora Ansichtssache?', in GELHAUS (ed) *Der Begriff Tempus – eine Ansichtssache?* 69–89. Düsseldorf: Schwann

(1969) 'Zum Tempussystem der deutschen Hochsprache', in GELHAUS (ed) *Der Begriff Tempus – eine Ansichtssache?* 5–22. Düsseldorf: Schwann

(1975) *Das Futur in ausgewählten Texten der geschriebenen deutschen Sprache der Gegenwart*. Munich: Hueber

(ed) (1969) *Der Begriff Tempus – eine Ansichtssache?* Wirkendes Wort, Beiheft 20. Düsseldorf: Schwann.

GERMER, R. (1961) 'Die Bedeutung einer guten Aussprache für Unterricht und Leben'. *Die Neueren Sprachen* 6, 512–19

GERSTENKORN, A. (1976) *Das 'Modal'-System im heutigen Deutsch*. Munich: Fink

GIPPER, H. (1972) *Gibt es ein sprachliches Relativitätsprinzip? Untersuchungen zur Sapir-Whorf-Hypothese*. Frankfurt/Main: Fischer

(1973) 'Der Inhalt des Wortes und die Gliederung des Wortschatzes', in *Duden, Grammatik*, ^{3}1973: 415–73

(1976) 'Die feldhafte Gliederung des Wortschatzes und das Problem ihrer Formalisierbarkeit', in MOSER (ed) *Probleme*, 1976: 26–49

GIPPER, H. and H. SCHWARZ (eds) (1962–6.) *Bibliographisches Handbuch zur Sprachinhaltsforschung*. Köln/Opladen: Westdeutscher Verlag

GLINZ, H. (1947) *Geschichte und Kritik der Lehre von den Satzgliedern in der deutschen Grammatik*. Dissertation Zurich.

(1952, ^{5}1968) *Die innere Form des Deutschen*. Bern: Franke

(1962) *Ansätze zu einer Sprachtheorie*. Wirkendes Wort Beiheft 2. Düsseldorf: Schwann

(^{3}1963) *Der deutsche Satz*. Düsseldorf: Schwann

(1969) 'Zum Tempus- und Modussystem des Deutschen', in GELHAUS (ed) *Der Begriff Tempus – eine Ansichtssache?* 5–58. Düsseldorf: Schwann

(1970) *Deutsche Grammatik I*. Frankfurt/Main: Athenäum Fischer

GRAF, R. (1977) *Der Konjunktiv in gesprochener Sprache*. Tübingen: Niemeyer

GREBE, P.: see *Duden*

GREIMAS, A. J. (1966) *Sémantique Structurale. Recherche de méthode*. Paris: Larousse

(1971) *Strukturale Semantik*. Braunschweig: Vieweg

GRIMM, J. (1819, ^{2}1822) *Deutsche Grammatik*. Göttingen

GROOT, A. W. DE (1949) *Structurele Syntaxis*. The Hague: Servire

GÜLICH, E. and W. RAIBLE (eds) (1972) *Textsorten. Differenzierungskriterien aus linguistischer Sicht*. Frankfurt/Main: Athenäum Fischer

(1977) *Linguistische Textmodelle. Grundlagen und Möglichkeiten*. Munich: Fink

HABERMAS, J. (1971) 'Vorbereitende Bemerkungen zu einer Theorie der kommunikativen Kompetenz', in HABERMAS, J. and N. LUHMANN (eds) *Theorie der Gesellschaft oder Sozialtechnologie*. Frankfurt/Main: Suhrkamp also in HOLZER, H. and K. STEINBACHER (eds) (1972) *Sprache und Gesellschaft*, 208–36. Hamburg: Hoffmann und Campe

HALLIDAY, M. A. K. (1969) 'Options and Functions in the English Clause'. *Brno Studies in English* 8, 81–8

(1970) 'Language structure and language function', in LYONS (ed) *New Horizons*, 1970: 140–65

(1973) 'The functional basis of language', in HALLIDAY *Explorations*, 1973: 22–47

(1973) 'Linguistic function and literary style: an inquiry into the language of William Golding's *The Inheritors*', in HALLIDAY *Explorations*, 1973: 103–40

(1973) 'Language in a social perspective', in HALLIDAY *Explorations*, 1973: 58–71

(1973) 'Relevant models of language', in HALLIDAY *Explorations*, 1973: 9–21

(1973) *Explorations in the Functions of Language*. London: Edward Arnold. *Explorations in Language Study*.

(1975) *Learning How to Mean: Explorations in the Development of Language*. London: Edward Arnold *Explorations in Language Study*.

HALLIDAY, M. A. K. and R. HASAN (1976) *Cohesion in English*. London: Longman

HAMANN, H. (1951) 'Funktionale Grammatik – eine neue Lehrweise?' *Die lebenden Fremdsprachen* 3, 19–24

HARTMANN, E. (1964) 'Bestehen Unterschiede zwischen der Affrikata /ts/ und der Lautfolge t+s? Eine phonetische Untersuchung'. *Zeitschrift für Phonetik, Sprachwissenschaft und Kommunikationsforschung* 18, 387–90

HARTMANN, P. (1971) 'Texte als linguistisches Objekt', in STEMPEL, W. D. (ed) *Beiträge zur Textlinguistik*, 9–29. Munich: Fink

HARTMANN, R. (1976) 'Über die Grenzen der kontrastiven Lexikologie' in MOSER (ed) *Probleme*, 1976: 181–99

HARWEG, R. (1968) 'Pronomina und Textkonstitution.' *Poetica Beiheft*, 2. Munich: Fink

HAUSER-SUIDA, U. and G. HOPPE-BEUGEL (1972) *Die Vergangenheitstempora in der deutschen geschriebenen Sprache der Gegenwart*, Heutiges Deutsch, Reihe I, vol. 4. Munich: Hueber, Düsseldorf: Schwann

HAYS, D. G. (1964). 'Dependency theory: a formalism and some observations'. *Language* 40, 511–25

HEGER, K. (1966) 'Valenz, Diathese und Kasus'. *Zeitschrift für romanische Philologie* 82, 138–70

(^{2}1976) *Monem, Wort, Satz und Text*. Tübingen: Niemeyer

HEIKE, G.(1969) *Suprasegmentale Analyse*. Marburg: Elwert

HEINRICHS, A., S. JÄGER, U. KNOOP, R. ZIMMERMANN and K. ERMERT (1974) 'Die Hessischen Rahmenrichtlinien "Deutsch"' Germanistische Linguistik (I and II)

HELBIG, G. (1970) 'Sind Negationswörter, Modalwörter und Partikeln im Deutschen besondere Wortklassen?'. *Deutsch als Fremdsprache* 7, 394–401

(1971) 'Theoretische und praktische Aspekte eines Valenzmodells', in HELBIG, G. (ed) *Beiträge*, 1971: 31–49

(1971) 'Zur Theorie der Satzmodelle'. *Biuletyn Fonograficzny* 11, 51–71

(1971) 'Zu einigen Spezialproblemen der Valenztheorie'. *Deutsch als Fremdsprache* 8, 269–82

(1973) *Die Funktionen der substantivischen Kasus in der deutschen Gegenwartssprache*. Halle/Saale: Niemeyer

(1974) *Geschichte der neueren Sprachwissenschaft*. Reinbek: Rowohlt

(ed) (1971) *Beiträge zur Valenztheorie*. The Hague: Mouton, Halle/Saale: Niemeyer

HELBIG, G. and J. BUSCHA (1974) *Kurze deutsche Grammatik für Ausländer*. Leipzig: VEB Enzyklopädie

HELBIG, G. and W. SCHENKEL (1968) *Wörterbuch zur Valenz und Distribution deutscher Verben*. Leipzig: VEB Bibliographisches Institut

HERDER, J. G. (1776) *Abhandlung über den Ursprung der Sprache*, in HERDER,

J. G. *Sprachphilosophische Schriften*, ed. E. HEINTEL, 1960: 3–90. Hamburg: Meiner

HERINGER, H. J. (1967) 'Wertigkeiten und nullwertige Verben im Deutschen'. *Zeitschrift für deutsche Sprache* 23, 13–34

(1968) 'Präpositionale Ergänzungsbestimmungen im Deutschen'. *Zeitschrift für deutsche Philologie* 87, 426–57

(1970) 'Zur Analyse von Sätzen des Deutschen auf der Unterstufe'. *Linguistik und Didaktik* 1, 2–28

(1970) *Deutsche Syntax*. Berlin, New York: Göschen

(1970) *Theorie der deutschen Syntax*. Munich: Hueber

(1974) *Praktische Semantik*. Stuttgart: Klett

(ed) (1974) *Der Regelbegriff in der praktischen Semantik*. Frankfurt: Suhrkamp

DER HESSISCHE KULTUSMINSTER (1972) *Rahmenrichtlinien Sekundarstufe I: Deutsch*. (= RRD). Frankfurt/Main: Diesterweg

HJELMSLEV, L. (1963) *Prolegomena to a Theory of Language*, trans F. WHITFIELD. Madison: University of Wisconsin Press

HOBERG, R. (1970) *Die Lehre vom sprachlichen Feld*. Düsseldorf: Schwann

HOLZ, G. (1956) 'Es kracht im Gebälk'. *Muttersprache* 61, 269–73

HOLZER, H. and K. STEINBACHER (eds) (1972) *Sprache und Gesellschaft*. Hamburg: Hoffmann und Campe

HORNBY, A. S., E. V. GATENBY and H. WAKEFIELD ([2]1963) *The Advanced Learner's Dictionary of Current English*. Oxford: Oxford University Press

HUDDLESTON, R. (1976) *An Introduction to English Transformational Syntax*. London: Longman

HUDSON, R. A. (1976) *Arguments for a Non-Transformational Grammar*. Chicago, London: University of Chicago Press

HÜLLEN, W. (1976) *Linguistik und Englischunterricht*, vol 2. Heidelberg: Quelle und Meyer

HUMBOLDT, W. VON (1810–11) 'Thesen zur Grundlegung einer allgemeinen Sprachwissenschaft' from *Einleitung in das Sprachstudium* in W. V. HUMBOLDT *Schriften zur Sprache*, ed M. BÖHLER, 1973: 12–21. Stuttgart: Reclam

(1820) 'Über das vergleichende Sprachstudium in Beziehung auf die verschiedenen Epochen der Sprachentwicklung', in HUMBOLDT *Werke III*, 1963: 1–25

(1827–9) 'Über die Verschiedenheit des menschlichen Sprachbaus', in HUMBOLDT *Werke III*, 1963: 144–367

(1830–5) 'Über die Verschiedenheit des menschlichen Sprachbaus und ihren Einfluss auf die geistige Entwicklung des Menschengeschlechts', in HUMBOLDT *Werke III*, 1963: 368–756

(1963) *Werke in fünf Bänden, Band III: Schriften zur Sprachphilosophie*, eds A. FLITNER and K. GIEL. Darmstadt: Wissenschaftliche Buchgesellschaft

HUNDSNURSCHER, F. (ed) ([3]1970) *Transformationelle Schulgrammatik*. Göppingen: Verlag Alfred Kümmerle

(1972) *Neuere Methoden der Semantik*. Tübingen: Niemeyer

HYMES, D. H. (1972) 'On Communicative Competence', in PRIDE, J. B. and J. HOLMES (eds) *Sociolinguistics*, 1972: 269–93. Harmondsworth: Penguin

INSTITUT FÜR SCHULPÄDAGOGIK (1975) *Curricularer Lehrplan für das Fach Englisch in der Orientierungsstufe*. Munich

IORDAN, I. and J. ORR (1970) *An Introduction to Romance Linguistics. Its Schools and Scholars*, rev with supplement by R. POSNER. Oxford: Blackwell

IPSEN, G. (1924) 'Der alte Orient und die Indogermanen', in *Stand und Aufgaben der Sprachwissenschaft, Festschrift für Wilhelm Streitberg*, 200–37. Heidelberg: Carl Winter

(1930), *Sprachphilosophie der Gegenwart*. Berlin: Junker und Dünnhaupt

IVIC, M. (1965) *Trends in Linguistics*. The Hague: Mouton

JACOBS, R. and P. ROSENBAUM (eds) (1970) *Readings in Transformational Grammar*. Waltham, Mass: Ginn

JÄGER, S. (1971) 'Sprachnormen und Schülersprache', in MOSER, H. (ed) *Sprache und Gesellschaft*, 1971: 166–233

(1971) 'Zum Problem der sprachlichen Norm und seiner Relevanz für die Schule'. *Muttersprache* 81, 162–75

(1971) *Der Konjunktiv in der deutschen Sprache der Gegenwart. Untersuchungen an ausgewählten Texten*. Munich: Hueber, Düsseldorf: Schwann

(1972) 'Sprachbarrieren und kompensatorische Erziehung: Ein bürgerliches Trauerspiel'. *Linguistische Berichte* 19, 80–99

(1973) *Sprechen und soziale Schicht*. Frankfurt: Athenäum

JANKOWSKY, K. P. (1972) *The Neogrammarians: A Re-evaluation of their Place in the Development of Linguistic Science*. The Hague: Mouton

JELLINEK, M. H. (1913) *Geschichte der neuhochdeutschen Grammatik von den Anfängen bis auf Adelung* I. Heidelberg: Carl Winter

JESPERSEN, O. (1886) 'Zur Lautgesetzfrage'. *Internationale Zeitschrift für Allgemeine Sprachwissenschaft* 3, 188–216

(1937) *Analytic Syntax*. Copenhagen: Munksgaard

JOAS, H. and A. LEIST (1971) 'Performative Tiefenstruktur und interaktionistischer Rollenbegriff. Ein Ansatz zu einer soziolinguistischen Pragmatik'. *Münchener Papiere zur Linguistik* 1, 31–54

JONES, D. (1957) *The History and Meaning of the Term 'Phoneme'*. London: International Phonetic Association

([14]1977) *English Pronouncing Dictionary*, rev A. C. GIMSON. London: Dent

KADE, O. (1968) *Zufall und Gesetzmässigkeit in der Übersetzung*, Beiheft zur Zeitschrift Fremdsprachen 1, Leipzig: VEB Verlag Enzyklopädie

KALLMEYER, W., W. KLEIN, R. MEYER-HERMANN, K. NETZER and H. J. SIEBERT (1974) *Lektürekolleg zur Textlinguistik I and II*. Frankfurt: Athenäum

KATZ, J. J. and J. A. FODOR (1963) 'The structure of a semantic theory'. *Language* 39, 170–210

KATZ, J. J. and P. POSTAL (1964) *An Integrated Theory of Linguistic Descriptions*. Cambridge, Mass: MIT Press

KAUFMANN, G. (1976) *Die indirekte Rede und mit ihr konkurrierende Formen der Redeerwähnung*. Munich: Hueber

KIPARSKY, P. (1966) 'Über den deutschen Akzent', in *Untersuchungen über Akzent und Intonation im Deutschen. Studia Grammatica VIII*, 69–98. Berlin: Akademieverlag

KIPARSKY, P. and C. KIPARSKY (1971) 'Fact', in STEINBERG, D. D. and L. A. JAKOBOVITS (eds) *Semantics*, 1971: 345–69

KLAUS, G. ([2]1969) *Semiotik und Erkenntnistheorie*. Berlin: Verlag der Wissenschaften (1964) *Die Macht des Wortes*. Berlin: das europäische Buch

KLIMA, E. S. (1964) 'Negation in English', in FODOR and KATZ (eds) *Structure*, 1964: 246–323

KLUGE, W. (1961) *Perfekt und Präteritum im Neuhochdeutschen*. (Dissertation, Münster)

(1969) 'Zur Diskussion um das Tempussytem', in GELHAUS (ed), 59–68. Düsseldorf: Schwann

KOCHAN, D. C. and W. WALLRABENSTEIN (eds) (1974) *Aussichten eines kommunikationsbezogenen Deutschunterrichts*. Kronberg: Scriptor Verlag

KOHLER, K. J. (1977) *Einführung in die Phonetik des Deutschen*. Berlin: E. Schmidt

KÖNIG, W. (1978) *dtv-Atlas zur deutschen Sprache. Tafeln und Texte*. Munich: dtv

KOLDE, G. (1970) 'Zur Funktion der sogenannten Modalwörter in der deutschen Sprache der Gegenwart' *Wirkendes Wort* 20, 116–25

KRAUS, C. J. (1787) 'Rezension des Allgemeinen Vergleichenden Wörterbuchs von Pallas'. *Allgemeine Literaturzeitung.*

LABOV, W. (1966) *The Social Stratification of English in New York City.* Washington DC: Center for Applied Linguistics

LAND, S. K. (1974) *From Signs to Propositions. The Concept of Form in Eighteenth-Century Semantic Theory.* London: Longman

LAZARUS, M. (1856–57) *Das Leben der Seele in Monographien,* 2 vols. Berlin

LEECH, G. (1969) *A Linguistic Guide to English Poetry.* London: Longman
(1969) *Towards a Semantic Description of English.* London: Longman
(1971) *Meaning and the English Verb.* London: Longman.
(1974) *Semantics.* Harmondsworth: Penguin

LEHMANN, W. P. (1964) *Historical Linguistics. An Introduction.* New York: Holt, Rinehart and Winston

LEHRER, A. (1974) *Semantic Fields and Lexical Structure.* Amsterdam: North Holland

LEISI, E. (⁴1971) *Der Wortinhalt.* Heidelberg: Quelle und Meyer

LENERZ, J. (1977) *Zur Abfolge nominaler Satzglieder im Deutschen.* Tübingen: TBL Günter Narr

LENNEBERG, E. H. (1967) *Biological Foundations of Language.* London: J. Wiley
(1971) 'Language and cognition', in STEINBERG, D. D. and L. A. JAKOBOVITS (eds) *Semantics,* 1971: 536–57

LINDGREN, K. B. (1957) *Über den oberdeutschen Präteritumsschwund.* Annales Academiae Scientiarum Fennicae Series B 112, Helsinki

LOCKE, J. (1690) *An Essay concerning Human Understanding,* ed P. H. NIDDITCH (1975). Oxford: Clarendon Press

LOCKWOOD, W. B. (1968) *Historical German Syntax.* London: Oxford University Press

LONGMAN DICTIONARY OF CONTEMPORARY ENGLISH (1978) London: Longman

LUND, H. C. (1958) 'Eine kritische Betrachtung der "Funktionalen Grammatik" '. *Die neueren Sprachen* 8, 475–83

LYONS, J. (1968) *Introduction to Theoretical Linguistics.* Cambridge: Cambridge University Press
(1970) *Chomsky.* London: Fontana
(1977) *Semantics* 2 vols. Cambridge: Cambridge University Press
(ed) (1970) *New Horizons in Linguistics.* Harmondsworth: Penguin

MAAS, U. (1974) 'Dependenztheorie' in ARNOLD, H. E. and V. S. SINEMUS (eds) *Grundzüge,* 1974, 257–75

MAAS, U. and D. WUNDERLICH (1972) *Pragmatik und sprachliches Handeln. Mit einer Kritik am Funkkolleg.* Frankfurt: Athenäum

MCCAWLEY, J. D. (1971) 'Where do noun phrases come from?' in STEINBERG, D. D. and L. A. JAKOBOVITS (eds) *Semantics,* 1971: 217–31

MANGOLD, M. (1974) *Duden-Aussprachewörterbuch.* Mannheim, Vienna, Zürich: Bibliographisches Institut

MARTINET, A. (1964) *Elements of General Linguistics.* London: Faber

MATHESIUS, V. (1947) 'O tak zvaném aktualnim členěm větném (On the so-called Functional Sentence Perspective)' in MATHESIUS, V. *Čeština a obecný jazykopyt (The Czech Language and General Linguistics)* 234–42

MAURER, F. (1934) 'Geschichte der deutschen Sprache', in *Germanische Philologie. Ergebnisse und Aufgaben. Festschrift für O. Behaghel,* 201–28. Heidelberg: Carl Winter

MEIER, G. F. (1959) 'Was versteht man unter marxistischer Sprachwissenschaft?' *Hochschulwesen* 7, 31–9
(1961) *Das Zéro-Problem in der Linguistik.* Berlin: Akademieverlag
(1964) 'Semantische Analyse und Noematik', *Zeitschrift für Phonetik, Sprachwissenschaft und Kommunikationsforschung* 17, 581–95

(1966) 'Noematische Analyse als Voraussetzung für die Ausschaltung der Polysemie', in MEIER, G. F. (ed) *Zeichen*, 1966: 117–45
(ed) (1966) *Zeichen und System der Sprache, Band III*. *Schriften zur Phonetik, Sprachwissenschaft und Kommunikationsforschung*. Berlin: Akademieverlag
MERINGER, R. (1898) 'Etymologien zum geflochtenen Haus', in *Abhandlungen zur germanistischen Philologie. Festgabe für R. Heinzel*, 177–92. Halle: Niemeyer
MORRIS, C. W. (1938) *Foundations of the Theory of Signs*. Chicago: University of Chicago Press
MOSER, H. (ed) (1962) *Das Ringen um eine neue deutsche Grammatik. Aufsätze aus drei Jahrzehnten (1929–1959)*. Darmstadt: Wissenschaftliche Buchgesellschaft
(ed) (1967) *Satz und Wort im heutigen Deutsch*, Düsseldorf' Schwann.
(ed) (1968) *Sprachnorm, Sprachpflege, Sprachkritik*. Düsseldorf: Schwann
(ed) (1971) *Sprache und Gesellschaft. Beiträge zur soziolinguistischen Beschreibung der deutschen Gegenwartssprache*. Düsseldorf: Schwann
(ed) (1976) *Probleme der Lexikologie und Lexikographie*. Düsseldorf: Schwann
MOTSCH, W. (1964) *Syntax des deutschen Adjektivs. Studia Grammatica III*. Berlin: Akademieverlag
(1967) 'Können attributive Adjektive durch Transformationen erklärt werden?'. *Folia Linguistica* 1, 23–48
(1974) *Zur Kritik des sprachwissenschaftlichen Strukturalismus*. Berlin: Akademieverlag
MOULTON, W. G. (1962) *The Sounds of English and German*. Chicago: University of Chicago Press
NAUMANN, H. (1923) 'Versuch einer Geschichte der deutschen Sprache als Geschichte des deutschen Geistes', in *Deutsche Vierteljahresschrift für Literaturwissenschaft und Geistesgeschichte* 1, 139–60
NEUBERT, A. (1966) 'Analogien zwischen Phonologie und Semantik', in MEIER, G. F. (ed) *Zeichen*, 1966: 106–16
(1968) 'Semantik und Übersetzungswissenschaft', in RŮŽIČKA, R. (ed) *Probleme*, 1968: 199–207
(1973) 'Invarianz und Pragmatik', in NEUBERT, A. and O. KADE (eds) *Beiträge*, 1973: 13–26
(ed) (1968) *Grundfragen der Übersetzungswissenschaft. Beiheft zur Zeitschrift Fremdsprachen*. Leipzig: VEB Verlag Enzyklopädie
NEUBERT, A. and O. KADE (eds) (1973) *Neue Beiträge zu Grundfragen der Übersetzungswissenschaft*. Frankfurt: Athenäum
NEUHOFF, R. (1959) 'Bemerkungen über den Konjunktiv'. *Deutschunterricht* 11, 68–87
O'CONNOR, J. D. (1973) *Phonetics*. Harmondsworth: Penguin
OEVERMANN, U. (1970) *Sprache und soziale Herkunft*. Frankfurt: Suhrkamp
OGDEN, C. K. and I. A. RICHARDS (⁴1936) *The Meaning of Meaning*. London: Kegan Paul
OKSAAR, E. (1958) *Semantische Studien im Sinnbereich der Schnelligkeit*. (Acta Universitatis Stockholmiensis) Stockholm: Almquist und Wiksell
OSTHOFF, H. and K. BRUGMANN (1878) *Morphologische Untersuchungen auf dem Gebiete der indogermanischen Sprachen*. Leipzig
PALMER, F. R. (1976) *Semantics*. Cambridge: Cambridge University Press
(ed) (1968) *Selected papers of J. R. Firth 1952–1959*. London: Longman (1974) *The English Verb*. London: Longman
PAUL, H. (⁵1920) *Prinzipien der Sprachgeschichte*. Halle: Niemeyer
PENZL, H. (1975) *Vom Urgermanischen zum Neuhochdeutschen. Eine historische Phonologie*. Berlin: E. Schmidt
PILCH, H. (1964) *Phonemtheorie I*. Basel: Karger
(1966) 'Das Lautsystem der hochdeutschen Umgangssprache'. *Zeitschrift für Mundartforschung* 33, 247–66

PINSKER, H. E. (³1969) *Historische englische Grammatik*. Munich: Hueber
POLENZ, P. VON (1964) 'Sprachnormung und Sprachentwicklung im neueren Deutsch'. *Deutschunterricht* 16, 67–91
(1969) 'Der Pertinenzdativ und seine Satzbaupläne' in *Festschrift für Hugo Moser zum 60. Geburstag am 19. Juni 1969*, 146–71. Düsseldorf: Schwann
(1972) 'Neue Ziele und Methoden der Wortbildungslehre'. *Paul und Braunes Beiträge* 94, 398–425
PORZIG, W. (1934) 'Wesenhafte Bedeutungsbeziehungen'. *Beiträge zur Geschichte der deutschen Sprache und Literatur* 5, 70–97
POSNER, R. (1972) *Theorie des Kommentierens. Eine Grundlagenstudie zur Semantik und Pragmatik*. Frankfurt/Main: Athenäum
POTTIER, B. (1964) 'Vers une semantique moderne'. *Travaux de Linguistique et de Litterature* 2, 107–37
PRIDE, J. B. and J. HOLMES (eds) (1972) *Sociolinguistics*. Harmondsworth: Penguin
PRISCIANUS (c 500) *Institutionum grammaticarum Libri XVIII*, ed H. M. HERTZ (1855–9). Leipzig
PUTSCHKE, W. (1969) 'Zur forschungsgeschichtlichen Stellung der junggrammatischen Schule'. *Zeitschrift für Dialektologie und Linguistik* 36, 19–48
QUIRK, R., S. GREENBAUM, G. LEECH and J. SVARTVIK (1972) *A Grammar of Contemporary English*. London: Longman
RADTKE, I. (1972) 'Soziolinguistik von Stadtsprachen. Tendenzen soziolinguistischer Forschungen in der BRD'. *Germanistische Linguistik* 4, 1974: 441–517
(1973) 'Die Umgangssprache. Ein weiterhin ungeklärtes Gebiet der Sprachwissenschaft'. *Muttersprache* 83, 161–71
RASK, R. (1818) *Undersogelse om det gamle Nordiske eller Islandske Sprogs Orprindelse*. Copenhagen
RAUMER, R. VON (1837) 'Die Aspiration und die Lautverschiebung', in RAUMER (1863) *Gesammelte Sprachwissenschaftliche Studien*, 1–104. Erlangen
RIES, J. (1894) *Was ist Syntax?* Marburg: Taussig und Taussig
ROBINS, R. H. (1964) *General Linguistics*. London: Longman
(1967) *A Short History of Linguistics*. London: Longman
ROBINSON, J. (1970) 'Dependency Structure and T-Rules'. *Language* 46, 259–85
ROHRER, C. (1971) *Funktionelle Sprachwissenschaft und Transformationelle Grammatik*. Munich: Fink
RÖHRL, E. (1962) 'Der Konjunktiv im heutigen Sprachgebrauch'. *Muttersprache* 72, 289–98
ROSS, J. R. (1970) 'On declarative sentences', in JACOBS, R. and P. ROSENBAUM (eds) *Readings*, 1970: 222–72
ROTH, E. (1971) *Transformationsgrammatik in der englischen Schulpraxis*. Frankfurt/Main: Diesterweg
RŮŽIČKA, R. (ed) (1968) *Probleme der strukturellen Grammatik und Semantik*. Halle/Saale: Niemeyer
SADOCK, J. M. (1968) 'Hypersentences'. (Dissertation.) Urbana: University of Illinois
SAUSSURE, F. DE (1916, 1973) *Cours de Linguistique Génerale*. Paris: Payot
SAVIGNY, E. VON (1974) *Die Philosophie der normalen Sprache*. Frankfurt/Main: Suhrkamp
SCHAFF, A. (1962) *Introduction to Semantics*. New York: Pergamon
SCHIPPOREIT, L. (1971) *Tenses and Time Phrases in Modern German*. Munich: Hueber
SCHIRMUNSKI, V. M. (1962) *Deutsche Mundartkunde*. Berlin: Akademieverlag
SCHLEGEL, A. W. (1818) *Observations sur la langue et la littérature provençales*. Paris
SCHLEICHER, A. (1861–2) *Compendium der vergleichenden Grammatik der indogermanischen Sprachen*. Weimar: Böhlau
SCHMIDT, F. (1970) *Symbolische Syntax*. Halle: Niemeyer, Munich: Hueber

SCHMIDT, J. (1872) *Die Verwandtschaftsverhältnisse der indogermanischen Sprachen*. Weimar: Böhlau

SCHMIDT, L. (ed) (1973) *Wortfeldforschung*. Darmstadt: Wissenschaftliche Buchgesellschaft

SCHMIDT, S. J. (1969) *Bedeutung und Begriff zur Fundierung einer sprachphilosophischen Semantik*. Braunschweig: Vieweg

(1973) *Texttheorie: Probleme einer Linguistik der sprachlichen Kommunikation*. Munich: Fink

(ed) (1974) *Pragmatik I*. Munich: Fink

SCHMIDT, W. (1965, ⁴1973) *Grundfragen der deutschen Grammatik*. Berlin: Volk und Wissen

(1969) 'Skizze der Kategorien und der Methode der funktionalen Grammatik'. *Zeitschrift für Phonetik, Sprachwissenschaft und Kommunikationsforschung* 19, 518–31

(1969) 'Zur Theorie der funktionalen Grammatik'. *Zeitschrift für Phonetik, Sprachwissenschaft und Kommunikationsforschung* 19, 135–51

(1974) 'Linguistische Positionen einer Theorie der muttersprachlichen Bildung und Erziehung'. *Zeitschrift für Phonetik, Sprachwissenschaft und Kommunikationsforschung* 24, 520–9

SCHNEIDER, G. (1973) *Zum Begriff des Lautgesetzes in der Sprachwissenschaft seit den Junggrammatikern*. Tübingen: TBL Narr

SCHNELLE, H. (1973) *Sprachphilosophie und Linguistik*. Reinbek: Rowohlt

SCHOTTEL, J. G. (1663) *Ausführliche Arbeit von der Teutschen Haubtsprache*. Repr. Tübingen 1967: Niemeyer

SCHUCHARDT, H. (1885) *Über die Lautgesetze. Gegen die Junggrammatiker*. Berlin: Oppenheim

SCHULZ, D. and GRIESBACH (¹⁰1976) *Grammatik der deutschen Sprache*. Munich: Hueber

SCHUMACHER, H. (1976) 'Ein Valenzwörterbuch auf semantischer Basis', in MOSER, H. (ed) *Probleme*, 1976: 275–300

(ed) (1976) *Untersuchungen zur Verbvalenz*. Tübingen: TBL Günter Narr

SCHWARTZ, U. (1973) *Modus und Satzstruktur: Eine syntaktische Studie zum Modussystem im Deutschen*. Kronberg: Scriptor Verlag

SEARLE, J. R. (1969) *Speech Acts. An Essay in the Philosophy of Language*. London: Cambridge University Press

(1971) 'What is a Speech Act' in SEARLE, J. R. (ed) *Philosophy*, 1971: 39–53

(ed) (1971) *The Philosophy of Language*. London: Oxford University Press

SEBEOK, T. A. (ed) (1974) *Current Trends in Linguistics*, Vol 12. The Hague: Mouton

SEIFFERT, L. (1968) *Wortfeldtheorie und Strukturalismus*. Stuttgart: Kohlhammer

SGALL, P., C. HAJIČOVÁ and E. BENEŠOVA (1973) *Topic, Focus and Generative Semantics*. Kronberg: Scriptor Verlag

SIEBS, T. (¹¹1915) *Deutsche Bühnenaussprache*. Bonn: Ahn

SITTA, H. and U. BRINKER (eds) (1973) *Studien zur Texttheorie und zur deutschen Grammatik. Festgabe für Hans Glinz zum 60. Geburtstag*. Düsseldorf: Schwann

STEGER, H. (1971) 'Soziolinguistik. Grundlagen, Aufgaben und Ergebnisse für das Deutsche', in MOSER, H. (ed) *Sprache*, 1971: 9–44

(1973) 'Soziolinguistik', in ALTHAUS, H. P., H. HENNE and H. E. WIEGAND (eds) *Lexikon*, 1973: 245–54

(ed) (1970) *Vorschläge für eine strukturale Grammatik des Deutschen*. Darmstadt: Wissenschaftliche Buchgesellschaft

STEINBERG, D. D. and L. A. JACOBOVITS (eds) (1971) *Semantics. An Interdisciplinary Reader in Philosophy, Linguistics and Psychology*. Cambridge: Cambridge University Press

STEINHEIL, F. C. VON (1812) *Lehrgebäude der deutschen Sprache*. Stuttgart

STEINTHAL, H. (1855) *Grammatik, Logik und Philosophie. Ihre Prinzipien und ihr Verhältnis zueinander.* Berlin: Dümmler

(1871) *Abriss der Sprachwissenschaft, 1. Teil: Einleitung in die Psychologie und Sprachwissenschaft.* Berlin: Dümmler

STEMPEL, W. D. (ed) (1971) *Beiträge zur Textlinguistik.* Munich: Fink

STICKEL, G. (1970) *Untersuchungen zur Negation im heutigen Deutsch.* Braunschweig: Vieweg

(1972) 'Ja und nein als Kontroll- und Korrektursignale'. *Linguistische Berichte* 17, 12–17

(1975) 'Einige syntaktische und pragmatische Aspekte der Negation' in WEINRICH, H. (ed) *Positionen der Negativität,* 17–38. Munich: Fink

STÖTZEL, G. (1970) *Ausdrucksseite und Inhaltsseite der Sprache. Methodenkritische Studien am Beispiel der deutschen Reflexivverben.* Munich: Hueber

STRAWSON, P. F. (1964) 'Intention and Convention in Speech Acts'. *The Philosophical Review* 73, 439–60

SÜSKIND, W. (1940) *Vom A-B-C zum Sprachkunstwerk. Eine deutsche Sprachlehre für Erwachsene.* Stuttgart, Berlin: Deutsche Verlagsanstalt

TESNIERE, L. (1953) *Esquisse d'une Syntaxe Structurale.* Paris: Klincksieck

(1959) *Élements de Syntaxe Structurale.* Paris: Klincksieck

THOMAS OF ERFURT (between 1300 and 1310) *Novi Modi Significandi.* Ed. G. L. BUR-SILL-HALL (1972) *Grammatica Speculativa of Thomas of Erfurt.* London: Longman

TRIER, J. (1931) *Der deutsche Wortschatz im Sinnbezirk des Verstandes.* Heidelberg: Carl Winter

(1932) 'Sprachliche Felder'. *Zeitschrift für deutsche Bildung* 8, 417–27

(1965) 'Unsicherheiten im heutigen Deutsch', in MOSER, H. (ed) *Sprachnorm,* 1968: 11–27

(1968) 'Altes und Neues vom sprachlichen Feld', in SCHMIDT, L. (ed) *Wortfeldforschung,* 1973: 453–64

TRUDGILL, P. (1974) *Sociolinguistics.* Harmondsworth: Penguin

(1975) *Accent, Dialect and the School.* London: Edward Arnold

ULLMANN, S. (1962, 1972) *Semantics. An Introduction to the Science of Meaning.* Oxford: Blackwell

UNGEHEUER, G. (1977) *Materialien zur Phonetik des Deutschen.* Hamburg: Buske

VACHEK, J. (1966) *The Linguistic School of Prague.* Bloomington: University of Indiana Press

(1972) 'The linguistic theory of the Prague School', in FRIED, V. (ed) *Prague School,* 1972: 12–28

VATER, H. (1973) *Dänische Subjekt- und Objektsätze.* Tübingen: Niemeyer

(1973) 'Towards a Generative Dependency Model.' Trier: Linguistic Agency, University at Trier

VENNEMANN, T. (1968) 'Die Affrikaten in der generativen Phonologie des Deutschen'. *Phonetica* 18, 65–76

(1974) 'Zur Theorie der Wortstellungsveränderung von SXV zu SVX über TVX' in DINSER, G. (ed) *Zur Theorie der Sprachveränderung,* 265–314. Kronberg: Scriptor Verlag

VERNER, K. (1877) 'Eine Ausnahme der 1. Lautverschiebung'. *Zeitschrift für vergleichende Sprachforschung* 23, 97–130

VIERECK, W. (ed) (1976) *Sprachliches Handeln – Soziales Handeln. Ein Reader zur Pragmalinguistik und Soziolinguistik.* Munich: Fink

VOSSLER, K. (1904) *Positivismus und Idealismus in der Sprachwissenschaft.* Heidelberg: Carl Winter

(1905) *Sprache als Schöpfung und Entwicklung.* Heidelberg: Carl Winter

(1921) *Frankreichs Kultur im Spiegel seiner Sprachentwicklung.* (²1929) as *Frank-*

reichs Kultur und Sprache: Geschichte der französischen Schriftsprache von den Anfängen bis zur Gegenwart. Heidelberg: Carl Winter

WÄNGLER, H. H. (1960) *Grundriss einer Phonetik des Deutschen.* Marburg: Elwert (⁶1976) *Atlas deutscher Sprachlaute.* Berlin: Akademieverlag

WEGENER, P. (1885) *Untersuchungen über die Grundfragen des Sprachlebens.* Halle: Niemeyer

WEINRICH, H. (1961) 'Phonologie der Sprechpause'. *Phonetica* 7, 4–18
(1964) *Tempus. Besprochene und erzählte Welt.* Stuttgart: Kohlhammer
(1964) *Linguistik der Lüge. Kann Sprache die Gedanken verbergen?* Heidelberg: Lambert Schneider
(1976) *Sprache in Texten.* Stuttgart: Klett
(ed) (1975) *Positionen der Negativität.* Munich: Fink

WEISGERBER, J. L. (1949, ²1954) *Von den Kräften der deutschen Sprache I: Die Sprache unter den Kräften des menschlichen Daseins.* Düsseldorf: Schwann
(1950) *Von den Kräften der deutschen Sprache II: Vom Weltbild der deutschen Sprache.* Düsseldorf: Schwann
(1953) *Von den Kräften der deutschen Sprache II/1: Die inhaltbezogene Grammatik.* Düsseldorf: Schwann
(1954) *Von den Kräften der deutschen Sprache II/2: Die sprachliche Erschliessung der Welt.* Düsseldorf: Schwann
(²1957) *Von den Kräften der deutschen Sprache. Die Muttersprache im Aufbau unserer Kultur.* Düsseldorf: Schwann
(1958), 'Der Mensch im Akkusativ', *Wirkendes Wort* 8, 193–205
(²1959) *Von den Kräften der deutschen Sprache. Die geschichtliche Kraft der deutschen Sprache.* Düsseldorf: Schwann
(1962) *Die ganzheitliche Behandlung eines Satzbauplanes, Beiheft zum Wirkenden Wort* 1
(1962) *Von den Kräften der deutschen Sprache. Grundzüge der inhaltbezogenen Grammatik.* Düsseldorf: Schwann
(1962) *Von den Kräften der deutschen Sprache. Die sprachliche Gestaltung der Welt.* Düsseldorf: Schwann
(1963) *Die vier Stufen in der Erforschung der Sprachen.* Düsseldorf: Schwann
(²1964) *Das Menschheitsgesetz der Sprache als Grundlage der Sprachwissenschaft.* Heidelberg: Quelle und Meyer
(1973) *Zweimal Sprache.* Düsseldorf: Schwann

WERLICH, E. (1975) *Stories and Reports.* Dortmund: Lensing
(1975) *Typologie der Texte.* Heidelberg: Quelle and Meyer
(1976) *A Text Grammar of English.* Heidelberg: Quelle and Meyer

WERNER, O. (1973) *Einführung in die strukturelle Beschreibung des Deutschen. Teil I.* Tübingen: Niemeyer

WEYDT, H. (ed) (1977) *Aspekte der Modalpartikeln.* Tübingen: Niemeyer

WHORF, B. L. (1956) *Language, Thought and Reality*, ed J. B. CARROLL, Cambridge, Mass MIT Press, New York: Wiley
(1956) 'Science and Linguistics', in WHORF, B. L. 1956, *Language*: 207–19

WILKINS, D. A. (1972) *Linguistics in Language Teaching.* London: Edward Arnold

WIMMER, R. (1974) 'Die Bedeutung des Regelbegriffs der praktischen Semantik für den kommunikativen Sprachunterricht', in HERINGER, H. J. (ed) *Regelbegriff*, 1974: 133–57

WINKLER, C. (1967) 'Zur Frage der deutschen Hochlautung', in MOSER, H. (ed) *Satz und Wort im heutigen Deutsch*, 1967: 313–18

WINTER, W. (1965) 'Transforms without Kernels'. *Language* 41, 484–9

WOTJAK, G. (1971) *Untersuchungen zur Struktur der Bedeutung.* Munich: Hueber
(1973) 'Zur Wahrung der semantischen Invarianz beim Übersetzen', in NEUBERT, A. and O. KADE (eds) *Beiträge*, 1973: 71–80

WUNDERLICH, D. (1969) 'Karl Bühlers Grundprinzipien der Sprachtheorie'. *Muttersprache* 79, 97–107
(1969) 'Unterrichten als Dialog'. *Sprache im technischen Zeitalter* 32, 263–87
(1970) 'Die Rolle der Pragmatik in der Linguistik'. *Deutschunterricht* 22, 5–41
(1970) 'Syntax und Semantik in der Transformationsgrammatik'. *Sprache im technischen Zeitalter* 36, 319–55
(1970) *Tempus und Zeitreferenz im Deutschen*. Munich: Hueber
(1971) 'Pragmatik, Spechsituation und Deixis'. *Zeitschrift für Literaturwissenschaft und Linguistik*, 153–90
(1974) *Grundlagen der Linguistik*. Reinbek: Rowohlt
(1974) 'Textlinguistik', in ARNOLD, H. L. and V. SINEMUS (eds) *Grundzüge*, 1974: 386–97
(1976) *Studien zur Sprechakttheorie*. Frankfurt: Suhrkamp
(ed) (1971) *Probleme und Fortschritte der Transformationsgrammatik*. Munich: Hueber
(ed) (1972) *Linguistische Pragmatik*. Frankfurt: Athenäum
WUNDT, W. (1900) *Völkerpsychologie*, Col I. Leipzig: Enyelm
ZEMB, J. M. (1972) *Satz, Wort, Rede. Semantische Strukturen des deutschen Satzes*. Freiburg: Herder
ZIMMERMANN, R. (1968) *Untersuchungen zum frühmittelenglischen Tempussystem*. Heidelberg: Groos

Index

Where more than one page reference is given **boldface** numbers indicate a major reference or the explanation of a technical term.